UTAH

In Demographic Perspective

UTAH

In Demographic Perspective

Regional and National Contrasts

Edited by

THOMAS K. MARTIN
TIM B. HEATON
STEPHEN J. BAHR

Printed in the United States of America

Library of Congress Cataloging in Publication Data:

Utah in demographic perspective.

Bibliography: p.
1. Utah—Population. 2. Utah—Social conditions.
I. Martin, Thomas K., 1952- II. Heaton, Tim B.
III. Bahr, Stephen J.
HB3525.U8U87 1986 304.6′09792 86-13930
ISBN 0-941214-44-3

CONTENTS

Preface 1

Chapter One: ABORTION 5

Chapter Two: TEENAGE PREGNANCY & OUT-OF-WEDLOCK BIRTHS 23

Chapter Three: FERTILITY 37

Chapter Four: MIGRATION 49

Chapter Five: MORTALILTY 59

Chapter Six: FAMILY FORMATION 71

Chapter Seven: FAMILY ECONOMICS 91

Chapter Eight: CHILD CARE 111

Chapter Nine: DIVORCE 121

Chapter Ten: NONTRADITIONAL FAMILIES 145

Chapter Eleven: FAMILY VIOLENCE 157

Chapter Twelve: ETHNIC GROUPS 165

Chapter Thirteen: THE DEMOGRAPHY OF UTAH MORMONS 181

Chapter Fourteen: EDUCATION 195

Chapter Fifteen: THE MONETARY EFFECTS OF EDUCATION 217

Chapter Sixteen: PUBLIC WELFARE 227

Chapter Seventeen: ALCOHOL CONSUMPTION AND ABUSE 245

Chapter Eighteen: ADOLESCENT DRUG USE 259

Chapter Nineteen: CRIME 277

Chapter Twenty: UTAH'S UNIQUE POPULATION STRUCTURE 289

Contributors 297

PREFACE

Utahns, it seems, are an often misperceived people. As heirs of the modern day Mormon zion of the Church of Jesus Christ of Latter-day Saints, many residents retain a zionist attitude, wanting to see only the positive aspects of their Rocky Mountain state. Others, of course, sometimes adopt an oppositionist stance, focusing on what they see as the shortcomings of the state and its people. And to those from outside the state, Utah is occasionally seen as a reclusive parochial state in the American hinterland consisting mostly of arid rundown towns where the biggest excitement is the weekly Mormon Tabernacle Choir broadcast.

The purpose of *Utah in Demographic Perspective* is to present, as far as possible, an objective description of Utah society and to compare it to that of the other mountain states and to the United States as a whole, using the most recent data available. We recognize that no single compilation of essays could capture the entire gamut of social life in Utah and have attempted to focus on some of the state's most timely and salient social and demographic features. We realize that many important aspects of Utah society are not addressed in this book. Still, we hope that the following twenty chapters will be enlightening to readers interested in catching a more accurate glimpse of Utah and its people.

A variety of demographic information was used in compiling the following chapters. In particular, the release of the 1980 U.S. census provided a rich source of data. Occasionally, however, the published census results proved too restrictive, and micro-files containing geographic samples of the individual respondents were obtained. A 5 percent sample of Utah, a 1 percent sample of the mountain states, and a .1 percent sample of the United States were used to create specialized tabulations where needed. Several chapters are based entirely on samples from the census returns, and any unreferenced census data came from this source.

Since census data are not appropriate for all issues, state reports, sample surveys, and agency statistics provided information for some chapters. Many of the questions about Utah which prompted this research were really aimed at Mormon/non-Mormon differences rather than interstate comparisons, but for most of the chapters, data which distinguish between the state's Mormon and non-Mormon populations were not available. Moreover, approximately one-third of Utah's population is non-Mormon. Thus caution is advised in generalizing the statistical patterns beyond the populations to which they specifically apply.

Several observations can be gleaned from the information which follows. For example, it will probably not be surprising to most readers to learn that Utah is characterized by a traditional family orientation. Marriage rates are high, and the average age at marriage is relatively young. Cohabitation is less common than nationally, as is divorce, and remarriage rates are higher. Fertility rates are well above national averages, and abortion rates are very low. Utahns also have a relatively conservative life-style; mortality rates are low; most types of crime occur less frequently than is true across the country; and the consumption of alcohol and illicit drugs is low. Finally, Utah is a relatively homogeneous state, a large percentage of the population belonging to one religious denomination. Racial and ethnic minorities are sparse. These and other findings tend to be interrelated; the traditional family orientation and conservative life-style go hand in hand, and homogeneity is an important factor underlying the conservative family oriented life-style.

These observations help to underscore the issues and challenges particular to Utah. Growth arising from high fertility will affect the state for years to come. Child care may be in short supply. Demands on a tight educational budget will increase. The supply of labor and associated demand for jobs will continue to grow. While earner income has been competitive in the state, per capita income is reduced by larger households, and caring for children on a modest budget will continue to be a major concern. At the same time, dealing with the growth of nontraditional families, especially single parent and step-parent families, will present new challenges. Perhaps because of the state's homogeneity, minorities and nonconformists have not fared well in Utah. For example, minorities have relatively high mortality rates, those who drink are more apt to be alcoholics, and those who marry at younger ages have higher divorce rates.

This book is an updated and revised edition of *Utah in Demographic Perspective: Regional and National Contrasts*, published in 1981 by the Family and Demographic Research Institute at Brigham Young University, Provo, Utah. The first edition was not widely circulated, and because of a number of false claims made about Utah—often in the face of contrary statistical evidence—it was concluded that the present edition should enjoy a wider distribution. The thirteen chapters of the first edition have herein been increased to twenty. Chapters in the first edition on bankruptcy, infant mortality, teenage suicide, and venereal disease have either been deleted or incorporated into other chapters. These topics are important, but in some instances qualified authors who were willing to take on the task of writing a chapter were unavailable. In other instances, it was decided that an earlier chapter would more appropriately fall within the range of a new, broader chapter. In the first edition, for example, two separate chapters were included on educational attainment and educational quality. In this edition, one chapter combines these two, and an entirely new essay was prepared on the monetary returns to education. Other new chapters on child care, drug use, ethnic groups, family economics, family formation, family violence, fertility, migration, nontraditional families, and religion were written specifically for this edition. The result, we believe, is the most up-to-date, thorough analysis of social conditions in Utah available in print.

Norene Petersen and Brenda Johnson typed the manuscript and provided other assistance. Michael Peterson helped with much of the computer analysis of the census micro-files. The Advisory Board of the Family and Demographic Research Institute gave several useful suggestions, while Anastasios Marcos and Shirley Ricks helped edit the chapters. We have tried in this edition to build upon the pioneering work of Howard M. Bahr, who edited the first edition. Research was funded by the Family and Demographic Research Institute and by the College of Family, Home, and Social Sciences at Brigham Young University.

Thomas K. Martin
Tim B. Heaton
Stephen J. Bahr

1.
ABORTION

Thomas K. Martin

In January 1980, *New York Times* reporter Leslie Bennetts noted that the "increasing political nature of abortion as a national issue is becoming apparent" (Bennetts, 22). Indeed, a cursory examination of major American newspapers reveals that abortion, besides being an important political controversy, is a major social, moral, and religious issue. As evidenced by the recent bombings of abortion clinics, few contemporary questions have caused such emotional responses as abortion.

Abortion became a prominent issue in national politics in January 1973 when the United States Supreme Court rendered landmark decisions in two different abortion cases. The high court ruled that a state acts unconstitutionally when, prior to the time a fetus can survive outside the womb, it interferes with a woman's decision to have an abortion. This ruling had an immediate effect on the abortion laws of most states, including Utah. Previously, Utah laws allowed abortions only if the life of the mother was threatened (Center for Disease Control 1974, Table 22).

Because few legal abortions were performed in Utah before 1973 and national figures prior to that time are incomplete at best, this chapter focuses on abortion in the United States, the mountain states, and Utah during the years 1973 to 1982.

Several measures can be used to describe the incidence of abortion. The most basic is the total number of abortions performed in a given population during a given year. However, because populations differ in size and other characteristics, the raw number of abortions may not always be a useful index. To place abortion in its context, it may also be helpful to consider additional measures. Since, for practical purposes, only women between the ages of 15 and 44 are likely to conceive, an examination of the number of abortions per 1,000 women in that age group may provide a better indication of the proportion of the eligible female population obtaining abortions. Thus, an abortion rate refers to the number of abortions per 1,000 women between the ages of 15 and 44 in a given population. An abortion ratio, on the other hand, refers to the number of abortions per 1,000 live births.

To appreciate abortion and its relationship to Utah society more fully, it is important to understand how subgroups within a population differ in regards to abortion. Thus, this chapter examines numbers of abortions, abortion rates, abortion ratios, and differences among certain groups in order to elucidate abortion in Utah.

NUMBER OF ABORTIONS

Few abortions were performed in Utah before 1973 because state officials restricted abortion to cases where the lives of the mothers were jeopardized. In 1973, the first year of legalized abortion, only 110 abortions were performed in the state (see Table 1). The following year the number increased more than twelvefold to 1,480 and continued to rise until 1980 when it peaked at 4,200. From 1980 to 1982, abortions leveled off at just over 4,000 per year. Thus, during the nine years from 1973 to 1982, the number of

TABLE 1.

Numbers of Abortions Performed, 1973-82

	REGION		
YEAR	UTAH	MOUNTAIN STATES	UNITED STATES
1973*	110	17,080	744,610
1974*	1,480	25,810	898,570
1975*	2,010	33,570	1,034,170
1976*	2,590	38,570	1,179,300
1977*	3,070	46,880	1,316,700
1978*	3,150	54,600	1,409,600
1979*	3,810	63,570	1,497,670
1980*	4,200	68,190	1,553,890
1981**	4,080	69,570	1,577,340
1982**	4,180	70,880	1,573,920

*Henshaw n.d., Table 10.
**Henshaw et al. 1984.

abortions in Utah jumped nearly 4,000 percent. However, because the initial number of abortions in Utah was so small, it may be more misleading than enlightening to discuss percentage increases.

Like Utah, the mountain states experienced rapid increases in the number of abortions during the years following the Supreme Court's 1973 ruling. Unlike Utah, however, the number of abortions in the region continued a steady climb through 1982, although this has slowed in recent years. In 1973, 17,080 abortions were performed in the eight states comprising the Mountain Region (see Table 1). A year later, 25,810 were performed, an increase of over 50 percent. The average annual increase in abortions during the seven years following 1973 was 25.1 percent. During the early 1980s, this dropped to 3.8 percent, but there is no evidence that the number has peaked. In 1982, the most recent year for which data are available, there were 70,880 abortions performed in the region.

The trend for the United States during the decade beginning in 1973 was similar to Utah's: a rapid increase during the late 1970s with a leveling off in the 1980s. Figures from the Alan Guttmacher Institute show that 744,610 abortions were performed in the United States in 1973 (see Table 1). Four

TABLE 2.

Abortion Rates Per 1,000 Women Ages 15 to 44, 1973-82

	REGION		
YEAR	UTAH	MOUNTAIN STATES	UNITED STATES
1973*	0.4	8.3	16.3
1974*	5.4	12.0	19.3
1975*	7.0	15.0	22.2
1976*	8.7	16.5	24.2
1977*	10.0	19.2	26.4
1978*	9.8	21.5	27.7
1979*	11.5	24.1	28.8
1980*	12.3	25.0	29.3
1981**	11.5	24.7	29.3
1982**	11.4	24.4	28.8

*Henshaw n.d., Table 11.
**Henshaw et al. 1984.

years later, 1,316,700 were performed, representing an average annual increase of 15.4 percent and a total increase of 76.8 percent. From 1977 to 1981, the number of abortions continued to rise, albeit at a considerably slower pace. In 1981, the peak year for abortions in the U.S., a total of 1,577,340 were reported, an increase of more than 111 percent since 1973 and more than 19 percent over 1977. However, the average annual increase from 1977 to 1981 dropped to 4.7 percent, and, in 1982, there was a slight decrease in the number of abortions performed nationally.

ABORTION RATES

During the first year of legalized abortion in Utah, less than one abortion was performed per 1,000 women between the ages of 15 and 44 (see Table 2). Subsequently, however, Utah's abortion rate climbed sharply from 1973 to 1979, except for a 2 percent decrease in 1978. By 1980, the peak year for Utah's abortion rate, 12.3 abortions were performed for every 1,000 women in the target age group. After 1980, the abortion rate declined for two consecutive years, dropping to 11.4 in 1982. As shown in Figure 1, Utah's abortion rate was small compared to regional and national figures, and, after the first couple of years, the annual rate of increase was less than those of either the region or the nation.

FIGURE 1.

Abortion Rates (per 1,000 women aged 15-44), 1973-1982.

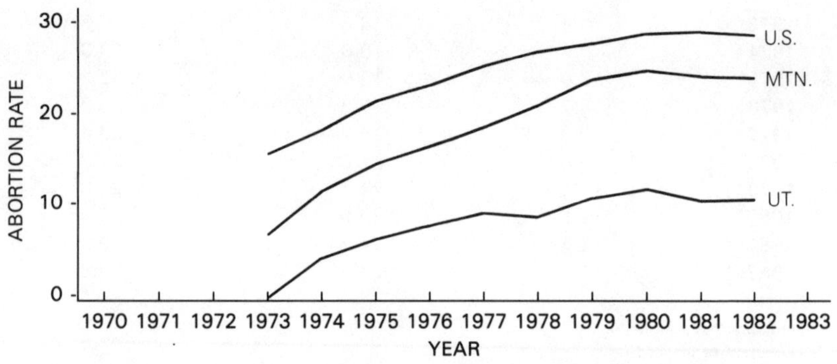

Until 1978, the trend in abortion rates for the Mountain Region paralleled those for Utah, though at a higher level (see Figure 1). From 8.3 abortions per 1,000 women in 1973, the regional abortion rate rose to a peak of 25 per 1,000 women in 1980. After 1980, the regional abortion rate stabilized at about 24 or 25 per 1,000 women.

Colorado, the most populous state in the Mountain Region, permitted legal abortions prior to 1973, diluting annual percentage increases for the region in subsequent years. However, a year-by-year comparison of regional abortion rates with Utah's shows that even after the two rates stabilized the regional rate was more than double Utah's (see Figure 1).

Of the nine geographical regions in the United States, the Mountain Region consistently ranked sixth or seventh in the number of abortions per 1,000 women 15 to 44 years old during the ten years from 1973 to 1983 (Henshaw n.d., Tables 10 and 11; Henshaw et al. 1984). Of the eight mountain states, Utah consistently ranked sixth or seventh. Along with Idaho and Wyoming, Utah's rates tended to be substantially lower than those for the other states.

The major difference between national rates and those for the Mountain Region or for Utah was simply that national rates were higher. Figure 1 shows

TABLE 3.

Abortion Ratio Per 1,000 Live Births, 1973-82

YEAR	UTAH	MOUNTAIN STATES	MOUNTAIN STATES WITHOUT UTAH	UNITED STATES
1973	4	103	123	237
1974	48	149	170	283
1975	62	190	219	328
1976	72	209	242	371
1977	79	239	279	395
1978	79	271	318	422
1979	91	294	344	428
1980	96	302	351	433
1981	97	300	345	434
1982	97	307	355	426

The figures are computed using the number of abortions from Table 1 and the number of live births in *Vital Statistics of the United States*.

the same trend nationally that was observed in Utah and in the mountain states. For the U.S. in 1973, 16.3 abortions were performed for every 1,000 women of childbearing age. From 1979 on, the national abortion rate remained fairly constant at about 29 per 1,000 women. The most recent data in Table 2 indicate that the abortion rate for the U.S. as a whole was about 18 percent higher than for the mountain states and about 150 percent higher than for Utah.

ABORTION RATIOS

As was the case with abortion rates, Utah's abortion ratio remained low compared to those for the mountain states and for the U.S. during the years 1973 to 1982. In 1973, only four abortions were performed in Utah for every 1,000 live births (see Table 3). By 1974, Utah's abortion ratio had increased twelvefold, to 48 per 1,000. The state's abortion ratio temporarily leveled off in 1977 and 1978 at 79 abortions per 1,000 live births before jumping again in 1979 and peaking just below 100 during the last three years for which data are available (see Figure 2).

The Mountain Region experienced both a much higher abortion ratio during the same period and a substantially higher rate of increase compared to Utah. The region had 103 abortions per 1,000 live births in 1973, more than 25 times higher than Utah's ratio. Figure 2 shows that Utah's rate of increase from 1973 to 1974 was about the same as that for the region. However, after 1974 the regional abortion ratio rose much higher than Utah's, roughly three times more each year.

Given that Utah's abortion ratio was considerably lower than the region's, it may be interesting to examine the regional rate exclusive of Utah. By removing Utah, the abortion ratio for the Mountain Region jumps an average of 16 percent per year over the ten years shown in Table 3, from 307 per 1,000 live births in 1982, for example, to 355.

National abortion ratios were, on the average, about 1.5 times higher than those for the mountain states during the decade following the Supreme Court decisions. From a low of 237 per 1,000 live births in 1973, the U.S. abortion ratio rose to a peak in 1981 of 434. From 1978 on, the national abortion ratio stayed between 420 and 435—almost one abortion for every two live births. This compares to less than one abortion for every three live births in the mountain states and to less than one abortion for every ten live births in Utah. Figure 2 shows that trends in U.S. abortion ratios and mountain states abortion ratios were about parallel and that both increased substantially faster than Utah's.

FIGURE 2.

Abortion Ratios (per 1,000 live births), 1973-1982. United States, Mountain States Region, & Utah.

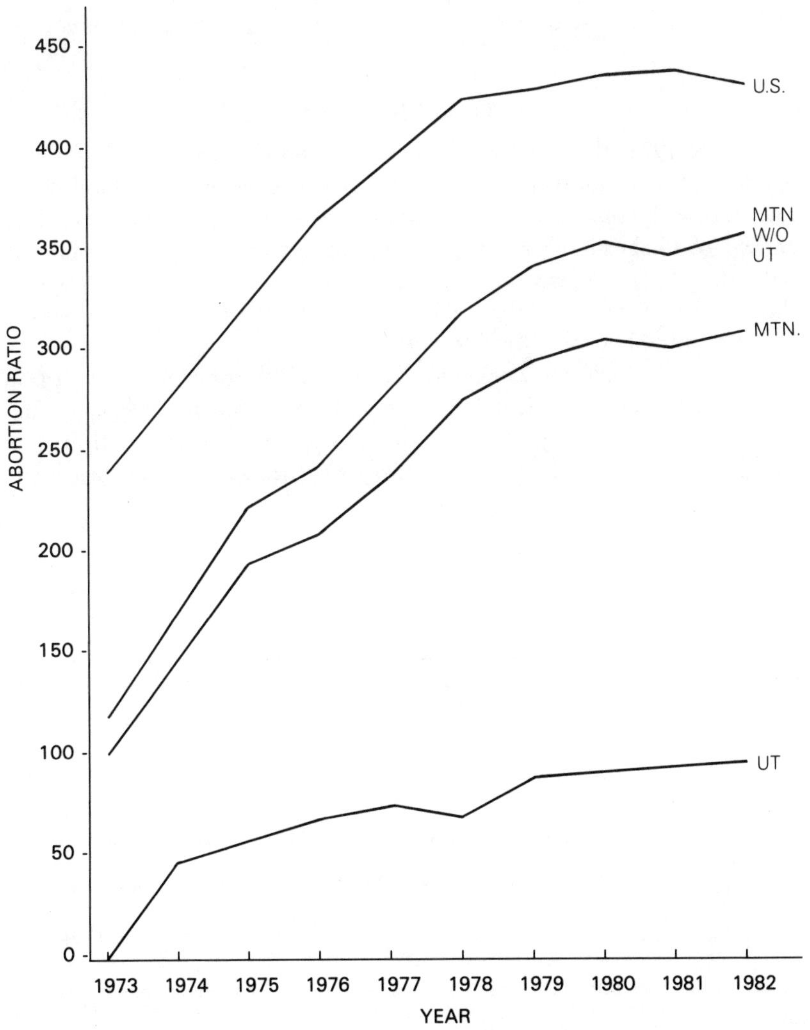

A comparison of abortion rates and abortion ratios makes it clear that Utah women obtained substantially fewer abortions than women in either neighboring states or the nation. The most likely explanation for this is the fact that nearly three-fourths of Utah's population are members of the Church of Jesus Christ of Latter-day Saints (Heaton 1986). As a matter of doctrine, the church opposes abortion except in cases where the life of the mother is threatened or because of rape. A related factor may be the absence of large numbers of minorities in the state.

STATE OF RESIDENCE

Prior to 1973, the number of legal abortions performed in Utah was negligible, and women seeking abortions had to go to other states. Table 4 shows that during the first year after the Supreme Court legalized abortion, 13.2 percent of all abortions involving Utah women were performed within the state. By 1974, the percentage of Utah women obtaining abortions within the state had increased to about 65 percent. Since then, less than 4 percent have obtained abortions in other states.

By comparison, more women in the Mountain Region and in the nation obtained abortions in their home states prior to and immediately following the Supreme Court ruling. In 1972, about 54 percent of women in the region and about 60 percent of women nationally obtained abortions in their home

TABLE 4.

Percentage of Legal Abortions Performed Within State of Residence, 1972-80*

	YEAR								
REGION	1972	1973	1974	1975	1976	1977	1978	1979	1980
Utah	0.0	13.2	65.4	97.3	95.7	97.4	97.3	96.6	96.1
Mountain States	53.5	66.7	84.0	88.2	92.9	95.4	93.2	94.5	94.1
United States	60.4	79.9	89.9	92.0	92.3	93.5	93.8	93.8	94.3

*Excluding abortions performed on women whose state of residence was unknown.
Source: Center for Disease Control 1972, 1973, 1974, 1975, 1976, 1977, 1978, 1979, 1980, Table 5.

states. By 1975, however, Utah exceeded both the region and the nation in the percentage of women staying within their state of residence to obtain abortions. Regionally and nationally about 7 percent of all women obtaining abortions from 1975 to 1980 left their state of residence for the procedure.

AGE, RACE, AND MARITAL STATUS

The national Center for Disease Control categorizes abortion data according to age, race, and marital status for each state and for the U.S. as a whole. Unfortunately, it does not publish regional data. Thus, only Utah and the U.S. can be compared, and in the latter case the number of states which reported relevant figures varied each year.

Age Differences

The data in Table 5 indicate that from 1973 to 1980 most abortions were performed on women between the ages of 20 and 24 both in Utah and in the United States. On the average, about 35 percent of all abortions were performed for women in the 20 to 24 year old age group. In addition, between 25 and 30 percent of all abortions involved women aged 15 to 19, while just under 20 percent were performed on 25 to 29 year-old women. Thus, on the average, women between the ages of 15 and 29 accounted for over 80 percent of all abortions performed in Utah and in the United States from 1973 to 1980. Slightly less than 10 percent were performed on women between the ages of 30 and 34, while women from 35 to 39 years old received less than 5 percent. Women in the under 15 and over 40 year age groups each received less than 2 percent of all abortions.

Although women in the under 15 year old age group had the smallest percentage of all abortions, they also experienced the fewest live births. Consequently, the abortion ratio for these women was the highest of all age groups (see Table 6). Nationally, women under 15 years of age had more abortions than live births for every year shown in Table 6. In Utah, the abortion ratio for the youngest group tended to fluctuate because of the small numbers involved. Although women under 15 years of age in Utah had higher abortion ratios than women of other ages, their abortion ratio was never as high as for the same group nationally. Still, no other group experienced more abortions than live births in any year covered in Table 6.

Throughout the United States women over 40 obtained the next highest abortion ratio, about four for every five live births in 1980. Women between the ages of 15 and 19 had the next highest abortion ratio. In 1980, women

TABLE 5.

Percentages of Abortions by Age Group, Utah and United States, 1973-80

REGION	YEAR	AGES OF FEMALES								NUMBER OF STATES REPORTING
		<15	15-90	20-24	25-29	30-34	35-39	>40	UNKNOWN	
Utah	1973	na	na	na	na	na	na	na	na	
	1974	0.8	27.8	35.2	16.8	8.2	5.0	1.9	4.1	
	1975	1.2	27.6	37.7	17.9	8.4	4.2	1.7	1.3	
	1976	1.1	29.3	35.8	17.7	8.5	3.7	1.7	2.2	
	1977	1.0	29.1	35.1	18.2	8.9	4.1	1.6	2.0	
	1978	0.4	21.9	37.4	22.3	8.8	4.4	1.5	3.2	
	1979	0.9	26.0	36.6	19.7	8.8	4.2	1.5	2.3	
	1980	0.9	24.6	35.1	22.2	10.1	3.9	1.1	2.1	
	Mean	0.9	26.6	36.1	19.3	8.8	4.2	1.6	2.5	
U.S.	1973	1.5	30.0	30.8	17.1	9.6	5.3	2.1	3.5	23
	1974	1.5	30.9	31.5	17.9	9.9	5.3	2.1	0.9	33
	1975	1.5	31.2	31.6	18.0	9.6	5.0	1.9	1.2	34
	1976	1.3	30.4	32.9	18.5	9.2	4.8	1.8	1.2	36
	1977	1.2	29.3	34.1	18.5	9.4	4.7	1.7	1.0	37
	1978	1.0	28.7	34.7	18.7	9.6	4.7	1.6	1.0	38
	1979	1.0	28.7	35.1	18.9	9.5	4.4	1.4	0.9	36
	1980	0.9	27.9	35.0	19.3	9.7	4.3	1.4	1.3	41
	Mean	1.24	29.6	33.2	18.4	9.6	4.8	1.8	1.4	

Source: Center for Disease Control 1973, 1974, 1975, 1976, 1977, 1978, 1979, 1980, Table 6.

TABLE 6.

Abortion Ratios by Age Group, Utah and United States, 1973-80*

		AGES OF FEMALES							
REGION	YEAR	<15	15-90	20-24	25-29	30-34	35-39	>40	NUMBER OF STATES REPORTING
Utah	1973	na	na	na	na	na	na	na	
	1974	435	115	48	32	34	50	82	
	1975	1,000	159	66	42	43	63	104	
	1976	1,034	195	69	42	44	57	118	
	1977	857	213	76	49	49	70	127	
	1978**	308	146	77	56	43	66	100	
	1979**	1,143	203	85	55	47	67	127	
	1980**	944	206	87	68	59	65	98	
U.S.	1973	1,237	539	294	207	280	451	648	23
	1974	1,156	491	263	184	224	389	585	33
	1975	1,193	542	289	192	250	422	668	34
	1976	1,208	582	320	198	241	419	712	36
	1977	1,123	568	326	199	230	424	755	37
	1978***	1,149	650	370	218	235	435	788	38
	1979***	1,196	676	380	221	228	407	746	36
	1980***	1,397	714	395	237	237	410	807	41

*Center for Disease Control 1973, 1974, 1975, 1976, and 1977, Table 7.
**Bureau of Health Statistics 1981, Table F.
***Center for Disease Control 1978, 1979, and 1980, Table 6.

in this category nationally obtained about seven abortions for every ten live births. The lowest abortion ratio for women nationally appeared among those between the ages of 25 and 30, about one abortion for every four or five live births.

By contrast, no age group of Utah women, except those under 15, had an abortion ratio as high as the lowest national ratio by age group. After the youngest age group, the next highest abortion ratios in Utah were among 15 to 19 year-old women. In 1980, this group received about one abortion for every five live births. Every other group of Utah women obtained less than one abortion for every ten live births.

TABLE 7.

Percentage of Abortions by Race, Utah and United States, 1973-80

		RACE			
	YEAR	WHITE	BLACK AND OTHER	UNKNOWN	NUMBER OF STATES REPORTING
Utah	1973	na	na	na	
	1974	85.5	9.2	5.3	
	1975	88.9	10.1	1.0	
	1976	87.8	11.1	1.1	
	1977	88.6	10.6	0.8	
	1978	90.7	5.4	3.9	
	1979	90.4	6.8	2.9	
	1980	88.4	8.2	3.5	
	Mean	88.6	8.8	2.6	
U.S.:	1973	67.7	25.7	6.6	21
	1974	67.2	29.2	3.7	28
	1975	65.3	31.0	3.7	31
	1976	63.3	31.8	5.0	33
	1977	63.5	32.2	4.3	33
	1978	64.5	31.8	3.7	33
	1979	65.8	29.7	4.5	30
	1980	66.2	28.5	5.4	34
	Mean	65.4	30.0	4.6	

Source: Center for Disease Control (1973, 1974, 1975, 1976, 1977, 1978, 1979, 1980), Table 8.

Racial Differences

Every year since 1973, the Center for Disease Control has reported the percentage of abortions performed on "white women" (i.e., caucasian, Mexican American, Puerto Rican, and Cuban) and on "black and other women" (i.e., Negro, American Indian, Chinese, Japanese, Hawaiian, and other). In the United States, the "black and other" group comprises about 17 percent of the total population, while in Utah it makes up only about 5 percent of the population (Jacobson 1986). Comparing these percentages with the those in Table 7 we find that Utah women in the "black and other" group tended to have more abortions than the proportion of the population they represent would have suggested, nearly 9 percent, on the average. Nationally, "black and other" women made up nearly 30 percent of all women having abortions. In both cases, the percentage was about 1.8 times greater than the percentage of the population represented.

According to the Center for Disease Control, abortion ratios from 1973 to 1980 for black and other women exceeded those for white women in Utah and the U.S. by about 170 percent. (In Utah, abortion ratios for black and other women averaged about 1.9 times higher than for white women.) White women in Utah had less than one abortion for every ten live births in 1980 and about one abortion for every three live births nationally. Black and other women in Utah had about one abortion for every five live births in 1980 and slightly more than one abortion for every two live births nationally. Thus, while abortion ratios for minority women in Utah were about double those of white women, both groups had abortion ratios substantially lower than white or minority women nationally.

Marital Differences

The majority of abortions, both in Utah and throughout the U.S., were performed for unmarried women (see Table 9). Averaging the percentages of abortions obtained by married and unmarried women from 1973 to 1980, about 72 percent of all abortions nationally were performed for unmarried women, while in Utah about 78 percent were for unmarried women, a difference of 6 percent. About one-half of this difference is attributable to better reporting measures in Utah, which left fewer women in the "unknown" category than nationally. Of all abortions performed in Utah, the Utah Bureau of Health Statistics (1981; 1983; 1984) attributed nearly 50 percent to never-married women between the ages of 15 and 24.

TABLE 8.

Abortion Ratios by Racial Group, Utah and United States, 1973-80*

REGION	YEAR	RACE OF FEMALES: WHITE	RACE OF FEMALES: BLACK AND OTHER	NUMBER OF STATES REPORTING
Utah	1973‡	na	na	
	1974	48	ca. 80†	
	1975	63	108†	
	1976	66	111†	
	1977	74	138†	
	1978	71**	123†	
	1979	79**	168†	
	1980	84**	192†	
U.S.	1973	326	420	18
	1974	270	421	26
	1975	277	476	27
	1976	289	530	29
	1977	268	490	31
	1978‡	297	497	33
	1979‡	311	506	30
	1980‡	332	543	34

*Center for Disease Control 1973, 1974,1975, 1976, 1977, Table 9.
**Utah Bureau of Health Statistics 1981, Table I.
†Computed by taking the numbers of abortions from Utah Bureau of Health Statistics, *Induced Abortions in Utah, 1974-77* (Table 6) and *1978-80* (Table I), dividing them by the numbers of live births from *Vital Statistics of the United States, Vol. 1, Natality,* Table 1-53, for the years 1974-80, and multiplying the quotient by 1,000.
‡Center for Disease Control 1978-80, Table 8.

The abortion ratios reported for "black and other" Utah women, 1974-77, are about half the size of those published by the Center for Disease Control. The CDC included abortions obtained by Hispanic women in the total number received by "black and other" Utah women. However, when abortion ratios were computed, live births to Hispanic women were not included in the total number of births for Utah's "black and other" women. As a result, the CDC overestimated abortion ratios for "black and other" Utah women by a factor of about two. Data are not available to evaluate CDC figures for other states, but abortion figures for minorities may be too high in general.

A comparison of abortion ratios for married and unmarried women suggests how large the differences between the two groups have been (see Table 10). In 1980, married women in Utah had about one abortion for every 40 live births. During the same year, however, unmarried women had slightly more abortions than live births, resulting in a 1980 abortion ratio more than 40 times that for married women. Nationally, this difference, while not as large, was still impressive. In 1980, married women nationally obtained about one abortion for every ten live births, while unmarried women had nearly 1.5 abortions for every live birth—an abortion ratio 14 times greater than for

TABLE 9.

Percentages of Abortions by Marital Status, Utah and United States, 1973-80

		MARITAL STATUS			
	YEAR	MARRIED	UNMARRIED	UNKNOWN	NUMBER OF STATES REPORTING
Utah:	1973	na	na	na	
	1974	22.2	77.7	0.1	
	1975	19.2	80.3	0.5	
	1976	20.2	78.8	0.9	
	1977	20.1	79.5	0.3	
	1978	20.1	79.2	0.7	
	1979	25.4	73.1	1.5	
	1980	25.5	73.8	0.7	
	Mean	21.8	77.5	0.7	
U.S.:	1973	25.6	69.7	6.5	23
	1974	26.7	70.9	2.4	30
	1975	25.6	72.7	1.7	31
	1976	24.0	73.5	2.5	34
	1977	23.7	73.9	2.4	34
	1978	25.9	72.2	1.9	32
	1979	24.2	73.9	1.9	31
	1980	21.7	72.4	5.9	37
	Mean	24.7	72.4	3.2	

Source: Center for Disease Control 1973, 1974, 1975, 1976, 1977, 1978, 1979, 1980, Table 9.

married women. Six years earlier, in 1974, the peak year for the abortion ratio of unmarried women in the U.S., women in this category had 1.6 abortions for every live birth—an abortion ratio more than 17 times greater than that of married women.

SUMMARY

Despite the rapidly increasing number of abortions during the early and mid-1970s, Utahns obtained substantially fewer abortions than did residents of either the Mountain Region or the United States as a whole. This was true regardless of whether one compares raw numbers of abortions, abortion rates, or abortion ratios.

TABLE 10.

Abortion Ratios by Marital Status, Utah and United States, 1973-80

	YEAR	MARRiED	UNMARRIED	NUMBER OF STATES REPORTING
Utah:	1973	na	na	
	1974	12	848	
	1975	14	1,322	
	1976	15	1,355	
	1977	17	1,340	
	1978**	20	1,008	
	1979**	23	1,103	
	1980**	25	1,083	
U.S.:	1973	76	1,398	21
	1974	95	1,675	29
	1975	96	1,610	31
	1976	95	1,570	33
	1977	93	1,480	32
	1978†	112	1,471	32
	1979†	106	1,429	31
	1980†	105	1,476	37

*Center for Disease Control 1973, 1974, 1975, 1976, 1977, Table 12.
**Utah Bureau of Health Statistics 1981, Table D.
†Center for Disease Control 1978, 1979, and 1980, Table 9.

Utah women who sought abortions were slightly more likely than women in the region or the nation to obtain them within their state of residence. Utah women between the ages of 15 and 29 accounted for about 85 percent of all abortions performed in the state. Black and other nonwhite Utah women were more likely to obtain abortions than white women. Unmarried women, particularly those who had never been married, were more likely to obtain abortions than married women in Utah.

REFERENCES

Bennetts, Leslie. "Abortion Foes Gird for Iowa Caucuses." *New York Times*, 13 Jan. 1980.

Bureau of Health Statistics. *Induced Abortions in Utah, 1978-80*. Salt Lake City: Utah Department of Health, 1981.

_____. *Induced Abortions in Utah, 1981*. Salt Lake City: Utah Department of Health, 1983.

_____. *Induced Abortion in Utah, 1982*. Salt Lake City: Utah Department of Health, 1984.

Center for Disease Control. *Abortion Surveillance, 1972*. Atlanta: U.S. Department of Health, Education, and Welfare, 1974.

_____. *Abortion Surveillance, 1973*. Atlanta: U.S. Department of Health, Education, and Welfare, 1975.

_____. *Abortion Surveillance, 1974*. Atlanta: U.S. Department of Health, Education, and Welfare, 1976.

_____. *Abortion Surveillance, 1975*. Atlanta: U.S. Department of Health, Education, and Welfare, 1977.

_____. *Abortion Surveillance, 1976*. Atlanta: U.S. Department of Health, Education, and Welfare, 1978.

_____. *Abortion Surveillance, 1977*. Atlanta: U.S. Department of Health, Education, and Welfare, 1979.

_____. *Abortion Surveillance, 1978*. Atlanta: U.S. Department of Health and Human Services, 1980.

_____. *Abortion Surveillance, 1979-1980*. Atlanta: U.S. Department of Health and Human Services, 1983.

Heaton, Tim B. "The Demography of Utah Mormons." *Utah in Demographic Perspective*. Salt Lake City: Signature Books, 1986.

Henshaw, Stanley K. "Abortion Services in the United States, Each State and Metropolitan Area, 1979-80." New York: Alan Guttmacher Institute: n.d.

_____, Jacqueline Darroch Forest, and Ellen Blaine. "Abortion Services in the United States, 1981 and 1982." *Family Planning Perspectives* 16 (May/June 1984): 119-27.

Jacobson, Cardell. "Ethnic Groups in Utah." *Utah in Demographic Perspective.* Salt Lake City: Signature Books, 1986.

2.

TEENAGE PREGNANCY AND OUT-OF-WEDLOCK BIRTHS

Bruce A. Chadwick

Considerable public attention has recently focused on teenage pregnancy as a critical social problem facing the nation. A 1976 pamphlet prepared by the Alan Guttmacher Institute, *Eleven Million Teenagers: What Can Be Done About the Epidemic of Adolescent Pregnancies in the United States?* exemplifies the alarm associated with this issue. The word "epidemic" implies a sudden, dramatic increase in teenage pregnancy sweeping the country. In addition, some researchers have asserted that teenage pregnancies can create serious health and social problems for both mother and child, including complications during pregnancy, long-range social and psychological impairment, and high infant mortality (Utah Department of Health 1980 and 1983; Kasun 1978).

Utah's teenage pregnancy rates have received special attention because of the state's emphasis on family life. In particular, the refusal of many Utahns to support the Equal Rights Amendment and their resistance to Planned Parenthood clinics have caused some critics to challenge the quality of family life in Utah. Newspaper headlines have periodically announced that Utah's teenage pregnancy is one of the highest in the United States.

The intent of this chapter is to determine the extent of teenage pregnancy in the state by comparing Utah's rates with national and regional rates. The impact of teenage abortion is also discussed, as is the extent to which teenage pregnancies result in out-of-wedlock births.

Contributing to the controversy over teenage pregnancy has been confusion regarding the difference between fertility rates and pregnancy rates. A population's fertility rate refers to the number of live births per 1,000 females—in this case, women between the ages of 15 and 19. A pregnancy rate is the number of live births and abortions per 1,000 women in the population. We will first examine the rates of live births (i.e., fertility), followed by rates of abortion, and then consider teenage pregnancy rates.

TEENAGE FERTILITY

Teenage fertility rates, or the number of live births per 1,000 women ages 15 to 19, for Utah and the nation from 1970 to 1982 are presented in Table 1 and are illustrated in Figure 1. Utah's teenage fertility rate has been higher than the national average, especially during the last three to four years. This is perhaps not unexpected since the state's largest religious denomination, the Mormon church, emphasizes parenthood and large families and discourages abortion. Thus the rate of teenage fertility in Utah increased 12 percent between 1970 and 1982, whereas the national rate decreased 5 percent during the same period. The major reason for this difference is that more teenagers outside the state terminated their pregnancies by abortion than did Utah adolescents.

Information for whites in the United States is also provided in Table 1 and Figure 1. Non-whites have significantly different patterns of fertility, but Utah's small 3 percent non-white population does not alter the state's rate. It may be more appropriate to contrast Utah's teenagers, most of whom are white, with white teenagers across the country. This increases the discrepancy between state and national fertility rates.

Table 1.

Teenage Fertility Rates for Utah and the United States, 1970-82

	UTAH		UNITED STATES	
YEAR	TOTAL	WHITE	TOTAL	WHITE
1970	58.9	58.9	68.3	57.4
1975	55.6	55.9	55.7	46.4
1976	56.9	57.2	52.8	44.1
1977	61.1	61.5	53.5	44.1
1978	62.6	63.0	51.5	42.9
1979	64.5	65.1	52.3	43.7
1980	65.2	65.4	53.4	44.6
1981	66.2	66.1	–	–
1982	66.0	65.9	–	–

Sources: National Center for Health Statistics 1975; Utah Department of Health 1983.

Since Utah's teenage fertility rate increased during the past decade while national rates declined, Utah's rate is now well above the national average. However, as Table 2 illustrates, this increase is part of an overall trend towards increasing fertility among Utah women of all ages. Indeed, the increase in teenage fertility is only about half that for some of the other age groups. For example, the largest increase was among women 35 to 39 years old (31 percent) and the smallest among women 25 to 29 years old (a 2 percent decrease). In other words, the increase in teenage fertility is part of a trend towards higher fertility among Utah women generally.

The fertility rates of the eight mountain states for 1977 and 1980 are shown in Table 3. Utah's rates are slightly different here from those reported

FIGURE 1.

Teenage Fertility Rates for Utah and the United States, 1970-1982.

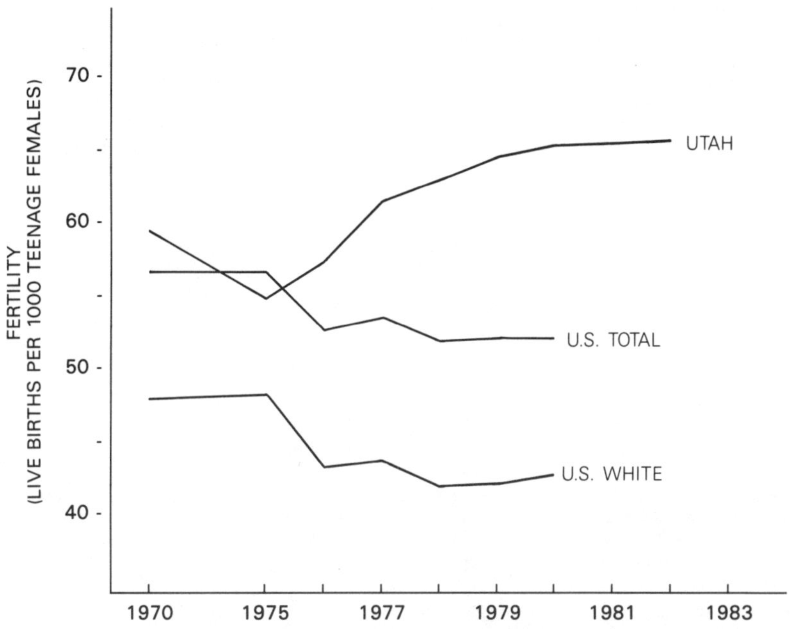

Table 2.

Fertility Rates of Women in Utah in Different Age Groups, 1975-81

	AGE					
YEAR	15-19	20-24	25-29	30-34	35-39	40-44
1975	55.6	186.3	184.2	107.5	44.2	10.8
1976	59.6	196.3	200.4	116.0	48.0	12.0
1977	61.1	201.3	200.6	124.4	50.5	11.9
1978	62.6	194.5	192.2	125.3	54.4	12.5
1979	64.5	196.8	196.3	126.7	57.8	12.2
1980	65.2	193.5	188.5	125.5	57.9	12.3
1981	66.2	187.5	179.1	121.1	52.0	11.7
Increase	19%	4%	-2%	17%	31%	14%

Table 3.

Teenage Fertility Rates for White Females* in the Mountain States, 1977 and 1980**

	RATE		PERCENT CHANGE
STATE	1977	1980	1977-1980
Arizona	54.1	61.4	+7.3%
Colorado	42.8	47.4	+4.6
Idaho	63.9	59.4	−4.5
Montana	37.7	43.3	+5.6
New Mexico	63.5	69.0	+5.5
Utah	69.7	64.6	−5.1
Wyoming	71.7	76.3	+4.6
United States	44.8	44.6	−.2

*Because of Utah's disproportionately low minority population, it is generally most useful to compare Utah's white population to white populations regionally and nationally. Still, interracial comparisons are sometimes made within this and following chapters and on subsequent tables.
**Figures for Nevada are absent from Tables 3, 5, 7 and 9. The relevant data were not available in state and federal reports.

Source: Utah Department of Health 1980, 1983.

in Table 1 probably because they were calculated using different population estimates. Although it is disconcerting to discover inconsistencies between statistics from different state-sponsored reports, the important trends and differences are nonetheless apparent. While Utah's 1980 rate is high, it is below Wyoming's and New Mexico's. Wyoming had the highest rate in the nation, and for some reason most of the mountain states had rates above the national average. The lowest rate in the U.S. was Connecticut's with 24.3 births per 1,000 teenage females. If we accept these data, it should be noted that Utah was one of only two mountain states to show a decline in fertility from 1977 to 1980. But if we substitute the 1977 rate from Table 1, then the state actually experienced a moderate increase. This regional comparison also suggests that while Utah's teenage fertility rate is high, it is compatible with that of other age groups in the state and with the teenage populations of neighboring states.

TEENAGE ABORTION

As noted in Chapter 1, about three-fourths of Utah's population belong to the Church of Jesus Christ of Latter-day Saints and are thus influenced to varying degrees by the church's opposition to abortion. LDS doctrine defines abortion, except in cases of rape, incest, or serious threat to the mother's

Table 4.

Teenage Abortion Rates in Utah and the United States, 1975-82

	UTAH		UNITED STATES	
YEAR	TOTAL	WHITE	TOTAL	WHITE
1975	9.3	9.0	28.2	24.5
1976	10.0	9.5	30.3	25.4
1977	11.7	10.9	32.8	27.5
1978	10.4	10.3	42.3	33.5
1979	12.7	12.4	42.0	34.1
1980	13.0	12.8	42.1	36.7
1981	13.1	12.6	—	—
1982	13.3	—	—	—
Increase	43%	40%	49%	50%

Source: Utah Department of Health 1983, 1984.

health, as a sin comparable to murder. This teaching has had a significant impact on the state's abortion rate. In 1973, when abortion was first legalized, Utah's abortion rate per 1,000 women ranked 41st in the nation and 47th in terms of abortions per 1,000 live births (U.S. Government Printing Office 1979). Teenage abortion rates in Utah and the United States from 1975 to 1982 are presented in Table 4. But while Utah's rate increased some 43 percent from 1975 to 1982, it has consistently been only about a third as high as national rates.

The mountain states had fairly low rates of abortion in 1980, as can be seen in Table 5, and Utah has been among the very lowest. Wyoming, with an rate of 10.0 among white teenagers, had a lower occurrence of abortion than Utah with a rate of 12.8. Utah's modest abortion rate has thus contributed to the state's high fertility, as relatively few pregnancies have been terminated by abortion.

TEENAGE PREGNANCY

Teenage pregnancy rates (i.e., the number of live births and abortions per 1,000 women between the ages of 15 and 19) for Utah and the United States, 1975 to 1981, are presented in Table 6 and Figure 2. As can be seen, Utah

Table 5.

Teenage Abortion Rates in Mountain States, 1980

STATE	RATE	
	WHITE	NON-WHITE
Arizona	21.3	34.6
Colorado	31.0	63.6
Idaho	15.4	28.9
Montana	29.1	35.8
New Mexico	23.5	18.7
Utah	12.8	29.4
Wyoming	10.0	19.1

Source: Utah Department of Health 1983.

Table 6.

Teenage Pregnancy Rates for Utah and the United States, 1975-81

YEAR	UTAH		UNITED STATES	
	TOTAL	WHITE	TOTAL	WHITE
1975	64.8	64.8	83.8	70.2
1976	66.9	66.7	80.2	69.4
1977	73.8	72.4	85.6	71.6
1978	73.0	73.3	90.1	76.4
1979	77.1	77.5	91.8	77.8
1980	78.1	78.2	113.7	80.5
1981	79.3	78.7	—	—
Increase	22.4%	21.5%	35.7%	14.5%

Source: Utah Department of Health 1983.

Table 7.

Teenage Pregnancy Rates in Mountain States, 1980

STATE	RATE	
	WHITE	NON-WHITE
Arizona	82.7	134.1
Colorado	78.3	152.0
Idaho	74.8	84.9
Montana	72.4	151.6
New Mexico	92.5	118.3
Utah	77.4	169.5
Wyoming	86.3	160.1

Source: Utah Department of Health 1983.

had a lower incidence of teenage pregnancies than nationally. The differenc between total populations (compared to white-only populations) is largei but this may be misleading since Utah has such a small number of non-white: Comparing white teenagers reveals that Utah had a lower rate of teenag pregnancy than the nation. But the gap seemed to be narrowing as whit teenage pregnancy in Utah increased approximately 21 percent compared t 14.5 for the country. Nevertheless, headlines to the contrary, Utah has no had one of the highest teenage pregnancy rates nationally, rather it has beer substantially below the national average.

Teenage pregnancy in the mountain states tended to be below the national average in 1980. The data in Table 7 reveal that New Mexico had the highest rate regionally and that Utah was third from the bottom, with only Idaho

FIGURE 2.

Teenage Pregnancy Rates for Utah and the United States, 1975-1981.

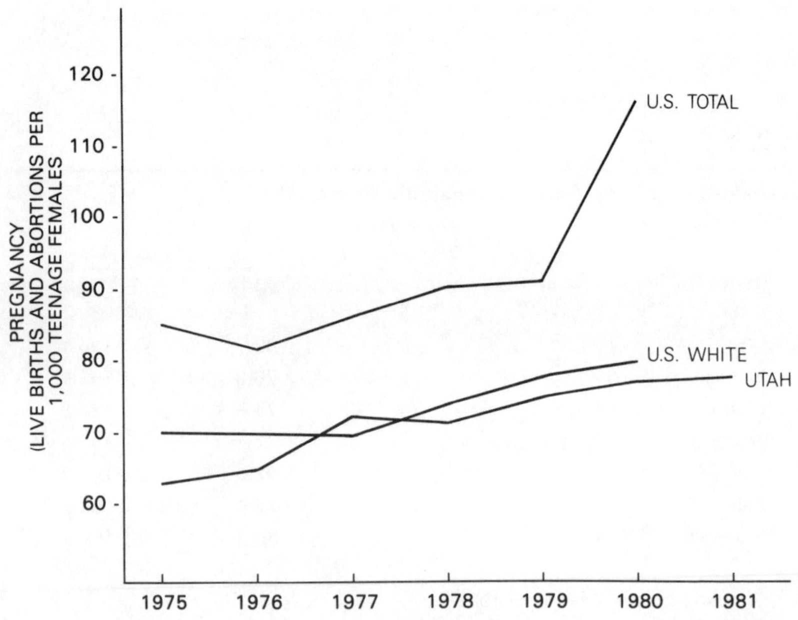

Table 8.

Pregnancy Rates for Females 15 to 17 and 18 to 19 Years of Age in Utah and the United States, 1975-81

	UTAH				UNITED STATES			
	WHITE		NON-WHITE		WHITE		NON-WHITE	
YEAR	15-17	18-19	15-17	18-19	15-17	18-19	15-17	18-19
1975	36.6	104.2	41.3	98.1	46.1	106.3	115.5	223.8
1976	38.9	104.6	40.8	122.1	44.3	106.6	113.7	221.2
1977	41.6	114.0	44.4	143.0	44.8	111.0	117.1	225.9
1978	40.3	116.3	37.4	110.5	47.7	186.6	113.2	233.2
1979	42.9	120.7	38.4	114.6	48.1	120.5	115.5	234.0
1980	45.1	118.2	50.4	115.6	50.0	123.8	116.0	232.6
1981	42.5	125.3	53.2	145.9	—	—	—	—
Increase	16%	20.2%	28.8%	48.7%	8.5%	16.5%	0%	3.9%

and Montana being lower. Thus, Utah's teenage pregnancy rate compared to the nation's or to neighboring states' has been well below the average.

TEENAGE PREGNANCY AND MARRIAGE

Teenage women are a diverse group, masking some important differences among peers. Single 15, 16, and 17 year-old girls still in high school who become pregnant are different from married 18 and 19 year-olds who have graduated from high school and who seek or, at least, accept pregnancy as a consequence of marriage. Thus, it is important to determine just which teenage women in Utah become pregnant.

The pregnancy rate for girls, ages 15, 16 and 17, is compared to that for 18 and 19 year-olds in Utah and the United States in Table 8. From 1975 to 1981 older Utah teenagers had a pregnancy rate nearly three times that of younger teenagers—a difference only twice as high nationally. These data might suggest that younger Utah girls are not as sexually active as their older sisters or girls the same age nationally. Most teenage pregnancies in Utah thus occur among older girls. The percentage increase for white girls in both age categories is a little higher in Utah than nationally, but this is partly because initial rates were lower and comparable increases resulted in higher percentages of change.

Table 9.

Percent of Births to White Teenage Mothers That Were Out-of-Wedlock in Mountain States, 1979

	PERCENT		
STATES	15-19 YEAR	15-17 YEAR	18-19 YEAR
Arizona	33.2	50.1	28.5
Colorado	35.9	54.0	29.2
Idaho	26.1	38.8	18.0
Utah	21.5	34.9	16.3
Wyoming	22.0	35.9	17.4

*Montana and New Mexico do not allow the collection of data regarding marital status on birth certificates.
Source: Utah Department of Health 1983.

Another consideration in assessing the seriousness of teenage pregnancy in Utah is how many of these occurred within marriage and how many occurred out-of-wedlock. The percentages of teenage illegitimate births for the mountain states in 1979 are presented in Table 9. Montana and New Mexico are missing because they do not record information about marital status on birth certificates. Only 21.5 percent of the live births to teenage mothers in Utah occurred outside of marriage. Among the older teenagers, who account for over two-thirds of the pregnancies, only 16.3 percent were illegitimate births. Among the mountain states, Utah had the lowest rate of illegitimacy. This has also been true nationally, as Utah has ranked at, or near, the bottom of the scale for illegitimate births over the years. In summary, the data in Tables 8 and 9 reveal that a majority of Utah's teenage pregnancies have occurred to older, married girls.

Undoubtedly some of these pregnancies occurred before marriage and, because of social pressures, led to "forced" marriages. According to 1975 Utah Department of Health figures, 60 percent of all teenage pregnancies in Utah were the consequence of premarital conception (Utah Department of Health 1980). While age-specific rates are not known, presumably premarital conception rates are much higher for younger brides. Still, if the 60 percent estimate is accepted, then a significant proportion of 18 and 19 year-old mothers also married after they became pregnant. However, a majority of the births to 18 and 19 year-old mothers could just as easily have resulted from conception following marriage.

Surprisingly, little research has assessed the long-range consequences of "forced" marriages. Systematic studies are needed to determine whether such marriages are eventually as satisfying and stable as marriages without premarital conception, or whether they evidence unhappiness, conflict, abuse, or a high divorce rate. It is possible that in some cases marriage may be an acceptable resolution to teenage premarital pregnancy.

Not all teenage pregnancies can be categorized as unwanted premarital conceptions. Certainly a large number of 18 and 19 year-old married mothers saw themselves as willing to bear children, and these "teenage pregnancies" in no way constituted a social problem. In addition, while some teenage pregnancies resulted in "forced" marriages, they may also have simply expedited marriage plans already in the making.

TEENAGE PREGNANCY AND THE HEALTH OF MOTHER AND CHILD

Several studies have suggested that the age of the mother is related to complications in pregnancy and to the infant's health (Simkins 1984). This position is perhaps most clearly stated by Baldwin and Cain (1980): "Teenage childbearing is associated with adverse, pervasive and long-lasting social and economic consequences for the young parents, especially adolescent mothers, who, at very young ages, also appear to be at higher risk of maternal morbidity and mortality." A review of teenage pregnancy in Utah similarly reported: "The younger the mother, the greater the risk of health associated consequences of pregnancy, low birth weight infants, and subsequent abnormal child development. Certainly delaying the first pregnancy until after the teenage years significantly diminishes these health risks" (Utah Department of Health 1980). And a later Utah report found that teenage birth was related to higher rates of low birth weights, congenital anomalies, and infant deaths during the first year of life (Utah Department of Health 1983).

On the other hand, studies testing the relationship among the age of mother, pregnancy risks, and infant health in Denmark and on American Indian reservations where medical care is available to all age groups, demonstrated that the younger the mother, the lower the risks and the healthier the baby (Kasun 1978). Kasun reviewed the contradictory findings and concluded that the youth of the mother may actually have been a favorable factor: "There is considerable evidence that youth and strength are on the side of the teenage mother and that, where she is not under an income handicap, her experience of motherhood has a high probability of success." And in a review of the literature from 1970 to 1980, Chilman (1980) echoed that "there appear to be no adverse effects associated with young maternal age if high quality prenatal and later health care are available." Finally, Cohen and her associates (1980) examined the relationship between maternal age and the intelligence of the child and reported that "there are no direct effects of teenage maternity on offspring intelligence, and that the observed negative relationship is primarily attributable to parental education."

The confusion generated by these inconsistent findings may be increased by the inappropriate use of statistical data to infer a causal relationship between the mother's age and health risks. Such a relationship may exist, but factors other than a mother's age may also cause health risks to her and her child. Factors such as marriage, the availability of health care, and the utilization of health care and nutrition are related both to the age of the mother and to health problems. Carefully controlled experiments are necessary to establish causal links between a mother's age and health problems.

Clearly, one should not unquestioningly assume that age itself results in a higher pregnancy risk or health hazard to the child. It may be that the two-thirds of Utah's teenage pregnancies among 18 and 19 year-old mothers occur at an optimum age as far as the health of the mother and child are concerned.

SUMMARY

Teenage pregnancy has been identified by those associated with public sex education and planned parenthood movements as a growing social problem in American society. Utah, because of its high teenage fertility, has sometimes been singled out for special attention. The data reveal that Utah has a high teenage fertility rate which has increased during the past decade. But this increase has been part of an overall trend towards increasing fertility among all Utah women and throughout the region as well.

One reason many states have had relatively low teenage fertility rates is because a large proportion of their teenage pregnancies were aborted. Utah has had a very low teenage abortion rate, only about one-third the national average. And when abortions are combined with live births to compute a pregnancy rate, Utah ranks well below the national average. In other words, Utah teenagers have not necessarily become pregnant more often than teenagers in other states, but because of religious or social values they have allowed their pregnancies to run full term, resulting in more live births, not more abortions. Over two-thirds of Utah's teenage pregnancies occur among 18 and 19 year-old women, most of whom have completed high school and are married at the time of delivery.

Finally, the evidence on the relationship between the age of the mother and the health of the child is inconsistent. However, some researchers suggest that young age at motherhood, in itself, poses little physiological threat to mother and child, and that the late teen years (ages 18-19) may, in fact, be an optimal time for childbirth. Of course, optimal age in terms of physiological readiness does not necessarily correspond with optimal age in terms of social or psychological readiness. The latter are issues that have not been raised in any systematic way by those studying teenage pregnancy and therefore deserve more attention.

While teenage pregnancy has been and will continue to be a problem in Utah, its significance should not be exaggerated. Utahns should not be too quick to judge their teenagers, whose rates of abortion and out-of-wedlock births are among the lowest in the nation. And a premature sense of crisis about teenage pregnancy should not be cited as a justification, in itself, for such remedies as mandatory sex education in public schools, planned parenthood clinics, or abortion clinics. In the long run, such programs, in my opinion, may not address the problems they are designed to alleviate.

REFERENCES

Alan Guttmacher Institute. *Eleven Million Teenagers: What Can Be Done About the Epidemic of Adolescent Pregnancies in the United States?* New York: Planned Parenthood Federation of America, Inc., 1976.

Baldwin, Wendy and Virginia S. Cain. "The Children of Teenage Parents." *Family Planning Perspectives* 12 (1980), 1:34-43.

Chilman, Catherine S. "Social and Psychological Research Concerning Adolescent Childbearing: 1970-80." *Journal of Marriage and the Family* 42 (1980), 4:793-805.

Cohen, Patricia, Lillian Belmont, Joy Drytoos, Zena Stein, and Susan Zayac. "The Effects of Teenage Motherhood and Maternal Age on Offspring Intelligence." *Social Biology* 27 (Summer 1980): 138.

Kasun, Jacqueline. "Teenage Pregnancy: Epidemic or Statistical Hoax?" *USA Today*, July 1978, pp. 31-32.

National Center for Health Statistics. *Vital Statistics of the U.S., 1970, Vol. 1, Natality*. Washington, D.C.: U.S. Department of Health, Education, and Welfare, 1975.

Simkins, Lawrence. "Consequences of Teenage Pregnancy and Motherhood." *Adolescence* 19 (1984), 73:41-54.

U.S. Government Printing Office. *Statistical Abstracts of the United States*. Washington, D.C.: U.S. Government Printing Office, 1979.

Utah Department of Health. *Adolescent Pregnancy in the 1970s*. Salt Lake City: Family Health Services Division, Bureau of Health Statistics, 1980.

_____ *Teenage Pregnancy in Utah, 1975-81*. Salt Lake City: Family Health Services Division, Bureau of Health Statistics, 1983.

_____. *Utah's Legally Induced Abortions, 1982*. Salt Lake City: Family Health Services Division, Bureau of Health Statistics, 1984.

3.
FERTILITY

Tim B. Heaton

Utah has long been noted for its higher than average rate of fertility (see Figure 1). Whereas Utah in the early 1970s experienced a decline in fertility, as was true nationally, by the mid-1970s its rate had turned around, increasing beyond 1970 levels while national rates had leveled off. Since 1980 Utah's rate has again dropped somewhat, but there is still a large difference between Utah and the nation.

A different picture emerges when one looks at age specific fertility rates for the 1980s. Here we see a net decline for Utah from the 1970 level; this matches the national decline in magnitude. Only at the youngest ages (15-19) are 1980 rates as high as 1970 rates. The disparity between national and Utah rates for women of all ages is due in part to an increase in younger couples in Utah. For example, the percentage of all couples under the age of 35 increased from 31.2 in 1970 to 40.3 in 1980. Thus, while actual family size declined in Utah during the 1970s, the state's fertility rate remained substantially higher than the national average.

In this chapter we explore some of the variables affecting fertility, comparing Utah to the Rocky Mountain states and to the nation. These variables include length of marriage, age at first marriage, wife's education, wife's labor force participation, and income of all family members except the wife. Two types of questions are raised. First, is Utah's fertility rate higher because of the state's demographic composition? (If so, then once the differences have been eliminated Utah's rates should compare to those regionally and nationally.) Second, are the effects of these variables the same in Utah as in the Rocky Mountains and the nation?

To address these questions we use information from the 1980 United States Census of Population. We have eliminated all nonwhite and Spanish-origin respondents from our analysis, and because marital disruption confounds

FIGURE 1.

Fertility Rates for Utah and the Nation

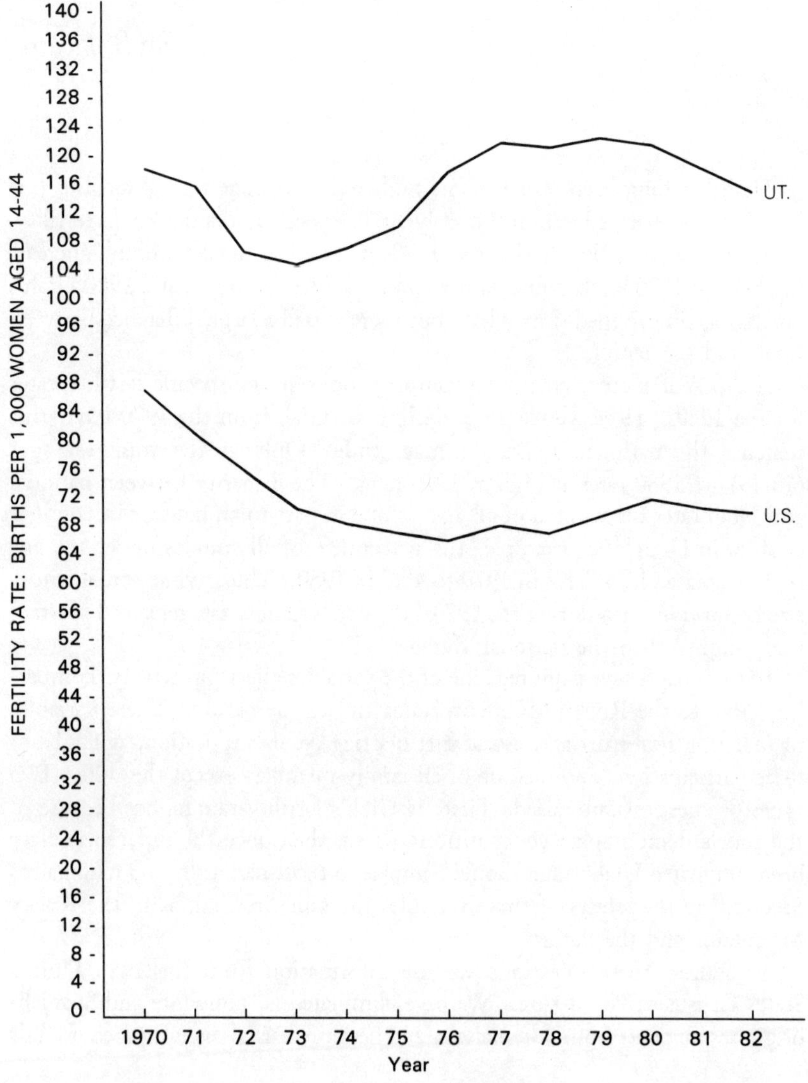

TABLE 1.

Children Ever Born per 1,000 Women in Utah and the United States, 1970 and 1980

AGE	UTAH				U.S.			
	1970		1980		1970		1980	
	ALL WOMEN	EVER-MARRIED WOMEN	ALL WOMEN	EVER-MARRIED WOMEN	ALL WOMEN	EVER-MARRIED WOMEN	ALL WOMEN	EVER-MARRIED WOMEN
15-19	65	560	111	618	76	636	94	583
20-24	686	1056	701	1100	683	1071	534	904
25-29	2073	2263	1697	1979	1743	1984	1166	1392
30-34	3206	3371	2583	2750	2599	2806	1815	1972
35-39	3749	3903	3292	3422	2984	3170	2406	2534

fertility, only women still in their first marriage are included. Because these variables can simultaneously affect fertility, we will use a multivariate statistical approach which takes into account the combined effects of these variables on fertility. The dependent variable in the following analysis is the number of children ever born.

FIGURE 2.

Children Ever Born by Duration Since Marriage: Adjusted Rates

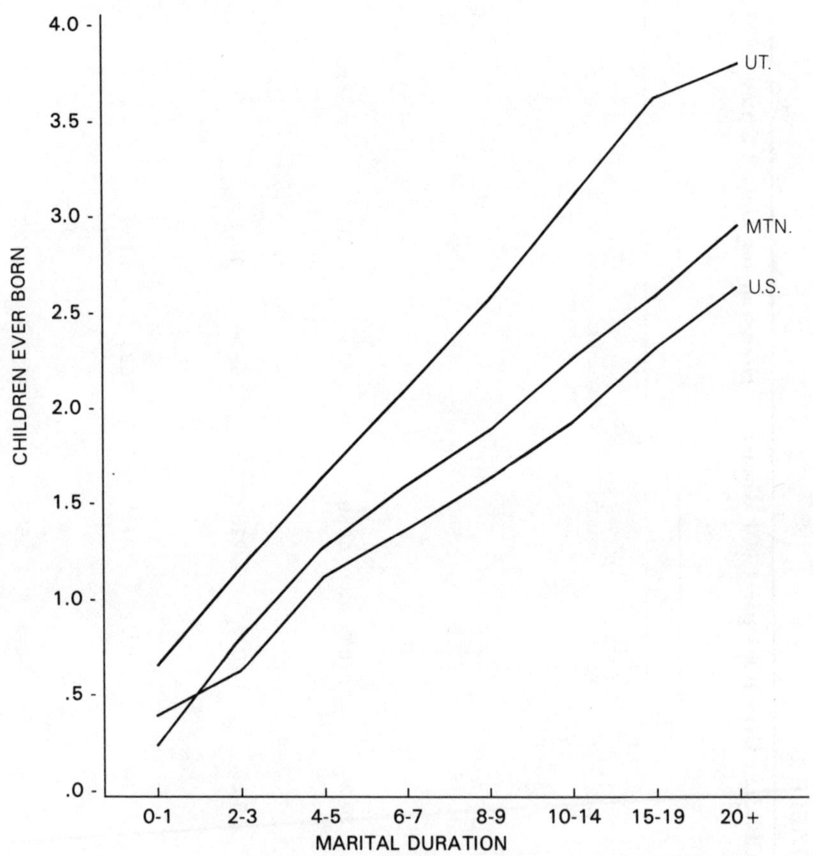

RESULTS

Table 1 reports the results of our analysis. The first column under each region (using unadjusted rates) reports the average number of children ever born for each subgroup. The second column (using adjusted rates) reports this rate when other variables are included.

The first variable considered is marital duration (see Figure 2). For each region, fertility increases with the length of time a couple remains married. This is no surprise since it takes time to bear children and most couples space

FIGURE 3.

Children Ever Born by Age at First Marriage: Adjusted Rates

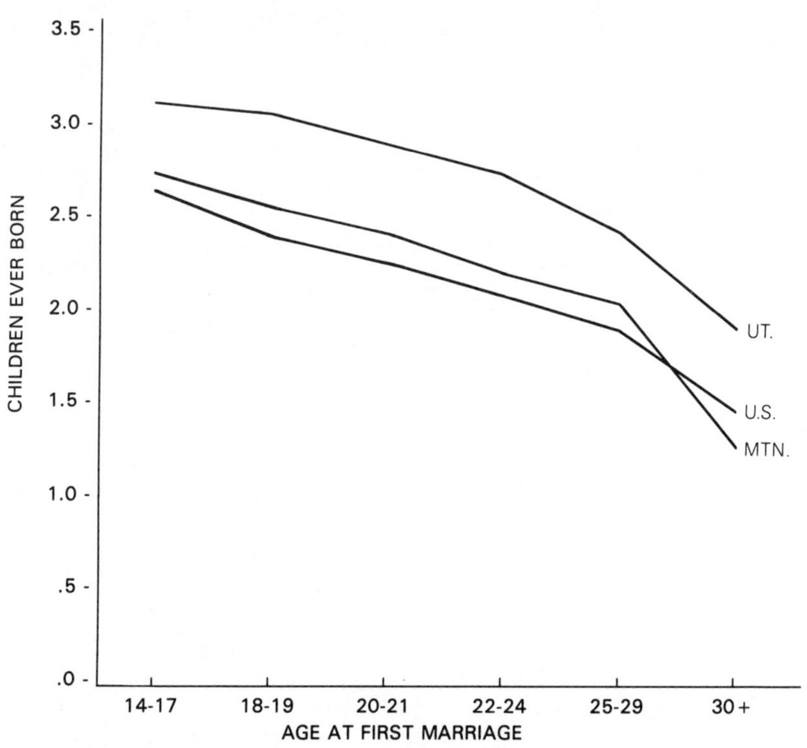

their children. Yet even in the earliest years of marriage, Utah rates are higher than those for the region or nation. Moreover, Utah's rate increases at a faster pace than do the other two rates. Apparently, Utahns begin bearing children at a faster pace and continue to do so throughout the childbearing years. As a result, they end up with families nearly one child larger than families in the Intermountain Region and more than one child larger than the national average. The pace of childbearing and ultimate family size are slightly greater in the Rocky Mountains than is true for the nation.

FIGURE 4.

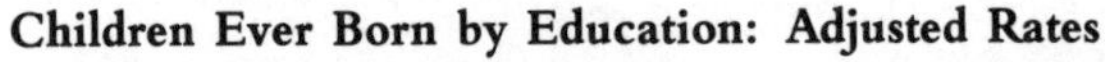

Children Ever Born by Education: Adjusted Rates

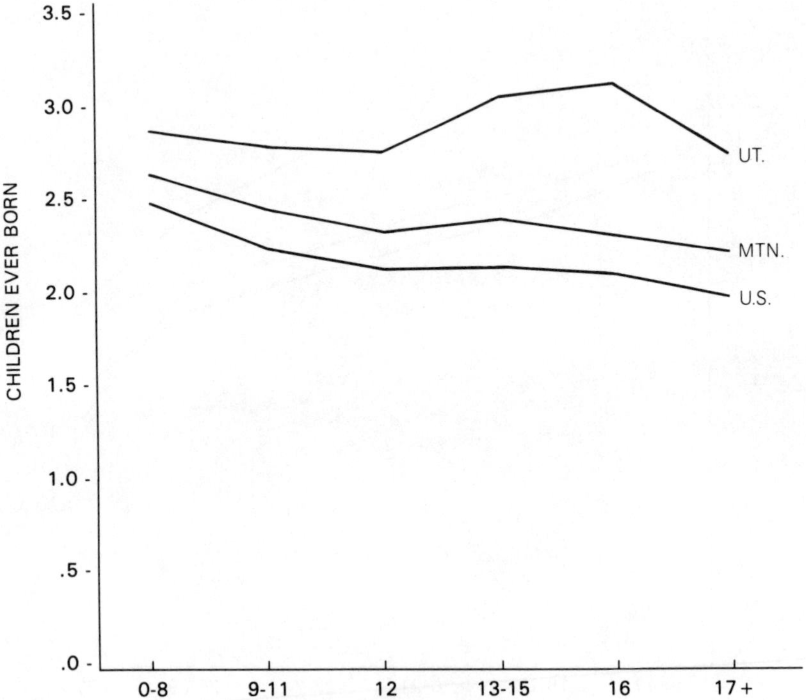

CHILDREN EVER BORN

3.5 -
3.0 -
2.5 -
2.0 -
1.5 -
1.0 -
.5 -
.0 -

UT.
MTN.
U.S.

0-8 9-11 12 13-15 16 17+

HIGHEST GRADE COMPLETED

The second variable considered is age at first marriage. The longer people wait to get married, the smaller their families. This is apparent in each of the three populations. While Utah fertility is higher than the region or nation regardless of the wife's age at marriage, it parallels regional and national fertility trends based upon age at marriage. For women married very young (before 18) or late (after 30) the Rocky Mountain states and the nation are similar, but for all other age groups the Rocky Mountains have a higher family size.

Generally, fertility decreases as the education of the wife increases. But this is not necessarily the case in Utah (see Figure 4). In fact, Utah women with undergraduate college experience have higher fertility rates than any other education group. Still, Utah fertility does drop off for women with post-graduate education. Utah fertility is higher than regional and national rates for each educational category, but the greatest differences are found among those with undergraduate college experience. For example, Utah women with no high school education have only about .4 children more than their national counterparts, whereas those with four years of college have nearly 1.0 children more than the national average. Evidently, education does not have the deterring effect on fertility in Utah that it is reported to have nationally. Rocky Mountain rates lie only slightly above national rates.

Female labor force participation is associated with lower fertility (Figure 5). This is especially true in Utah where the difference in fertility rates between those in and out of the labor force is .5 children. This difference is only .21 children in the Rocky Mountains and .17 children in the U.S. But again Utah women have higher fertility rates whether or not they are in the labor force.

The final variable considered is family income. The wife's income has been excluded from our analysis to remove the confounding effects of female employment and income. Except for a slight increase in fertility levels for the lowest income groups, the general pattern is for income to be positively associated with fertility: the better off a family is financially, the more likely it is to have additional children. This pattern is evident in the Rocky Mountains, the U.S., and in Utah. The one anomaly is that the highest income group ($50,000+) in the Rocky Mountain region actually has lower fertility rates than the next highest income group ($30,000 to $49,999). With this one exception the patterns for our three populations are similar. But even though the rates are parallel, Utah fertility is substantially higher at each income level than either the region or the nation.

TABLE 2.

Children Ever Born by Demographic Characteristics: Multiple Classification Analysis

CHARACTERISTIC	UTAH		ROCKY MOUNTAIN		U.S.	
	UNADJUSTED	ADJUSTED*	UNADJUSTED	ADJUSTED*	UNADJUSTED	ADJUSTED*
Marital Duration:						
0-1	.39	.61	.28	.44	.29	.48
2-3	1.00	1.11	.77	.86	.61	.73
4-5	1.65	1.67	1.21	1.27	1.05	1.14
6-7	2.19	2.12	1.59	1.62	1.40	1.44
8-9	2.64	2.54	1.92	1.92	1.67	1.71
10-14	3.11	3.03	2.27	2.26	2.04	2.05
15-19	3.72	3.68	2.72	2.69	2.47	2.44
20+	3.87	3.86	3.00	2.96	2.80	2.76
beta		.56		.47		.44
Age at First Marriage:						
14-17	3.28	3.19	2.88	2.68	2.79	2.66
18-19	3.07	3.06	2.50	2.50	2.35	2.38
20-21	2.86	2.89	2.30	2.33	2.23	2.24
22-24	2.63	2.68	2.06	2.14	2.02	2.07
25-29	2.44	2.41	1.86	1.92	1.86	1.86
30+	1.86	1.82	1.36	1.25	1.35	1.27
beta		.14		.18		.19

TABLE 2. CONTINUED

Education:						
0-8	3.52	2.89	3.06	2.58	2.87	2.49
9-11	3.08	2.77	2.66	2.45	2.50	2.26
12	2.91	2.77	2.34	2.25	2.18	2.17
13-15	2.80	3.02	2.15	2.32	1.97	2.15
16	2.76	3.08	1.94	2.25	1.76	2.09
17+	2.19	2.66	1.73	2.02	1.57	1.92
beta		.06		.06		.07
Labor Force:						
In	2.47	2.59	2.06	2.18	1.95	2.10
Out	3.18	3.09	2.52	2.39	2.41	2.27
beta		.12		.06		.05
Family Income (excluding wife):						
$ 1-999	2.40	2.83	1.97	2.18	1.94	2.03
2000-4999	2.22	2.63	2.16	2.09	2.15	1.96
5000-9999	2.29	2.67	1.97	2.10	2.02	2.03
10000-14999	2.38	2.82	1.99	2.21	1.90	2.09
15000-19999	2.77	2.87	2.17	2.27	1.98	2.13
20000-29999	3.26	2.93	2.50	2.39	2.31	2.26
30000-49999	3.67	3.06	2.81	2.51	2.65	2.44
50000+	3.80	3.15	2.72	2.41	2.74	2.53
beta		.06		.07		.09
R^2		.382		.293		.276
(N)	(12,520)		(17,064)		(36,207)	

*Adjusted for all other variables in the Table.

A closer examination of each variable gives some indication of its relative importance in accounting for variations in fertility. Marital duration is the single most important variable in each population, but it is more important in Utah than in the other two populations. This result, in turn, is a function of the link between marital duration and family size in higher fertility populations. Age at marriage is the second most important variable in each group. In Utah, labor force participation is the next most important variable, followed by education and income. In the Rocky Mountain region and the U.S.,

FIGURE 5.

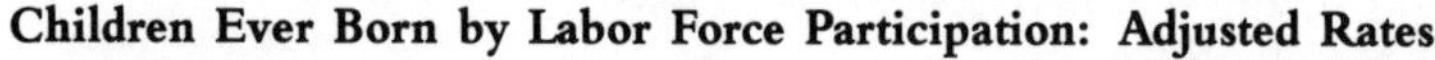

Children Ever Born by Labor Force Participation: Adjusted Rates

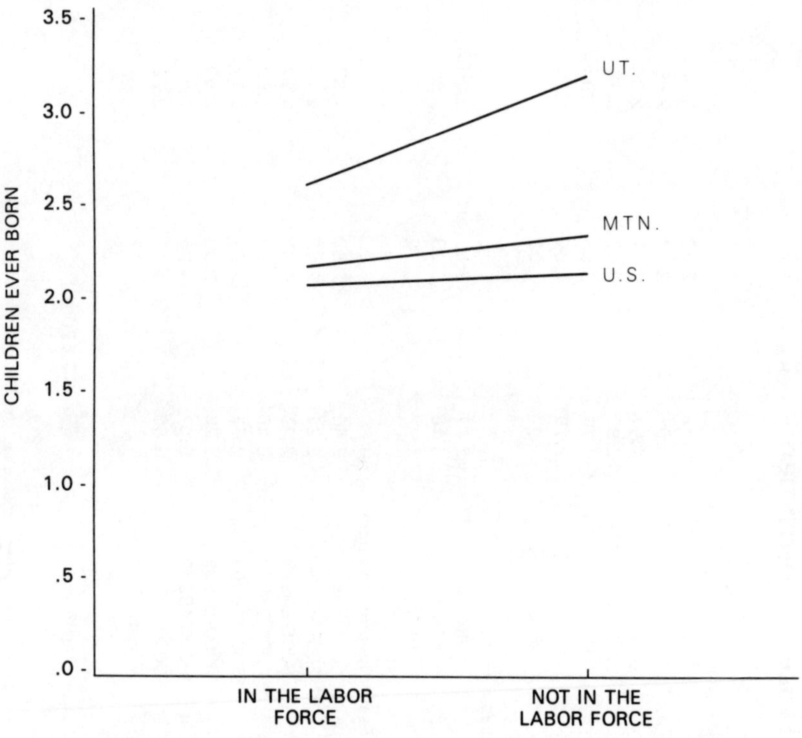

however, education, income and labor force participation are approximately equal in importance. Moreover, the influence of education and income is about equal in each of our three groups.

SUMMARY

Utah fertility is higher than regional or national levels in every category of every variable considered. Although the Rocky Mountain region has higher

FIGURE 6.

Children Ever Born by Family Income (excluding wife's income): Adjusted Rates

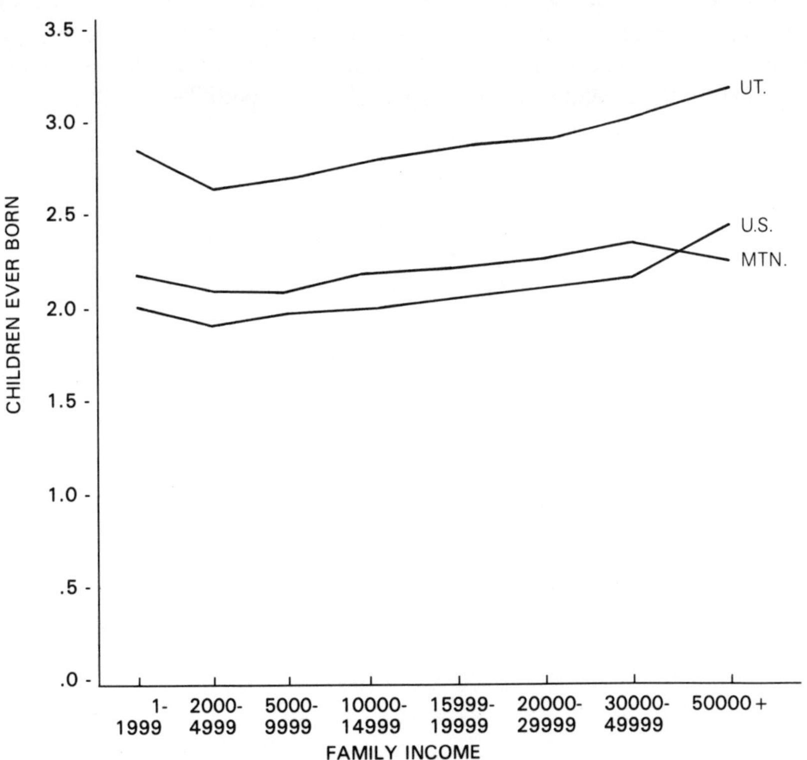

fertility than the nation, the gap between Utah and the region is much greater than that between the region and the nation. Because Utah continues to be distinctive, regardless of the variable considered, there may be some factor explaining Utah's high rate which we have not considered.

The pattern of relationships between variables is generally similar in Utah, the Rocky Mountains, and the nation. Two interesting exceptions are education and labor force participation. Labor force participation reduces fertility more in Utah than in the other two groups. Also, undergraduate college experience appears to enhance fertility in Utah but reduces fertility in the other populations.

As a possible explanation for these patterns, we point to the dominance of Mormon culture in Utah. The traditional family emphasis and associated high fertility rates of Mormons are well documented. The LDS church also encourages the desirability of educational achievement and traditional female roles. Thus it would not be surprising to find an educated female population with low labor force participation and high fertility. Additional information supporting this claim follows in other chapters, but incomplete data unfortunately make a comprehensive analysis almost impossible.

4. MIGRATION

Tim B. Heaton

Migration often serves to maintain a balance between regional resources and a population with different economic and social characteristics. Generally, immigration implies that an area is relatively well off, whereas emigration can indicate the reverse. In addition, the selective migration of people with particular attributes can alter the demographic composition of regions. In the first section of this chapter we examine patterns of migration in Utah, the Intermountain Region, and the nation, comparing metropolitan and nonmetropolitan areas. The second section focuses on the characteristics of immigrants as they compare with residents.

TRENDS

The volume and rate of migration from 1970 to 1980 are reported in Table 1. According to these figures the United States was witness to considerable immigration over the decade. These numbers, however, must be interpreted with some caution. Migration is computed as the population in 1980 minus the population in 1970, minus the total number of births, plus the total number of deaths between 1970 and 1980. In 1980 the census improved its procedures so that a larger fraction of the total population was counted. Because of this improvement in counting migration estimates are inflated. Unfortunately, more accurate migration estimates for each region are not available. Thus we must allow for some inflation of migration figures.

Nonetheless, migration rates indicate that Utah is experiencing much higher growth through migration than is the case nationally. And the Rocky Mountain region as a whole is growing at an even higher rate.

In Utah, as in the Rocky Mountains and the nation, metropolitan areas gained more immigrants in raw numbers than did nonmetropolitan areas. Of course, metropolitan areas had a higher fraction of the population to begin with. Migration rates indicate that in Utah, as in the nation, nonmetropolitan areas grew at a faster pace in terms of percentages than metropolitan areas. In the region, however, metropolitan areas had a slight advantage. Utah's metropolitan areas grew faster than the national average but slower than the regional average. In contrast, Utah's nonmetropolitan areas grew faster than either regional or national averages. In short, Utah attracted many immigrants, especially in its nonmetropolitan areas.

Migration rates for each county in Utah are reported in Table 2. A wide range of rates is evident. A handful of counties lost some residents, but a majority experienced an influx. Mining accounts for some of the fastest growing counties, but no simple explanation can be given for the diversity of migration patterns throughout the state.

Estimates of migration since 1980 yield conflicting reports. Federal figures indicate a net immigration of 51,000 people between 1980 and 1983 (Bureau of the Census 1984), but estimates based on state reports (Bureau of Health Statistics 1984 and 1985) suggest a more modest figure of 13,000. In either case, it appears that net immigration has slowed since 1980. There may even have been net emigration in recent years.

TABLE 1.

Volume and Rate of Net Immigration, 1970-80, in Metropolitan and Nonmetropolitan Areas

	UTAH	ROCKY MOUNTAIN REGION	U.S.
Volume (in 1000s)			
Total	149.0	1,879.0	9,252.0
Metropolitan	107.0	1,304.0	5,005.0
Nonmetropolitan	42.0	575.0	4,247.0
Rate (per 1,000)			
Total	11.8	13.4	4.3
Metropolitan	10.7	14.3	3.1
Nonmetroplitan	16.0	11.9	8.1
Percent Metropolitan	76.5	65.2	75.7

CHARACTERISTICS OF IMMIGRANTS

A comparison of immigrants to the population based on information from the 1980 census provides some insight as to who is being attracted to a given area. To the degree that immigrants differ from local residents the area in question is being altered by migration patterns. Unfortunately, census files do not contain as much information on emigrants. Thus, we will only be able to focus on immigrants. Immigrants are compared to the resident populations of Utah, the Rocky Mountains, and the U.S. on a variety of characteristics, and the results are presented in Table 3.

The ratio of immigrants to residents is .226 in Utah—about one immigrant for every five residents. This is lower than the ratio for the Rocky Mountains, .304, but higher than the national ratio, .130. These figures tend to support our observation that Utah attracts proportionately more people than the national average but fewer than its neighboring states.

Migration is most common among individuals in their 20s and early 30s, and Utah is no exception. In fact, Utah has a slightly higher percentage of immigrants in the 20 to 34 year-old age group (61.9 percent of men, 59.6

TABLE 2.

Rates of Net Immigration (per 1,000 Population), 1970-80, for Utah Counties

COUNTY	RATE	COUNTY	RATE
Beaver	−.4	Piute	5.4
Box Elder	−.3	Rich	10.1
Cache	7.4	Salt Lake	11.4
Carbon	21.6	San Juan	−.1
Daggett	−2.2	Sanpete	16.2
Davis	17.7	Sevier	21.4
Duchesne	24.3	Summit	39.5
Emery	58.2	Tooele	1.1
Garfield	1.4	Uintah	25.1
Grand	6.4	Utah	15.8
Iron	12.8	Wasatch	18.7
Juab	3.1	Washington	43.2
Kane	32.1	Wayne	12.8
Millard	9.1	Weber	−3.2
Morgan	3.8		

TABLE 3.

Demographic Characteristics of Immigrants (from a Different State) and Residents in Utah, The Rocky Mountain Region, and the United States, Males and Females

	UTAH				ROCKY MOUNTAIN				UNITED STATES			
	MALES		FEMALES		MALES		FEMALES		MALES		FEMALES	
CHARACTERISTICS	I	R	I	R	I	R	I	R	I	R	I	R
Age: 14-19	10.9	11.9	13.4	10.7	10.0	10.8	9.5	10.2	10.6	10.3	9.4	9.3
20-24	26.2	13.2	27.4	13.7	20.0	11.7	19.8	11.5	20.5	12.1	19.2	11.0
25-29	22.4	12.8	18.7	12.1	19.9	11.2	19.3	10.3	20.8	10.7	19.9	10.1
30-34	13.3	11.2	13.7	10.0	14.3	10.4	13.7	9.4	14.4	10.3	15.1	9.6
35-44	14.1	14.8	12.3	14.7	15.2	15.9	14.5	15.3	15.3	15.2	13.8	14.5
45-54	7.1	12.7	6.2	12.7	7.7	14.3	7.8	13.3	7.8	14.3	8.0	13.6
55-64	3.4	12.0	3.7	11.2	6.8	12.5	8.0	13.2	5.4	13.5	6.9	13.8
65-74	1.7	7.5	3.0	8.9	4.7	8.5	4.4	9.7	3.9	8.7	4.6	10.5
75+	1.0	3.8	1.6	6.0	1.4	4.6	2.9	6.6	1.5	4.9	3.1	7.6
Total	100.0	100.0	100.0	100.0	100.0	100.0	100.0	100.0	100.0	100.0	100.0	100.0
Race (%): White	86.5	94.3	88.2	94.4	87.7	82.1	87.5	82.1	79.0	82.4	80.0	81.4
Black	2.5	.4	1.0	.4	2.9	2.0	2.4	1.9	8.0	10.4	7.2	11.6
Hispanic	5.0	3.5	3.9	3.2	6.5	12.3	6.1	12.4	7.5	5.5	7.0	5.3
American Indian	1.9	.8	2.3	1.0	1.3	3.0	1.6	2.9	.7	.6	.7	.5
Other	4.1	.9	4.6	.9	1.6	.6	2.4	.8	4.8	1.1	5.1	1.2
Total	100.0	100.0	100.0	100.0	100.0	100.0	100.0	100.0	100.0	100.0	100.0	100.0

TABLE 3. CONTINUED

Marital Status (%):												
Currently Married	59.1	69.5	57.5	65.4	57.1	65.8	61.6	60.8	55.1	63.5	58.8	56.1
Divorced/Separated	6.7	5.3	8.9	7.9	9.1	7.8	10.7	10.0	8.3	7.1	11.1	9.8
Widowed	.7	1.7	4.1	9.6	1.0	2.4	5.2	11.0	1.1	2.9	5.8	13.3
Never Married	33.5	23.5	29.5	17.1	32.8	24.0	22.6	18.2	35.5	26.6	24.3	20.7
Total	100.0	100.0	100.0	100.0	100.0	100.0	100.0	100.0	100.0	100.0	100.0	100.0
Education (%):												
0-8	4.5	6.0	4.9	6.0	6.1	12.3	5.4	11.3	8.5	16.5	9.8	15.9
9-11	11.6	20.3	13.7	19.6	12.9	19.1	14.4	19.2	12.7	20.2	13.6	20.7
12	28.8	32.1	32.7	40.8	31.9	32.8	37.3	39.2	30.0	32.5	32.7	37.3
13-15	31.6	23.2	32.1	22.8	25.6	19.2	24.4	19.3	21.6	15.8	23.6	15.6
16	11.3	8.8	11.3	7.3	11.0	8.4	11.6	6.7	13.0	7.6	12.4	6.4
17+	12.3	9.6	5.2	3.4	12.4	8.2	6.9	4.4	14.1	7.3	7.8	4.1
Total	100.0	100.0	100.0	100.0	100.0	100.0	100.0	100.0	100.0	100.0	100.0	100.0
Employment (%):												
Labor Force	68.9	75.9	46.9	46.0	66.6	71.6	49.4	46.9	63.5	69.2	48.6	45.9
Military	5.6	.3	2.9	2.6	8.1	.5	.8	0.0	11.2	.4	1.2	0.0
Unemployed	4.8	4.2	.4	0.0	5.1	4.1	3.8	2.6	4.6	4.8	4.1	3.2
Not in Labor Force	20.8	19.7	49.8	51.4	20.3	23.8	46.0	50.4	20.7	25.5	46.1	50.8
Total	100.0	100.0	100.0	100.0	100.0	100.0	100.0	100.0	100.0	100.0	100.0	100.0
Occupation (%):												
Managerial/Prof.	25.0	22.7	20.1	18.3	25.8	22.0	22.9	18.7	30.7	19.8	23.9	19.0
Tech, Sales, Support	20.3	18.4	44.5	46.8	20.2	17.0	44.9	46.6	19.3	17.8	43.5	43.8
Service	12.2	8.5	21.8	19.7	11.7	10.3	21.9	21.9	10.2	10.1	19.4	20.1

TABLE 3. CONTINUED

Farming	3.1	4.0	1.1	1.0	3.8	7.7	1.1	1.6	3.4	5.2	1.0	1.3
Production, Craft, Labor, Operators	39.4	46.4	12.6	14.3	38.5	43.0	9.1	11.2	36.4	47.2	12.3	15.9
Total	100.0	100.0	100.0	100.0	100.0	100.0	100.0	100.0	100.0	100.0	100.0	100.0
Industry (%):												
Agriculture	3.6	4.1	1.3	1.2	4.4	7.7	1.6	2.4	3.6	4.9	1.3	1.5
Mining	4.4	4.5	.3	.5	4.9	4.4	.7	1.0	1.8	1.5	.3	.3
Construction	11.2	12.8	1.9	1.5	12.1	13.5	1.8	1.7	9.7	10.3	1.2	1.2
Manufacturing	17.0	16.9	11.4	13.2	15.4	14.4	9.2	9.9	23.7	27.0	14.7	17.7
Transportation, Communication, Utilities	7.5	10.5	3.7	3.7	8.0	9.6	3.9	4.3	8.0	9.6	3.7	3.8
Trade	20.8	18.9	26.7	27.7	19.6	18.8	25.8	26.3	19.1	19.2	25.0	23.9
Finance, Business, Personal Service	11.0	9.8	16.0	16.5	14.6	11.6	21.0	18.1	12.7	10.4	17.1	16.3
Entertainment, Recreation	1.2	1.2	1.6	1.3	2.4	1.7	2.3	1.9	1.9	1.2	1.3	1.1
Prof., Public Adm.	23.5	21.2	37.1	34.4	18.6	18.3	33.6	34.4	19.5	15.8	35.5	34.3
Total	100.0	100.0	100.0	100.0	100.0	100.0	100.0	100.0	100.0	100.0	100.0	100.0
Income (%):												
$ 1- 1999	9.8	7.1	29.9	23.7	7.1	7.7	21.8	21.6	8.9	7.6	21.6	19.4
2000- 4999	16.5	11.5	28.7	28.9	13.8	12.7	27.2	28.3	12.4	13.8	28.3	28.8
5000- 9999	21.7	17.2	26.2	27.4	23.1	18.6	30.1	26.3	24.3	18.9	28.4	27.6
10000-14999	18.6	17.2	10.5	12.6	19.2	17.2	13.3	14.5	17.8	17.4	13.2	14.5
15000-19999	13.3	17.6	2.9	4.8	12.9	15.4	4.6	5.8	12.8	15.1	5.2	5.7
20000-29999	12.7	20.2	1.2	2.0	15.1	18.6	2.2	2.7	14.3	17.6	2.5	3.0
30000-49999	6.1	7.2	.3	.4	6.8	7.1	.5	.6	6.8	6.9	.5	.7
50000+	1.3	2.0	.2	.2	1.9	2.5	.4	.2	2.6	2.6	.3	.3
Total	100.0	100.0	100.0	100.0	100.0	100.0	100.0	100.0	100.0	100.0	100.0	100.0

TABLE 3. CONTINUED

Residence (%):												
Metropolitan	87.0	85.7	87.3	85.5	67.2	60.2	67.8	61.7	78.7	74.0	78.6	75.1
Nonmetropolitan	13.0	14.3	12.7	14.5	32.8	39.8	32.2	38.3	21.3	26.0	21.4	24.9
Total	100.0	100.0	100.0	100.0	100.0	100.0	100.0	100.0	100.0	100.0	100.0	100.0
Return Migrant (%):												
No	96.0	—	96.6	—					97.9	—	98.4	—
Yes	4.0	—	3.4	—					2.1	—	1.6	—
Total	100.0		100.0						100.0		100.0	

The I column is for immigrants; the R column is for residents.

percent of women) than the region (54.2 percent of men, 52.8 percent of women) or the nation (55.7 percent of men, 54.2 percent of women). Although Utah has been termed a good retirement state, it attracts a proportionately lower percentage of immigrants in the older age groups.

Just as Utah is ethnically homogeneous (i.e., white nonhispanic), so are most of its immigrants. Over 86 percent are white nonhispanic. Still, minority immigrants, including blacks, Hispanics, American Indians, and other ethnic groups, actually comprise a larger percentage of the total immigrant population than they do of the state's resident population. This is an interesting contrast to the Rocky Mountain region where only blacks and Asians are overly represented. Another pattern is observed nationally where Hispanics and others are overly represented.

Regionally and nationally, immigrants are more likely than residents to be unmarried and are somewhat more likely to be divorced or separated. Utah, though not unique in this regard, is unusual in one respect: 12.4 percent more immigrant females have never been married than is true for residents. This compares to 4.4 percent for the Rocky Mountains and 3.6 percent for the nation. Part of this is because the percentage of residents who have never married is lower in Utah than regionally or nationally, but immigrants to Utah are actually more likely to have never been married than immigrants elsewhere. Thus, immigration is increasing the proportion of single, never married females in the state.

On the average, immigrants tend to be better educated than residents. This can be observed in Utah, the region, and the nation. In fact, a larger portion of immigrants to Utah have had some college experience than immigrants regionally and nationally. The percentage of male immigrants to Utah with college experience is 55.2 compared to 49.0 for the Rocky Mountains and 48.7 across the country. The comparable percentages for women are 48.6 in Utah, 42.9 in the Rocky Mountains, and 43.8 in the nation. But if one focuses only on those with four or more years of college, Utah does not rank above the region or the nation. In fact, Utah does not appear to be highly attractive to immigrants with post-graduate experience.

In terms of employment, male immigrants to Utah are similar to their regional and national counterparts. The one difference is that military employment is less common and civilian employment more common among Utah migrants. The reverse is true for female migrants: those coming to Utah are relatively (when compared to the state and region) more inclined to be employed in the military than in the civilian labor force. Female immigrants to Utah are also less likely to report being unemployed but are more apt to be out of the labor force than their regional and national counterparts.

Corresponding to their higher educational achievement, immigrants are more likely to be in professional occupations than residents. But immigrants to Utah and the Rocky Mountains are less likely to be professionals than is the case nationally. The more immigrants tend to be professionals, the less likely they are to be in blue collar occupations. This is more noticeable in Utah and the Rocky Mountains, however, than is true nationally. Overall, occupational differences in migration are not large.

Industries employing immigrants reflect areas of the economy which are growing. A comparison of immigrants by industry indicates rough similarities among the state, the region, and the nation. Mining and construction are over-represented among migrants to Utah and the Rocky Mountains compared to the national average. Also, Utah immigrants are over-represented in professional services and public administration. Manufacturing is less common among immigrants to Utah and to the region than for the nation as a whole. In comparing immigrants with residents, professional service and public administration appear to be growing sectors in Utah. But transportation, communications, and utilities are areas where the influx of immigrants is higher than the percentage of residents in the same industry. Still, these differences are not large, suggesting that the state's industrial structure is not being dramatically altered by immigration.

Utah immigrants do not compare favorably with other groups in terms of income. For example, 20.1 percent of the men moving to Utah reported incomes greater than $20,000. This compares with 23.8 percent in the Rocky Mountains and with 23.7 percent in the nation. Of female immigrants, 15.1 percent of those moving to Utah had incomes greater than $10,000 compared to 21.0 percent regionally and to 21.7 percent nationally. Moreover, in Utah the gap between immigrant and resident income is greater than in the Rocky Mountains or the nation. For example, among Utah men the percentage of immigrants reporting an income less than $15,000 is 12.6 points greater than for residents. This difference is only 7.0 percentage points for the Rocky Mountains and 5.7 percentage points for the United States as a whole. For women, a similar gap exists which is greater for Utah than for the region or nation. In short, Utah does not appear to do as well in attracting immigrants with higher incomes as do other states in the Rocky Mountains or in the nation as a whole.

Immigrants to Utah overwhelmingly select metropolitan destinations: nearly 90 percent moved to one or another of the state's major urban centers. This percentage is even greater than those for the nation and substantially larger (by 20 percentage points) than for the Rocky Mountains, and reflects the urban character of Utah's population. In fact, the destination of immigrants to Utah more closely corresponds to the distribution of residents than is the case for either the region or the nation.

Finally, in considering return migration (i.e., migration to one's state of birth), fewer than 5 percent of Utah's immigrants are returnees. However, this is about twice the national rate. Perhaps because of its position as the cultural center of Mormonism, Utah has an above average rate of return migration.

SUMMARY

Utah has been growing, in part, because of its ability to attract immigrants. Migration is substantially higher in Utah than nationally but a little lower than in the Rocky Mountain region. Mining, more than any other single factor, accounts for the rapid growth in some Utah counties. Growth due to migration has slowed since 1980. Immigrants to Utah are different from residents in some respects. For example, they are younger, less ethnically homogeneous, more apt to be single, more highly educated, and more likely to have professional occupations. But in terms of income, immigrants to Utah do not compare favorably with immigrants to other states. Utah appears to be a desirable destination for native Utahns who are living outside the state. In sum, while broad similarities between Utah and the region exist, several distinctive patterns can nonetheless be observed.

REFERENCES

Bureau of the Census. *Estimates of the Population of Utah Counties and Metropolitan Areas. Current Population Reports, Series P. 26, No. 83-44C*. Washington, D.C.: U.S. Government Printing Office, 1984.

Utah Bureau of Health Statistics. *Utah Vital Statistics*. Salt Lake City: Utah Department of Health, 1984.

_____. *Utah Vital Statistics*. Salt Lake City: Utah Department of Health, 1985.

5.

MORTALITY

James E. Smith

Low mortality, like high fertility, is another of the distinctive features of Utah's population. In 1980 the Utah crude death rate, or CDR, was 5.6 deaths per 1,000 residents, the third lowest in the United States. As shown in Table 1, most states' CDRs ranged from 8.0 to 10.0, fully 40 percent higher than Utah's.

Utah's CDRs have been significantly lower than overall U.S. crude death rates for at least four decades, as indicated in Figure 1. Although the trends in CDRs, pictured in Figure 1, might give the impression that there has been little reduction in mortality during this period, this is not the case. The problem is that CDRs are not good indicators of actual life expectancy in a population.

In the absence of life expectancy figures for Utah, the infant mortality rate can be used to infer levels and trends in life expectancy. Reductions in infant mortality are strongly correlated with improvements in life expectancy in the U.S. during the period from 1940 to 1980. Therefore, we can appropriately infer from the infant mortality trends presented in Figure 1 that life expectancy in Utah has been consistently higher than for the U.S. and has followed the same increasing trend.

The most obvious reason for Utah's low mortality is the lower risk of death from certain major diseases. Death rates according to cause are illustrated for Utah, the mountain states, and the U.S. in Figure 2. Utah death rates for the two leading causes of death, heart disease and cancer (i.e., malignant neoplasms), are more than 40 percent lower than U.S. rates. Moreover, for each of the ten leading causes of death, except suicide, the Utah rate is lower than the U.S. rate.

Part of the reason for Utah's low death rates is its location among the mountain states. For all but three of the ten leading causes of death, mountain states death rates are lower than U.S. rates. And for the three leading causes of death, rates for the mountain states are considerably lower than U.S. rates. Thus, Utah's low mortality is partly due to favorable conditions in the Mountain Region and partly to favorable conditions within Utah itself.

One apparent anomaly in Utah's otherwise enviable mortality situation is the state's high suicide rate. However, it should be noted that the mountain states suicide rate exceeds both U.S. and Utah rates. This suggests that whatever factors affect suicide rates in the mountain states also operate in Utah, albeit to a lesser extent.

From this regional and national comparison of death rates we can see that Utah's death rates are always lower than those for the mountain states and are usually lower than U.S. death rates. For the two leading causes of death, heart disease and cancer, Utah death rates are significantly lower than both mountain states and U.S. rates, although these remain the leading causes of death within Utah. Only in the case of suicide does Utah's rate exceed that for the U.S., though it still does not reach the mountain states rate.

The death rates presented so far do not take into account the different population compositions of Utah, the mountain states, and the U.S. With the youngest population of any state, Utah would be expected to have a low death rate for heart disease because a large percentage of Utah's population is children and young adults. On the other hand, Utah's infant death rate (i.e., infant

TABLE 1.

Distribution of State Crude Death Rates, 1980

DC	11.	1																
MO, PA, FL	10.	1	4	7														
	9.	0	0	1	1	2	2	3	3	3	4	4	5	6	6	8	8	9	9
	8.	1	1	1	1	2	2	3	3	5	5	5	6	6	7	8	9		
	7.	0	2	4	6	7	9	9	9										
CO, WY	6.	6	9																
HI, UT	5.	2	6																
AK	4.	3																	

Digits to right of vertical line are tenths; e.g. Alaska = 4.3, Utah = 5.6. Four states have CDRs of 8.1, etc.
Source: United States Bureau of the Census 1983, 76.

deaths per total population, as opposed to infant mortality rate which is infant deaths compare to infant births) is 12.9 per 100,000 residents, the highest in the nation, because infants make up such a large part of the state's population.

One way to take population composition into account when measuring mortality is to use age-specific death rates, measuring one death rate for each age group for each cause of death. But it can be cumbersome to work with so many different death rates, especially when comparing rates among populations. A single age-adjusted rate can be computed from a set of age-specific rates to simplify comparisons. But in any case, it is necessary to begin by examining mortality according to age.

Table 2 presents Utah's death rates for the five leading causes of death for each age group and for all age groups combined. Here, it is easy to see a general progression from certain causes of death in infancy to other causes as individuals age. Not surprisingly, "problems of early infancy"

FIGURE 1.

Mortality Trends, Utah and U.S., 1940-1980

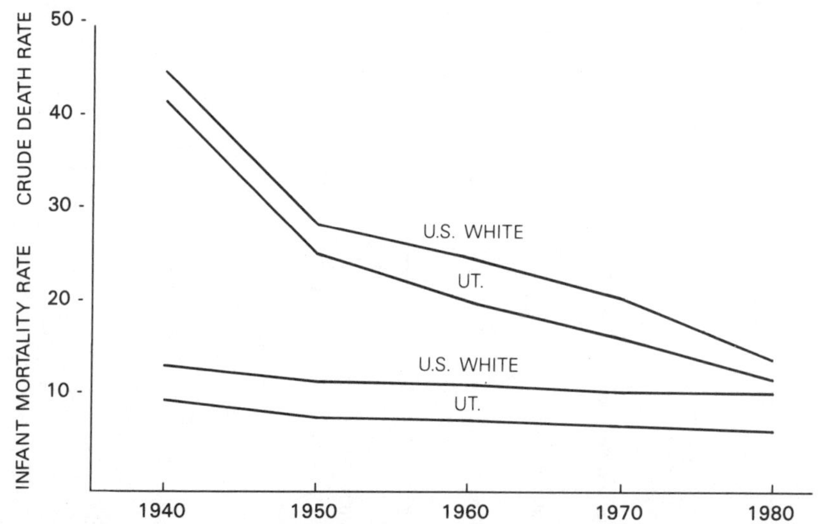

Source: *Statistical Abstract of the United States.*

FIGURE 2.

Comparison of Utah, Mountain States, and U.S. Mortality, Ten Leading Causes of Death, 1980

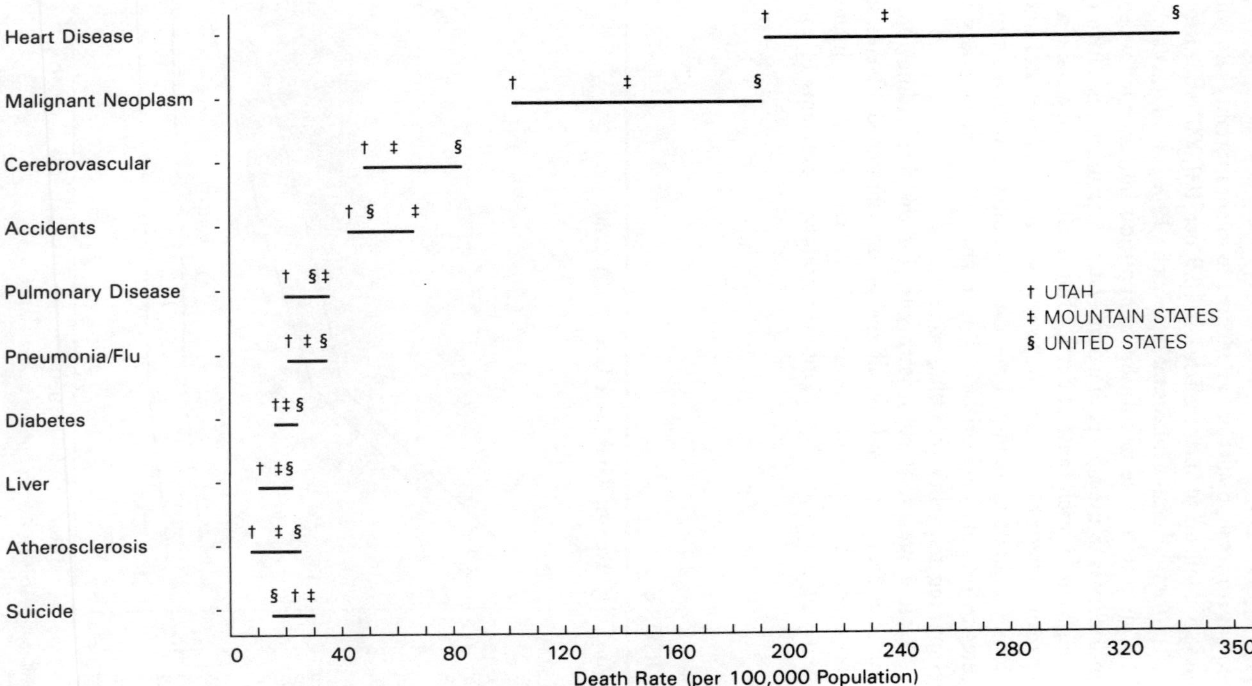

TABLE 2.

Rank and Death Rate (per 100,000) of Leading Causes of Death, by Age Group, Utah, 1978-82

	AGE GROUP						
	LESS THAN 1 YR	1-14 YR	15-24 YR	25-44 YR	45-64 YR	65+ YR	ALL AGES
Problems of early infancy	1 630.8						5 18.3
Congenital Anomalies	2 266.6	3 4.6					
Non motor vehicle accidents	3 20.4	1 10.5	3 14.0	5 15.3	4 23.0	—	4 19.9
Pneumonia/flu	4 15.6					4 182.2	
Infectious and parasitic	5 8.5						
Motor vehicle accidents		2 8.9	1 42.9	1 25.1			3 23.7
Cancer		4 3.5	5 5.4	2 21.1	2 195.3	2 779.3	2 94.3
Homicide		5 1.7	4 5.8				
Suicide			2 14.1	3 19.4			
Heart/Stroke				4 16.0	1 290.1	1 2566.2	1 239.0
Liver					3 31.1		
Pulmonary					5 23.0	3 186.0	
Diabetes						5 108.4	
	941.9	29.2	82.2	96.9	562.5	3822.1	

Source: Utah Department of Health 1984, 35.

and "congenital anomalies" disappear as leading causes of death after the youngest ages. In contrast, non-motor-vehicle accidents remain among the five leading causes of death until age 64. Pneumonia and influenza are major causes of infant mortality, but disappear until old age when they emerge again.

The leading causes of death for certain "middle age groups," as identified in Table 2, are motor vehicle accidents (ages 1-44), homicide (ages 1-24), suicide (ages 15-44), and liver disease (ages 45-64). But none of these are among the five leading causes of death among infants (under 1 year) or the elderly (65 years or more). Significantly, each of these leading causes of death has a strong behavioral component, such as liver disease, which is caused mainly by alcohol consumption. It is not surprising that in the ages when one's biological constitution is the strongest that these "behavioral" factors should emerge as leading causes of death.

Of the two overall leading causes of death (cancer and heart disease/stroke), cancer surfaces the earliest as a leading cause. Cancer is ranked fourth or fifth among the young (ages 1-24), then becomes the second leading cause of death for all subsequent ages. Heart disease, on the other hand, emerges in later years but quickly assumes first rank by age 45 and continues to be the leading cause of death thereafter.

TABLE 3.

Expected Years of Life Lost to Major Causes of Death, Utah, 1981

CAUSE OF DEATH	NUMBER OF DEATHS	EXPECTED YEARS OF LIFE LOST PER DEATH*	PERCENT OF TOTAL YEARS OF LIFE LOST*
All causes	8502	20.6	100.0
Heart/Stroke	3606	12.1	24.9
Cancer	1460	18.0	15.0
MV accidents	325	47.1	8.8
Other accidents	273	34.9	5.4
Pulmonary	90	16.5	.9
Pneumonia/Flu	232	13.1	1.7
Diabetes	184	15.9	1.7
Liver	110	23.2	1.5
Suicide	203	38.6	4.5

Source: Utah State Department of Health 1984, 20.

One way to summarize the impact of various causes of death is to look at expected years of life lost due to each cause. This is done with approximate computations in Table 3. The expected years of life lost per death is the average number of years a person who died from a specific cause would have otherwise been expected to live according to a life table. (A more precise computation would require that an entirely new life table be produced by excluding the specific cause of death and then performing the computation.)

In terms of expected numbers of years of life lost per death, accidents (motor vehicle and other) and suicide are the leading causes. This follows from the fact that they are leading causes of death in the younger to middle age groups where expected years of remaining life is otherwise high.

In contrast, heart disease/stroke, which has been termed the leading cause of death nationally, has the least impact in terms of shortening an individual's life. Only about twelve years of life are lost on the average when a person dies of heart disease or a stroke. This number would undoubtedly be higher if heart disease were considered independently of strokes, but such data are not available. In any case, it is not surprising that both heart disease/stroke and cancer rank low in terms of the numbers of years of life lost per death since these types of death tend to occur at older ages.

Another perspective on years of life lost is presented in Table 3. The percentage of years lost expresses the loss in years due to a given cause as a percentage of the total number of years lost for all deaths. Heart disease/stroke and cancer appear as the leading causes of death because the sheer numbers of deaths due to each of these offset the relatively low number of years of life lost per death.

The analysis presented in Table 3 demonstrates that there is no single "calculus of mortality" which is satisfactory for all purposes. The policy maker, for example, faces a dilemma in trying to decide whether to invest resources in reducing accidental and suicide deaths because of the high number of expected years of life lost *per death*, or whether to invest in the reduction of heart/stroke and cancer deaths because of the large total number of years of life lost to these causes. Viewing Utah mortality from various demographic perspectives helps to illuminate but not to resolve these questions.

Still another perspective from which one can analyze Utah's mortality is that of mortality differentials among the different population groups. The two major mortality differentials discussed by demographers are those of gender and race.

In the United States, as in all human populations, male death rates generally exceed those for females. As shown in Table 4, U.S. white male mortality for all causes combined is 1.8 times higher than for females. For Utah, the male/female mortality ratio is only 1.26. Thus, while males have higher mortality rates than females in both U.S. and Utah populations, they are relatively low in Utah. It should be noted that the Utah ratios in Table 4 are not age adjusted, whereas those for the U.S. are. Adjusting for age would cause the Utah ratio to be slightly higher.

In the U.S. the most dramatic male/female mortality differentials are for accidental deaths and suicides, with pulmonary diseases next. In Utah the suicide and pulmonary disease ratios are even higher, but the ratios for accidental deaths are lower. Nevertheless, the general U.S. pattern of higher male mortality rates for these causes holds true for Utah.

Because more deaths in the U.S. are caused by heart disease/stroke than any other cause, this plays a leading role in depressing Utah's sex differentials. Among U.S. whites, 89 percent more males than females die because of heart disease/stroke, whereas in Utah the excess is only 16 percent. Likewise,

TABLE 4.

Ratio of Male to Female Mortality Rates, Utah (1978-82) and U.S. (1981)

	UTAH	U.S. WHITE AGE-ADJUSTED
All causes	1.26	1.80
Heart/Stroke	1.16	1.89
Cancer	1.12	1.48
MV accidents	2.21	2.85
Other accidents	2.27	3.10
Pulmonary	3.05	2.73
Pneumonia/Flu	1.02	1.73
Diabetes	.71	1.11
Liver	1.79	2.21
Suicide	4.00	3.15

Source: National Center for Health Statistics 1984, Table 7; Utah Department of Health 1984, Table 12.

48 percent more men than women die from cancer in the U.S. compared to only 12 percent in Utah.

It is difficult to determine the specific reasons for Utah's reduced male/female mortality ratios for these two leading causes of death (i.e., heart disease/stroke). It may have something to do with the behavioral components of these diseases, particularly tobacco consumption, which is low in Utah because of the state's largely Mormon population. This causes death rates due to these to be low (see Figure 1) and, at the same time, eliminates much of the male/female behavioral differences for smoking. These speculations require further analysis than we can present here.

Racial differences in death are also known to be important in the U.S. One feature of U.S. black/white mortality differentials is that when age adjustments are not made it appears that blacks have the same overall mortality rate as whites, and have lower mortality rates for the major causes (see Table 5). In fact, there are significant differences in the age structures of the U.S. black and white populations, with blacks typically being younger than whites. Thus, seemingly equal mortality rates between blacks and whites are more a function of the young age of the black population than any real equality in death rates.

TABLE 5.

Ratio of Black to White Mortality Rates, Utah (1978-82) and U.S. (1981)

	UTAH	U.S. UNADJUSTED	U.S. AGE-ADJUSTED
Male			
All causes	.82	1.03	1.47
Heart/Stroke	.62	.99	1.26
Cancer	.84	.82	1.47
Female			
All causes	1.00	.88	1.49
Heart/Stroke	.64	.79	1.54
Cancer	1.45	.79	1.19

Source: National Center for Health Statistics 1984, Table 7; Utah Department of Health 1984, Table 12.

Adjusted and unadjusted black/white mortality ratios are presented in Table 5 for the U.S. together with unadjusted ratios for Utah. Because of the small number of blacks in Utah, and therefore the small number of black deaths, only the major causes of death can be represented. It appears that black males have an advantage in Utah, with an overall death rate about 18 percent lower than whites, whereas in the U.S. the unadjusted ratio shows blacks at about the same mortality level as whites. (Age adjusted black/white ratios cannot be computed from present Utah data.)

For black females mortality in Utah appears to be worse, relative to whites, than in the U.S. This is largely due to the high incidence of cancer among Utah's black women. It is unclear why black females in particular should experience 45 percent more deaths due to cancer than white females in Utah, and it is unlikely that adjustments for age would significantly reduce this ratio. It is possible that Utah's black population tends to belong to religious denominations other than Mormonism and that the state's predominantly Mormon female population is more likely than Utah's men to adhere to Mormon behavioral norms. Black women would therefore stand out more than black men in terms of smoking and cancer. Again, however, these speculations require analyses beyond the scope of this chapter.

TABLE 6.

Indian and Non-Indian Infant Mortality Rates (Per 10,000 Live Births), Utah, 1968-75

	INFANT MORTALITY RATE		
YEAR	NON-INDIAN	INDIAN	INDIAN LIVE BIRTHS
1968	16.8	73.9	352
1969	15.3	44.8	357
1970	14.9	22.9	393
1971	13.9	13.6	440
1972	13.2	25.5	431
1973	12.5	21.8	451
1974	11.8	34.9	487
1975	12.8	33.8	503

Source: Meaux 1978, 16.

Another important racial difference in Utah is that of the state's Indian and non-Indian populations. Data on Indian mortality in Utah are rare and deal with a relatively small population. But for one important indicator of life expectancy—infant mortality rates—Indian and non-Indian data can be compared. Table 6 shows that Utah's Indian population is seriously disadvantaged in terms of life expectancy. In general, Indian infant mortality rates are two to three times higher than non-Indian rates.

Although Utah mortality compares favorably with that of the mountain states and the U.S., one should not forget that there are significant minorities, such as blacks and Indians, who do not benefit from Utah's generally advantageous mortality situation. This does not mean that they are worse off in Utah than in other parts of the country, only that they are not better off in Utah relative to the majority population.

In summary, Utah's overall mortality level is low. This is due in part to the young age of Utah's population and partly to low risks of death due to leading diseases, such as heart disease/stroke and cancer. For all leading causes of death, Utah's mortality is lower than that of the mountain states and, with the exception of suicide, than that of the U.S. Age patterns of mortality are generally the same in Utah as in the U.S. Sex differences follow the same patterns as they do nationally but with more equal male/female mortality ratios. Racial differences also exist in Utah, our limited data revealing more favorable mortality conditions for whites than for black or Indian minorities.

REFERENCES

Meaux, Ele. *Health Status of American Indians in Utah as Indicated by Vital Statistics Data, Supplement 1973-75*. Salt Lake City: Utah State Division of Health, 1978.

National Center for Health Statistics. ''Advanced Report, Final Mortality Statistics, 1981.'' *Monthly Vital Statistics Report 33 (3), Supp. DHHS Pub. No. (PHS) 84-1120*. Hyattsville, MD: Public Health Service, 22 June 1984.

U.S. Bureau of the Census. *Statistical Abstract of the United States, 1984*. 104th Edition. Washington, D.C.: 1983.

_____. *Statistical Abstract of the United States, 1985*. 105th Edition. Washington, D.C.: 1984.

Utah Department of Health. *A Statement of Health Policy*. Salt Lake City: Utah Department of Health, 1984.

6.
FAMILY FORMATION

Stephen J. Bahr

The family is, without question, ɔne of our most fundamental social institutions. In every society, some type of family system regulated by custom and law exists (Lee 1977; Leslie 1982). The most socially acceptable way to begin a family is by a public ritual, or marriage ceremony. Family relationships may also be formed by cohabitation or by bearing children.

Many cohabiting couples function in marriage-like situations even though they have not gone through the legal process of marriage. In recent years the number of cohabiting couples in the United States has increased substantially. According to recent census data, almost two million "unmarried couples" were living in the United States in 1984—almost four times as many as in 1970 (U.S. Bureau of the Census, *Statistical Abstract*, 1984).

Another way in which families are formed is through the birth of a child. Parents, whether married or not, are the legal guardians of their children and are responsible for their care and socialization. The federal government treats this parent-child unit as a family having the same rights and legal protections as a family created by marriage (Brieland and Lemmon 1985).

This chapter examines family formation in Utah and compares it to family formation in the Intermountain Region and in the United States.

Three demographic variables are related to family formation: age, gender, and ethnic group. As age increases, so does the number of people who marry and have children (U.S. Bureau of the Census 1976 and *American Women*, 1983). Women tend to marry at earlier ages than men (U.S. Bureau of the Census 1976). And blacks typically have higher fertility rates than whites (U.S. Bureau of the Census, *Statistical Abstract*, 1984). The data for this analysis are taken from the 1980 samples of the United States census published in 1983. Three different samples were used: a .1 percent sample of all persons in the United States; a 1 percent sample of all persons in the mountain states (i.e., Arizona,

Colorado, Idaho, Montana, Nevada, New Mexico, Utah, and Wyoming); and a 5 percent sample of adults in Utah. A complete description of the data can be found in the technical documentation published by the U.S. Bureau of the Census, *Population and Housing* (1983).

MARRIAGE

Table 1 shows the percentage of Utahns who have ever been married, according to gender, ethnic group, and age, as of 1980. For both sexes and all ethnic groups, approximately 95 percent marry sometime during their lives. Women marry earlier than men within all ethnic groups. For example, 8.6 percent of white males, ages 18-19, were married in 1980 compared to 26.5 percent of white females. However, this difference decreases with age. By age 40 there is no difference between the proportion of males and females who have ever married.

Hispanics marry at earlier ages than other ethnic groups, while whites have the second highest early marriage rate. For example, 30 percent of Hispanic women have married by age 19 compared to almost 27 percent among whites and only 7 percent among Asians. Almost 80 percent of Hispanic and white females have married by age 25 compared to about 67 percent among black and Asian women and just over 60 percent among Native American women. Among males, two-thirds of Hispanics, Native Americans, and whites have married by age 25 compared to one-half of the Asians and 42 percent of blacks.

Table 2 shows the percentage of intermountain residents who have been married at least once, according to gender, ethnic group, and age, for 1980. A comparison of Tables 1 and 2 reveals that marriage tends to occur earlier in Utah than in the Intermountain Region. For example, in Utah 26.5 percent of white females have married by age 19 compared to only 23 percent for intermountain females. Similarly, over 30 percent of Utah Hispanic females have married by age 19 compared to 21 percent in the Intermountain Region. By age 21 almost one-half of white females in Utah have married compared to 43 percent for the region.

Utah Asians contradict this trend. For both men and women, Asians in Utah tend to marry later than in the Intermountain Region. For example, only 7.4 percent of Asian females in Utah have married by age 19 compared to 21 percent of Asian females in the region.

For men and women over age 40, there is little difference among the ethnic groups or between Utah and the Intermountain Region, with one exception.

TABLE 1.

Percent Ever Married by Gender, Ethnic Group, and Age—Utah 1980

		AGE									
GENDER	ETHNIC GROUP	12-17	18-19	20-21	22-23	24-25	26-27	28-29	30-34	35-39	40 +
Male	White	0.8	8.6	30.4	50.5	67.6	78.6	84.4	91.3	95.5	97.1
	Black	—	7.4	3.8	38.5	42.1	64.3	90.0	92.0	84.6	93.0
	Native	—	9.4	21.7	42.3	68.4	65.0	83.3	87.0	95.5	96.3
	Asian	—	4.8	24.0	21.7	50.0	50.0	79.2	78.9	84.6	92.4
	Hispanic	1.3	10.3	25.4	55.1	68.7	76.6	88.5	90.1	88.3	96.0
Female	White	6.2	26.5	49.2	69.5	78.1	86.3	89.8	93.8	95.9	97.5
	Black	—	22.2	33.3	33.3	66.7	80.0	80.0	100.0	75.0	96.1
	Native	6.3	17.1	23.1	44.4	62.5	71.4	84.2	80.0	90.0	97.0
	Asian	5.0	7.4	24.1	54.8	67.9	84.0	88.5	90.9	94.1	96.0
	Hispanic	9.4	30.2	56.8	57.7	79.2	75.5	89.8	92.7	97.2	95.0

TABLE 2.

Percent Ever Married by Gender, Ethnic Group, and Age—Intermountain Region 1980

		AGE									
GENDER	ETHNIC GROUP	12-17	18-19	20-21	22-23	24-25	26-27	28-29	30-34	35-39	40+
Male	White	1.1	7.5	23.0	42.6	56.2	67.9	78.5	87.8	93.7	96.3
	Black	—	7.6	18.8	32.9	38.6	59.7	69.8	81.8	81.8	93.9
	Native	2.3	11.1	29.0	45.7	74.1	60.3	76.4	80.9	82.8	93.4
	Asian	—	—	22.7	29.2	30.8	60.0	66.7	87.0	96.6	94.7
	Hispanic	1.9	8.2	27.8	49.4	69.7	75.0	78.3	88.2	91.9	94.1
Female	White	5.5	23.0	43.3	62.8	73.2	83.2	87.3	92.5	96.2	84.4
	Black	1.7	13.6	20.0	41.5	65.5	74.5	80.0	84.7	95.4	96.5
	Native	5.6	19.8	43.0	53.1	67.2	76.9	81.8	87.7	84.5	95.4
	Asian	6.3	21.1	40.0	83.3	82.1	77.1	89.5	91.4	95.0	100.0
	Hispanic	9.1	21.1	42.5	63.5	75.8	80.9	86.9	92.3	95.4	96.2

TABLE 3.

Percent Ever Married by Gender, Ethnic Group, and Age—United States 1980

		AGE									
GENDER	ETHNIC GROUP	12-17	18-19	20-21	22-23	24-25	26-27	28-29	30-34	35-39	40+
Male	White	1.1	5.7	20.9	37.5	54.9	67.1	76.4	86.6	91.8	94.2
	Black	1.1	3.1	9.3	22.4	38.2	59.8	63.3	77.9	85.1	90.5
	Native	6.4	12.2	22.6	51.9	50.0	57.1	66.7	80.7	87.2	91.9
	Asian	—	—	7.2	17.9	46.2	48.8	66.7	82.0	90.0	93.1
	Hispanic	2.5	6.2	28.0	48.4	58.3	74.3	78.5	87.6	88.6	93.0
Female	White	4.6	18.8	37.4	58.5	69.8	80.4	86.5	91.3	94.7	94.8
	Black	1.6	7.2	20.8	34.6	52.4	59.9	68.5	79.0	86.3	92.4
	Native	6.1	37.2	39.3	40.9	70.8	75.0	82.6	88.3	93.6	92.2
	Asian	3.3	8.3	27.9	50.9	62.8	78.5	84.0	90.0	90.1	95.4
	Hispanic	7.9	23.1	42.7	57.3	75.2	80.3	82.5	88.1	92.8	93.3

More than 97 percent of white females in Utah over age 40 have been married compared to 84 percent in the Intermountain Region.

The percentage of couples ever married in the United States, according to gender, ethnic group, and age, is shown in Table 3. A comparison of Tables 2 and 3 reveals that early marriage tends to be more common in the Intermountain Region than in the United States. A comparison of Tables 1 and 3 reveals that teenage marriage occurs more frequently in Utah than in the United States. For example, almost 9 percent of white males in Utah have married by age 19 compared to less than 6 percent nationally. Similarly, 27 percent of white females in Utah have married by age 19 compared to less than 19 percent nationally. The exceptions to this trend are that Asian and Native American women in Utah marry later than nationally.

Again, these differences tend to decrease with time. By age 40 over 90 percent of all men and women in Utah and the United States have married. Still, the proportion who never marry is twice as high in the United States as in Utah. Among whites over age 40, 2.5 percent of Utah women have never married compared to 5.2 percent of United States females. For males, the comparable percentages are 2.9 for Utah and 5.8 for the United States.

REMARRIAGE

Remarriage is another way in which families are formed. Divorce rates increased dramatically during the 1960s and 1970s, and, consequently, remarriage has become common. Recent estimates indicate that over 40 percent of existing marriages will eventually end in divorce (Norton and Glick 1979; Preston 1975). For the past decade there have been more than a million divorces per year in the United States (National Center for Health Statistics 1986; U.S. Bureau of the Census, *Statistical Abstract*, 1984). Over three-fourths of divorced persons eventually remarry (Glick 1980), and in 20 percent of marriages at least one spouse has been divorced (Cherlin and McCarthy 1985).

Table 4 shows the percentage of ever married Utahns who have remarried, according to gender, race, and age. Remarriage rates appear similar for men and women, although men tend to remarry later than women. First marriage is also later for males than females, as shown in Table 1. It is also common for older men to marry younger women. Asians tend to remarry less frequently than other ethnic groups, while blacks and Native Americans remarry more often. For example, among black and Native American women, ages 30 to 34, 25 percent of those who have ever married have married at least twice. The comparable percentages for whites, Hispanics, and Asians are

TABLE 4.

Percent of Ever Married that have Remarried by Gender, Ethnic Group, and Age—Utah 1980

		AGE					
GENDER	ETHNIC GROUP	12-19	20-25	26-29	30-34	35-39	40+
Male	White	3.4	5.1	10.5	16.9	22.9	22.7
		(119)	(2083)	(2035)	(2295)	(1729)	(8273)
	Black	—	7.1	11.1	26.1	27.3	35.0
			(14)	(18)	(23)	(11)	(40)
	Native	—	10.3	8.7	15.0	23.8	34.6
			(29)	(23)	(20)	(21)	(52)
	Asian	—	0.0	15.2	13.3	4.5	9.1
			(19)	(33)	(45)	(22)	(110)
	Hispanic	—	2.8	9.5	21.1	23.5	24.4
			(107)	(95)	(109)	(68)	(238)
Female	White	3.5	7.2	14.4	20.4	22.2	22.5
		(431)	(2859)	(2116)	(2302)	(1753)	(9366)
	Black	—	0.0	0.0	25.0	—	34.7
			(12)	(12)	(12)		(49)
	Native	—	8.3	0.0	25.0	11.2	37.0
			(24)	(31)	(28)	(18)	(65)
	Asian	—	2.3	4.5	12.5	15.6	11.8
			(43)	(44)	(40)	(32)	(119)
	Hispanic	3.1	8.5	16.0	20.8	27.2	25.0
		(32)	(129)	(81)	(101)	(70)	(248)

TABLE 5.

Percent of Ever Married that have Remarried by Gender, Ethnic Group, and Age—Intermountain Region 1980

		AGE					
GENDER	ETHNIC GROUP	12-19	20-25	26-29	30-34	35-39	40 +
Male	White	4.2	6.5	13.2	20.6	26.0	25.7
		(142)	(2139)	(2513)	(3303)	(2699)	(14091)
	Black	—	9.2	9.5	22.3	26.6	34.0
			(65)	(74)	(99)	(60)	(262)
	Native	—	4.2	16.3	20.4	20.8	24.8
			(95)	(80)	(123)	(77)	(309)
	Asian	—	0.0	3.8	5.0	3.6	12.2
			(16)	(26)	(40)	(28)	(90)
Female	White	3.0	9.2	17.9	22.2	26.7	21.3
		(466)	(3137)	(2800)	(3431)	(2662)	(15727)
	Black	—	8.7	11.4	27.7	27.4	35.5
			(69)	(70)	(83)	(62)	(304)
	Native	9.5	9.9	20.2	17.8	28.1	25.2
		(21)	(111)	(104)	(107)	(82)	(353)
	Asian	—	6.0	4.5	15.7	31.6	16.2
			(50)	(44)	(64)	(38)	(154)
	Hispanic	0.0	8.2	13.6	18.7	15.9	18.5
		(95)	(429)	(403)	(492)	(377)	(1600)

TABLE 6.

Percent of Ever Married that have Remarried by Gender, Ethnic Group, and Age—United States 1980

		AGE					
GENDER	ETHNIC GROUP	12-19	20-25	26-29	30-34	35-39	40+
Male	White	1.7	4.5	10.6	16.6	19.6	19.6
		(230)	(3654)	(4341)	(6123)	(5102)	(29783)
	Black	0.0	4.1	6.8	15.1	18.4	25.1
		(24)	(342)	(511)	(664)	(538)	(2935)
	Native	—	6.9	12.5	28.2	24.4	29.8
			(29)	(24)	(46)	(41)	(148)
	Asian	—	0.0	1.2	5.7	4.4	8.6
			(47)	(83)	(123)	(135)	(418)
	Hispanic	0.0	3.3	7.0	11.7	11.3	18.2
		(28)	(427)	(374)	(487)	(405)	(1415)
Female	White	2.0	13.2	13.9	17.8	21.1	18.7
		(751)	(5426)	(5093)	(6479)	(5408)	(35700)
	Black	0.0	3.9	8.2	12.0	14.9	23.2
		(56)	(589)	(622)	(799)	(667)	(3872)
	Native	0.0	13.5	18.9	22.7	34.1	34.4
		(18)	(37)	(37)	(53)	(44)	(166)
	Asian	—	1.1	3.8	4.2	9.4	11.3
			(94)	(130)	(189)	(128)	(516)
	Hispanic	1.0	4.4	10.3	13.4	17.7	17.7
		(100)	(540)	(409)	(526)	(401)	(1398)

20, 21, and 13, respectively. Among males 30 to 34 years old, 26 percent of blacks and 21 percent of Hispanics have remarried. In comparison, 15 percent of Native American males, 17 percent of white males, and only 13 percent of Asian males, ages 30 to 34, have remarried.

Data on remarriage in the Intermountain Region and in the United States are shown in Tables 5 and 6. Among whites, the proportion remarrying is higher regionally than in Utah and higher in Utah than nationally. For example, among white females, ages 30 to 34, the proportion remarrying in Utah is 20 percent compared to 22 percent regionally and 18 percent nationally.

COHABITATION

As noted earlier, cohabitation is an increasing way in which families are formed. There is not much reliable data on cohabitation, but some information has been collected by the U.S. Bureau of the Census since 1970. They refer to cohabitants as "unmarried couples," defined as two unrelated adults of the opposite sex who share the same household. Regional data are not available, which limits our comparisons to Utah and the United States.

In 1980 the Census Bureau identified 6,951 "unmarried couples" in Utah, almost half of whom had never been married, while 43 percent had been divorced. Five percent were separated from their spouses, and 3 percent were widowers. Nationally in 1980 there were 1.8 million "unmarried couples," more than three times as many as in 1970, and by 1984 this number had increased to almost two million (U.S. Bureau of the Census, *Statistical Abstract*, 1984).

In the United States widows and separated persons comprised a higher proportion of "unmarried couples" than in Utah (see Table 7). For example, more than 10 percent of cohabitants in the United States were married but separated from their spouses compared to only 5 percent in Utah. Similarly, 8 percent of cohabitants in the United States were widows compared to only 3 percent in Utah.

In this chapter we have defined a family as an "unmarried couple" *or* two or more persons living in the same household who are related by birth, marriage, or adoption. To be a family there must be a parent and child, a husband and wife, or a cohabiting couple. In 1980 1.9 percent of all Utah families could be termed "unmarried couples." By comparison, 2.9 percent of all families in the United States were "unmarried couples" (U.S. Bureau of the Census, *Census of the Population*, 1983 and 1984). Thus, cohabitation is more common in the United States than in Utah. However, cohabitants in Utah are more likely to have a dependent child in the household. In Utah 34 percent of all unmarried couples have at least one child under fifteen in the household compared to 30 percent in the United States.

CHILDBEARING

Childbearing, particularly the birth of a first child, is an important aspect of family formation. Among the unmarried, it creates a family, socially if not legally; among the married, it expands the family. Table 8 shows the percentage of never married Utah women who are parents, according to ethnic group and age. Among Asians childbearing outside of marriage is negligible. For nonmarried whites, childbearing is small among all age groups and never exceeds 2 percent. Childbearing outside of marriage, while higher among Hispanics and Native Americans, is highest among blacks. Among single women, ages 12 to 19, 5 percent of Hispanics are mothers compared to almost 10 percent of Native Americans and 16 percent of blacks. Among all ethnic groups the proportion of never married females with children decreases after age 23.

TABLE 7.

Unmarried Couples by Marital Status of Householder—Utah and United States, 1980

	UTAH		UNITED STATES	
MARITAL STATUS	NUMBER	PERCENT	NUMBER	PERCENT
Never Married	3386	48.7	814,237	46.2
Divorced	2966	42.7	616,541	35.0
Married, Spouse Absent	374	5.4	185,719	10.5
Widowed	225	3.2	147,483	8.4
Total	6951	100.0	1,763,980	100.1

	UTAH	UNITED STATES
Percent of all Families that are Unmarried Couples	1.9	2.9

Source: U.S. Bureau of the Census, *Census of the Population*, 1983 and 1984.

TABLE 8.

Percent of Never-Married Females with Children by Ethnic Group and Age—Utah 1980

	AGE							
ETHNIC GROUP	12-19	20-21	22-23	24-25	26-29	30-34	35-39	40+
White	1.6	2.0	1.2	1.2	1.1	0.4	0.1	0.0
	(2471)	(483)	(1471)	(1418)	(2407)	(2453)	(1828)	(9611)
Black	15.8	—	—	—	6.7	0.0	—	0.0
	(19)				(15)	(12)		(51)
Native	10.4	15.4	16.7	6.3	7.5	11.4	—	3.0
	(67)	(26)	(18)	(16)	(40)	(35)		(67)
Asian	—	—	—	—	—	—	—	—
Hispanic	5.3	8.1	15.4	8.3	4.1	2.8	1.4	1.1
	(150)	(74)	(52)	(72)	(98)	(109)	(72)	(261)

TABLE 9.

Percent of Never-Married Females with Children by Ethnic Group and Age—Intermountain Region 1980

	AGE							
ETHNIC GROUP	12-19	20-21	22-23	24-25	26-29	30-34	35-39	40+
White	2.1	2.7	2.2	1.1	1.2	0.7	0.5	0.0
	(3206)	(1778)	(1762)	(1722)	(3286)	(3710)	(2767)	(16226)
Black	16.8	34.5	20.8	14.5	9.9	6.1	4.6	2.9
	(119)	(55)	(53)	(55)	(91)	(98)	(65)	(315)
Native	11.8	6.3	14.1	14.1	9.2	5.7	8.2	2.4
	(170)	(79)	(64)	(64)	(131)	(122)	(97)	(370)
Asian	2.9	0.0	0.0	0.0	0.0	0.0	0.0	0.0
	(35)	(30)	(18)	(28)	(54)	(70)	(40)	(154)
Hispanic	5.3	9.9	8.0	4.3	4.8	3.0	1.8	0.8
	(645)	(294)	(301)	(281)	(480)	(533)	(395)	(1663)

TABLE 10.

Percent of Never-Married Females with Children by Ethnic Group and Age—United States 1980

	AGE							
ETHNIC GROUP	12-19	20-21	22-23	24-25	26-29	30-34	35-39	40+
White	1.6	2.8	2.4	2.0	1.4	0.7	0.4	0.2
	(6288)	(3392)	(3315)	(3180)	(6108)	(7094)	(5713)	(37675)
Black	15.3	27.3	31.6	25.7	18.5	12.8	8.3	3.9
	(1245)	(583)	(534)	(540)	(971)	(1012)	(773)	(4192)
Native	6.6	17.9	0.0	8.3	8.5	5.0	2.1	2.2
	(76)	(28)	(22)	(24)	(47)	(60)	(47)	(180)
Asian	2.3	2.3	1.8	0.0	1.3	1.0	0.0	0.5
	(133)	(43)	(55)	(86)	(160)	(210)	(142)	(541)
Hispanic	4.8	10.0	8.9	8.0	7.4	5.4	3.5	2.3
	(650)	(309)	(337)	(286)	(503)	(597)	(432)	(1712)

A comparison of Tables 8 and 9 shows that parenthood among single blacks and whites tends to be more common in the Intermountain Region than in Utah. For example, 2.7 percent of intermountain whites, ages 20 to 21, are mothers compared to 2.0 percent among Utah whites. Among Native Americans, Asians, and Hispanics there are no consistent differences between Utah and the Intermountain Region in parenthood outside of marriage.

Relevant figures for the United States are shown in Table 10. Parenthood outside of marriage is lower in Utah than in the United States. Among white and black teenagers who have never married, a greater proportion are parents in the Intermountain Region than in the United States. However, for those older than 20 the Intermountain Region witnesses less childbearing outside of marriage than the United States. And at all age levels rates are less in Utah than regionally or nationally. This finding holds for whites and blacks but not for other ethnic groups. Among Asians, Hispanics, and Native Americans, for example, parenthood outside of marriage does not vary consistently among Utah, the Intermountain Region, and the United States.

Childbearing within marriage is shown in Tables 11, 12, and 13. Since fertility is covered in a previous chapter, only brief mention of married parenthood is given here. Among whites, childbearing within marriage is higher in Utah than regionally and higher regionally than nationally. For example, among married whites, ages 20 to 21, 29 percent are parents in Utah, 22 percent are parents in the Intermountain Region, and 18 percent are parents in the United States. At every age level more married couples are parents in Utah than in the region or in United States. For other ethnic groups the trends are not as consistent or as striking.

SUMMARY

Utahns tend to marry earlier and in greater proportions than is the case regionally or nationally. Indeed, the proportion of men and women never marrying is half as large in Utah as in the United States. Remarriage is more common in the Intermountain Region than in Utah and is higher in Utah than in the United States. Cohabitation is less common in Utah than in the United States; only 2 percent of Utah families are "unmarried couples" compared to 3 percent of United States families. Fewer children are born outside of marriage in Utah, where more are born to married couples than regionally or nationally.

TABLE 11.

Percent of Ever-Married Females with Children by Ethnic Group and Age—Utah 1980

	AGE							
ETHNIC GROUP	12-19	20-21	22-23	24-25	26-29	30-34	35-39	40+
White	9.3	28.5	46.0	61.6	75.4	84.5	91.2	91.2
	(2471)	(1483)	(1471)	(1418)	(2407)	(2453)	(1828)	(9611)
Black	0.0	—	—	—	0.0	75.0	—	82.4
	(19)				(15)	(12)		(51)
Native	4.5	15.4	38.9	50.0	65.0	77.1	85.0	88.1
	(67)	(26)	(18)	(16)	(40)	(35)	(20)	(67)
Asian	0.7	13.8	25.8	46.4	70.6	81.8	91.2	86.3
	(43)	(29)	(31)	(28)	(51)	(44)	(34)	(124)
Hispanic	12.0	37.8	46.2	62.5	74.5	84.4	88.9	89.3
	(150)	(74)	(52)	(72)	(98)	(109)	(72)	(261)

TABLE 12.

Percent of Ever-Married Females with Children by Ethnic Group and Age—Intermountain Region 1980

	AGE							
ETHNIC GROUP	12-19	20-21	22-23	24-25	26-29	30-34	35-39	40+
White	6.5	22.0	37.3	45.5	62.0	77.5	87.6	86.0
	(3206)	(1778)	(1762)	(1722)	(3286)	(3710)	(2767)	(16226)
Black	2.5	16.4	24.5	49.1	59.3	75.5	92.3	79.0
	(119)	(55)	(53)	(55)	(91)	(98)	(65)	(315)
Native	7.1	40.5	46.9	60.9	74.8	84.4	82.5	87.3
	(170)	(79)	(64)	(64)	(131)	(122)	(97)	(370)
Asian	11.4	26.7	44.4	42.9	61.1	75.7	87.5	83.1
	(35)	(30)	(18)	(28)	(54)	(70)	(40)	(154)
Hispanic	9.1	26.2	49.2	61.2	73.1	86.7	90.9	90.3
	(645)	(294)	(301)	(281)	(480)	(533)	(395)	(1663)

TABLE 13.

Percent of Ever-Married Females with Children by Ethnic Group and Age—United States 1980

	AGE							
ETHNIC GROUP	12-19	20-21	22-23	24-25	26-29	30-34	35-39	40+
White	5.5	18.2	32.1	43.2	59.6	76.9	86.6	83.3
	(6288)	(3392)	(3315)	(3180)	(6108)	(7094)	(5713)	(37675)
Black	2.9	15.6	24.7	42.0	53.8	71.1	79.0	75.5
	(1245)	(583)	(534)	(540)	(971)	(1012)	(773)	(4192)
Native	4.5	14.3	31.8	70.8	74.5	83.3	91.5	78.9
	(76)	(28)	(22)	(24)	(47)	(60)	(47)	(180)
Asian	14.5	14.0	30.9	33.7	51.3	71.4	77.5	85.0
	(133)	(43)	(55)	(86)	(160)	(210)	(142)	(541)
Hispanic	9.2	26.5	43.0	56.6	69.4	79.2	87.0	85.0
	(650)	(309)	(337)	(286)	(503)	(597)	(432)	(1712)

REFERENCES

Brieland, Donald and John Allen Lemmon. *Social Work and the Law.* 2nd Edition. St. Paul: West Publishing Co., 1985

Cherlin, Andrew and James McCarthy. "Remarried Couple Households: Data from the June 1980 Current Population Survey." *Journal of Marriage and the Family* 47 (1985): 23-30.

Glick, Paul C. "Remarriage: Some Recent Changes and Variations." *Journal of Family Issues* 4 (1980): 455-78.

Lee, Gary R. *Family Structure and Interaction: A Comparative Analysis.* Philadelphia: J. B. Lippincott Co., 1977.

Leslie, Gerald R. *The Family in Social Context.* 5th Edition. New York: Oxford University Press, 1982.

National Center For Health Statistics. "Births, Marriages, Divorces, and Deaths for 1985." *Monthly Vital Statistics Report. Vol. 34, No. 12.* DHHS Publication No. (PHS) 86-1120. Hyattsville, MD: Public Health Service, March 24, 1986.

Norton, Arthur J. and Paul C. Glick. "Marital Instability in America: Past, Present, and Future." In Levinger, G. and O. C. Moles, eds., *Divorce and Separation: Context, Causes, and Consequences*, New York: Basic Books, 1979, pp. 6-19.

Preston, Samuel H. "Estimating the Proportion of American Marriages that End in Divorce." *Sociological Methods and Research* 3 (1975): 435-60.

U.S. Bureau of the Census. "Number, Timing, and Duration of Marriages and Divorces in the United States: June 1975." *Current Population Reports, Series P-20, No. 297.* Washington, D.C.: Government Printing Office, 1976.

_____. *American Women: Three Decades of Change.* Washington, D.C.: Government Printing Office, 1983.

_____. *Census of the Population, Vol. 1, Characteristics of the Population, Chapter D, Detailed Population Characteristics, Part 46, Utah, PC80-1-D46.* Washington, D.C.: Government Printing Office, 1983.

_____. *Census of the Population and Housing, 1980: Public-Use Microdata Samples Technical Documentation.* Washington, D.C.: Government Printing Office, 1983.

_____. *Census of the Population, Vol. 1, Characteristics of the Population, Chapter D, Detailed Population Characteristics, Part 1, United States Summary, Section A, PC80-1D1-A.* Washington, D.C.: Government Printing Office, 1984.

_____. *Statistical Abstract of the United States, 1985.* 105th Edition. Washington, D.C.: Government Printing Office, 1984.

7.

FAMILY ECONOMICS

Jerry Mason

To appreciate more fully family economics in contemporary American society, one must examine labor force participation, educational achievement, poverty status, and family income. While the broad focus of this chapter is family economics in the United States, its main objective is to examine the economic well-being of Utah families. Because national and state averages can mask important differences among segments of a population, much of the following analysis considers five ethnic groups: whites, blacks, American Indians, Asians, and Spanish Americans. Such detail provides both a clearer understanding of trends over time and a better picture of the current status of families in the major ethnic groups.

INCOME

One of the more interesting numbers used to measure the economic status of families is per capita income. One frequently reads news releases in which per capita income for Utahns ranks near the bottom among the fifty states. Yet such rankings are to be expected because the number of children born to Utah women, ages 15 to 44, is among the highest in the nation. For whites, the dominant ethnic group in Utah, the number of persons per household and number of persons per family are above national averages. Since Utah's families are larger, per capita income would be smaller if family income in Utah were identical to the national average. However, median income for white, American Indian, and Asian families in Utah is also below the national average. Just the opposite is true for both black and Spanish American families in Utah. Persons per household and persons per family (see Table 1) are below national figures for blacks and Spanish Americans, while median family income is higher (see Table 2). Thus, per capita income is actually above national averages for Utah's black and Spanish American families. But per capita income

American families. But per capita income for Utah generally is below U.S. averages, because the data for the small populations of black and Spanish American families do not offset those for white, Indian and Asian families.

Increasingly, women are entering the labor force. As Table 3 indicates, husbands earn a higher income in families where the wife is not employed. But what is of greater interest is the percentage of total family income contributed by the wife. In both Utah and national data, when husband and wife are employed, the wife contributed between 25 to 33 percent of the family income in 1979. As a result, total family income in two-earner families was usually higher than in families where the wife did not work. However, it is unknown whether families where both spouses are employed enjoy a significantly higher level of living due to greater expenses incurred for child care, taxes, food, and transportation. In many instances, a wife may seek

TABLE 1.

Number of Persons per Living Unit—1980

	PER HOUSEHOLD	PER FAMILY
White		
U.S.	2.65	3.16
Utah	3.19	3.66
Black		
U.S.	3.07	3.72
Utah	2.75	3.49
Indian		
U.S.	3.36	3.89
Utah	3.97	4.43
Asian		
U.S.	3.34	4.05
Utah	3.28	4.03
Spanish		
U.S.	3.48	3.92
Utah	3.39	3.85

Source: U.S. Bureau of the Census 1983, vol. 1, Chapter B, Part 1, Tables 47, 49; Part 46, Tables 22, 24.

TABLE 2.

1979 Per Capita and Median Family Income by Ethnic Origin

	INCOME PER CAPITA				
	WHITE	BLACK	INDIAN	ASIAN	SPANISH
U.S.	$7,808	$4,545	$4,577	$7,037	$4,586
Utah	6,415	4,856	3,126	4,959	4,628
	MEDIAN FAMILY INCOME				
U.S.	$20,835	$12,598	$13,724	$22,713	$14,712
Utah	20,205	15,041	11,855	17,500	16,499

Source: U.S. Bureau of the Census 1983, vol. 1, Chapter C, Part, 1, Tables 128, 138; Part 46, Tables 81, 91.

TABLE 3.

1979 Mean Earnings for Married Couples

	U.S.	UTAH
Husband Worked, Wife Did Not		
Family Income	$22,580	$21,822
Husband and Wife Usually Work Full Time		
Family Income	27,644	25,855
Husband	18,605	18,021
Wife	9,039	7,834
*	33	30
Husband and Wife Worked, But One or Both Worked Part Time		
Family Income	24,766	21,583
Husband	17,881	16,274
Wife	6,885	5,309
*	28	25

*Wife's earnings as a percent of family earnings.

Source: U.S. Bureau of the Census 1984, vol. 1, Chapter D, Part 1, Table 300; 1983, vol. 1, Chapter D, Part 46, Table 241.

employment more as a necessity to help keep her family from falling behind economically than to enable it to enjoy a higher standard of living.

Families with children where the husband is absent receive a significantly lower income than families where the husband is present (see Table 4). This finding, which is neither new nor unexpected, is nonetheless dramatic, because families without a husband receive only a fraction of the income they do when the husband is present. This financial crisis is worse for families with children under age six when the husband is absent. Median income for such families is similar for all ethnic groups both in Utah and nationally. (The plight of female-headed families is explored in greater detail in the section on poverty.)

Median income for Utah families is below national averages in most cases for white, Indian, and Asian families, but is above average for Spanish American families. A wife's earnings, whether the husband is absent or present, does not alter this finding.

BANKRUPTCY

The rate of bankruptcy filings in Utah during the last fifty years is not unlike national rates based on a per capita filing basis. As the data in Table 5 indicate, filings in Utah were above the national average in three of the five years reported. Because such differences are not large, they are probably due to economic conditions that affect areas of the nation differently. Business and individual filings are examined together since separate data are not always available. Business filings usually account for 10 to 15 percent of all bankruptcy filings, the majority of which involve farmers, professionals, and other sole proprietorships.

More interesting than the differences between filing rates for Utah and the United States is the trend towards increased filings per capita during the last fifty years. Although it is impossible to account fully for the increase in filings, several factors have contributed to the rise. For example, bankruptcy seems to have lost much of its social stigma; apparently, it is more acceptable today than in the past. In addition, two new developments have also been credited with the greater number of filings. The 1978 Bankruptcy Reform Act greatly strengthened the debtor's position in bankruptcy proceedings and liberalized the amount of assets not subject to liquidation by the courts. (However, the 1978 law allowed states to set stricter exemption levels, which most have done, and a 1984 amendment tightened certain exemptions available to debtors.) About the same time, lawyers began advertising for bankruptcy cases. This has been considered by some to account, at least partially, for the increased filings.

TABLE 4

1979 Median Family Income By Age of Children and Presence of Husband in the Family

CHILDREN UNDER 18

HUSBAND PRESENT

	WHITE	BLACK	INDIAN	ASIAN	SPANISH
U.S.	$23,147	$19,036	$16,874	$25,034	$17,180
Utah	21,793	19,273	14,701	18,062	19,572

HUSBAND ABSENT

	WHITE	BLACK	INDIAN	ASIAN	SPANISH
U.S.	9,138	6,448	6,618	9,370	5,948
Utah	8,862	5,568	7,017	7,969	6,012

CHILDREN UNDER 6

HUSBAND PRESENT

	WHITE	BLACK	INDIAN	ASIAN	SPANISH
U.S.	20,057	16,991	14,704	22,484	15,219
Utah	19,099	14,976	12,810	15,878	16,631

HUSBAND ABSENT

	WHITE	BLACK	INDIAN	ASIAN	SPANISH
U.S.	5,805	4,711	5,000	6,378	4,581
Utah	5,966	4,727	4,643	4,816	4,492

Source: U.S. Bureau of the Census 1983, vol. 1, Chapter C, Part 1, Tables 128, 138; Part 46, Tables 81, 91.

TABLE 5.

Trend in Bankruptcy Filings Since 1940*

	TOTAL FILINGS		FILINGS AS A PERCENTAGE OF THE POPULATION	
	U.S.	UTAH	U.S.	UTAH
1980	360,957	2,109	.159	.144
1970	194,399	1,377	.095	.129
1960	110,034	577	.061	.064
1950	33,392	168	.022	.024
1940	52,577	203	.039	.037

*The 1978 law changed the way bankruptcy estates are filed for married couples. The prior law required husbands and wives to file separately. The new law allows them to file jointly. The total number of estates filing for bankruptcy in 1980 is understated since about 160,000 filings, as reported above, are joint filings. Filings for Utah have not been adjusted upward to account for the joint filings.

Source: Administrative Office of the United States Courts 1941, 1951, 1961, 1980, 1982

TABLE 6.

Percentage of Bankrupts Filing Under Selected Chapters in the Bankruptcy Code

		CHAPTER 7	CHAPTER 13	OTHER
1980	U.S.	76	22	2
	Utah	87	9	4
1970	U.S.	84	16	0
	Utah	97	2	1
1960	U.S.	87	12	1
	Utah	100	0	0
1950	U.S.	80	18	2
	Utah	100	0	0
1940	U.S.	87	6	7
	Utah	84	1	15

Sources: Administrative Office of the United States Courts 1941, 1951, 1961, 1980, 1982.

Just as bankruptcy statistics are divided into business and non-business filings, records are also kept on the type of filing. For example, although bankruptcy can be filed under several chapters in the bankruptcy law, most are under Chapter 7 (see Table 6), which supervises the liquidation of individual or business assets to pay creditors. However, as previously noted, debtors are now allowed to exempt some of their assets from creditor claims. For example, persons filing under Chapter 7 cannot have their wages garnished to pay creditors, who can only look to the liquidation of assets to pay their secured or unsecured claims.

Chapter 13 is often called the wage-earner plan. Under a Chapter 13 filing, a repayment program is worked out over a two-year period to satisfy creditor claims out of the debtor's income. (Just as the debtor's income is not available under Chapter 7 to pay creditor claims, debtor assets are not available under Chapter 13 to pay creditor claims.) Rarely, however, does a debtor repay all creditors 100 percent under Chapter 13. If at least 10 percent of the amount owed is expected to be paid during the two years, the courts will usually approve the repayment plan. And the balance owed to a creditor that has not been repaid at the end of the two-year period is usually cancelled. Historically,

TABLE 7.

Percentage of Labor Force Participation Ages 20-64

	U.S.	UTAH
Male		
Employed	80.3	84.0
Unemployed*	5.0	4.0
Not in Labor Force	14.7	12.0
Female		
Employed	56.4	53.0
Unemployed*	3.5	2.5
Not in Labor Force	40.1	44.5

*These figures, which may appear low, are usually computed as percentages of those in the labor force and not, as I have done, as percentages of the total adult population.

Source: U.S. Bureau of the Census 1983, vol. 1, Chapter C, Part 1, Table 103; Part 46, Table 67.

Utahns have not filed under Chapter 13 until recently. Lawyers prefer Chapter 7 filings, but it is surprising that more debtors have not filed under Chapter 13, which, because it often enables the debtor to pay off more of his or her debts, can be considered a more "responsible" way to go bankrupt.

LABOR FORCE PARTICIPATION

Labor force statistics can be used as well as abused by persons trying to support a particular position or belief. Too often, only part of the picture is presented. For example, in a political campaign, one candidate may emphasize unemployment rates, while his or her opponent may limit debate to the number of people employed. In discussing labor force participation rates, it is helpful to examine employment and unemployment rates together. Table 7 provides an overview of labor force participation among adults, ages 20 to 64, as of 1980. In Utah, 84 percent of all males within this age group were employed, 4 percent were unemployed but looking for work, and 12 percent were either in school, disabled, or had given up looking for work. Over 50 percent of women between the ages of 20 and 64 were employed. A comparison of the statistics for Utah and the United States shows that the percentage of adults employed is about the same, with Utah males having slightly higher employment rates and Utah females having slightly lower rates.

It is interesting to note labor force participation rates for married couples of all ages (see Table 8). No doubt a large majority of couples not employed

TABLE 8.

Percentage of Labor Force Participation for Married Couples

	U.S.	UTAH
Husband, wife usually worked full time	33	29
Husband and wife worked, but one or both worked part time	18	23
Wife worked, husband did not work	4	3
Husband worked, wife did not work	33	36
Husband and wife did not work	12	9

Source: U.S. Bureau of the Census 1984, vol. 1, Chapter D, Part 1, Table 300; 1983, vol. 1, Chapter D, Part 46, Table 241.

were retired. Adding together all categories where the wife works (i.e., the first three listed on Table 8), 55 percent of married women in Utah and in the United States were employed in 1980. Employment is a significant factor in terms of participation rates and family income (see Table 3).

Cross-sectional data collected at one time do not reveal major trends taking place in the labor force. For example, most people recognize that more women are employed today than in the past (see Table 9). While the employment rate for women is higher today than in 1940, it has changed very little for white males, ages 20 to 54, during the same period. (Rates have decreased for white men over 55, however, probably because of better disability and retirement benefits.) But rates for black males have declined for all ages during this forty-year period. Since labor force participation rates for black and white men over age 20 were similar in 1940, one can only speculate as to the reasons for the decline among black males. Is it possible that women have taken jobs away from black men? Over the last forty years, the percentage of women, most of whom are white, in the labor force has greatly increased, while rates have held steady for white men and declined for blacks.

Because ethnic differences have been documented in labor rates and the racial mix in Utah differs from national proportions, employment and

TABLE 9.

Percentage of Adult Population in Labor Force

	MALE				FEMALE			
	WHITE		BLACK		WHITE		BLACK	
AGES	1940	1980	1940	1980	1940	1980	1940	1980
16-19	46.4	55.5	59.5	36.5	26.7	49.0	28.6	30.3
20-24	88.0	84.3	88.5	73.5	45.7	69.5	44.9	61.4
25-34	95.4	94.3	92.4	83.5	31.7	64.2	46.1	71.6
35-44	94.9	95.2	92.4	86.3	25.1	64.0	45.1	71.0
45-54	92.2	91.3	89.9	81.0	20.9	58.5	40.0	61.7
55-64	83.9	72.2	84.6	62.3	15.8	41.4	31.1	44.1
Over 64	41.2	19.4	49.0	17.7	5.6	8.0	12.5	10.4

Source: U.S. Bureau of the Census 1983, vol. 1, Chapter C, Part 1, Table 87.

unemployment statistics have been separated into five major ethnic groups in Table 10. As a general observation, employment and unemployment figures for men in Utah and in the United States are similar for all five groups except for blacks. It is surprising that both rates for black men are lower in Utah than nationally. In Utah, as in the United States, white, Spanish American, and Asian men all have much higher employment rates than blacks and Indians. Lower employment rates and higher unemployment figures are often related to discrimination and lower levels of education, although they may only partially explain differences in the data.

As noted in Table 10, labor force participation rates for Utah women are slightly below U.S. averages for most categories. These numbers group together single and married women and those with and without children.

Those labor statistics usually receiving considerable attention document the employment levels of women with minor children at home, with or without a husband present. As noted in Table 4, family income for families when the

TABLE 10.

Percentage of Adult Population Ages 20-64 Employed and Unemployed in 1979

		MALE		FEMALE	
		EMPLOYED	UNEMPLOYED	EMPLOYED	UNEMPLOYED
White	U.S.	82.2	4.5	56.5	3.0
	Utah	84.7	3.9	53.0	2.4
Black	U.S.	66.9	8.4	57.1	6.4
	Utah	54.6	4.6	56.4	7.5
Indian	U.S.	66.4	10.0	48.6	5.9
	Utah	69.2	8.9	42.2	6.0
Asian	U.S.	79.7	3.1	60.8	3.1
	Utah	80.3	3.8	57.5	2.8
Spanish	U.S.	78.6	4.8	50.0	4.9
	Utah	78.4	6.9	54.8	4.3

Source: U.S. Bureau of the Census 1983, vol. 1, Chapter C, Part 1, Tables 124, 134; Part 46, Tables 77, 87.

husband is absent is very low. In such families one would expect the labor force participation rate for women to be higher than when the husband is present. This is borne out by the data in Table 11, except for black families, where the higher rate for women tends to occur when the husband is present.

The labor force participation rate for women with children under age 6 is much lower than for women with older children. Many women with young children seem to prefer staying home to be with their preschoolers. Others find it is uneconomical to work when they must also pay for child care. Some cannot find adequate child care and will not leave their children to go to work.

TABLE 11

Percentage of Women in the Labor Force Who Have Children at Home

	WHITE	BLACK	INDIAN	ASIAN	SPANISH
CHILDREN UNDER 18					
HUSBAND PRESENT					
U.S.	59	70	57	67	55
Utah	60	83	43	72	64
HUSBAND ABSENT					
U.S.	79	68	64	76	59
Utah	86	61	55	75	77
CHILDREN UNDER 6					
HUSBAND PRESENT					
U.S.	42	66	45	51	43
Utah	35	47	40	43	46
HUSBAND ABSENT					
U.S.	59	51	47	58	41
Utah	61	53	53	61	43

Source: U.S. Bureau of the Census 1983, vol. 1, Chapter C, Part 1, Tables 124, 134; Part 46, Tables 77, 87.

In Utah the labor force participation rate for women with children when the husband is absent is generally higher than national figures.

Are these higher rates related to the Protestant work ethic—that is, are women determined to support themselves and their children when the husband is absent? Or do the higher employment rates reflect the inadequate transfer of payments from government and private assistance programs, as well as inadequate child support and alimony payments? Since median family income, presented in Table 4, was low when the husband was absent, the answer to all these and related questions may be yes.

To explain partially why the employment statistics of women who head families do not contribute more to family income, we must consider full-time vs. part-time employment. Although 25 percent of Utah women work all year, only 19 percent work 35 or more hours per week (see Table 12). Thus less than one-fifth of Utah women work full time. Although the statistics for the United States are higher, over one-half of employed women in Utah and in the United States work part-time. In addition, part-time employment in Utah is apparently at higher levels than nationally.

TABLE 12.

1979 Labor Force Participation Rate by Women over 15

	NUMBER OF WEEKS WORKED			
	50-52 WEEKS	27-49 WEEKS	1-26 WEEKS	EMPLOYED DURING THE YEAR
U.S.	28%	14%	13%	55%
Utah	25	16	18	59

	NUMBER OF WEEKS WORKED WHERE THE WORK WEEK IS 35 HOURS OR MORE		
U.S.	23%	9%	6%
Utah	19	9	8

Source: U.S. Bureau of the Census 1983, vol. 1, Chapter C, Part 1, Table 106; Part 46, Table 80.

Labor force participation rates for the five different ethnic groups in Utah do not vary greatly from national figures. Rates for women have been steadily increasing throughout the past half century, and the rate of women when the husband is present is about the same as for all women. However, the rate for women with minor children when the husband is not present is much higher. Still, the majority of employed women only work part time.

POVERTY

The incidence of poverty, as related to ethnic backgrounds, has long been explored. As the data in Table 13 document, a higher percentage of blacks, Indians, and Spanish Americans in . he United States are likely to be classified

TABLE 13.

Percentage of Total Population in 1979 Below Poverty Level by Ethnic Origin

	U.S.	UTAH
White	9.4	9.3
Black	29.9	29.4
American Indian	27.5	37.2
Asian	13.1	22.7
Spanish	23.5	18.5
	100.0	100.0

Percentage of Total Population at or Below Poverty Level by Family Status

	65+		FEMALE FAMILY HEAD WITH CHILDREN UNDER 18		FAMILIES	
	U.S.	UTAH	U.S.	UTAH	U.S.	UTAH
White	12.8	11.3	32.1	33.2	7.0	6.9
Black	35.2	24.7	52.6	54.6	26.5	18.2
Indian	32.0	37.5	51.7	58.4	23.7	32.6
Asian	14.4	14.8	34.8	39.2	10.7	18.4
Spanish	25.6	23.7	56.2	54.2	21.3	16.5

Source: U.S. Bureau of the Census1983, vol. 1, Chapter C, Part 1, Tables 129, 139; Part 46, Table 104.

as poor than are whites and Asians. National and Utah data are similar for whites and blacks, with about one in ten whites at or below the poverty line and about 30 percent of all blacks classified as poor in 1980.

While a larger percentage of Asians and Indians are classified as poor in Utah than in the United States, such findings may not be too surprising. Utah has only a small Asian population, but it experienced a large influx of refugees from Cambodia, Vietnam, and Laos during the 1970s. Upon arrival, most of these immigrants were poor. Although upward mobility is expected for most, when the census was taken in 1980, many were classified as poor. Because a high percentage of Asians were employed but median family income remained low, one could expect that most Asians in Utah in 1980 had low-paying jobs. However, it is more difficult to explain the higher-than-average incidence of poverty among Indians in Utah, many of whom live on reservations. Indians who stay on reservations may be economically worse off than mobile Indians, who achieve a higher standard of living when they move to urban centers. A smaller percentage of Spanish Americans in Utah is classified as poor than nationally. Although Spanish American employment statistics are about the same in Utah as in the United States, median family income is higher in Utah, indicating that Spanish American families have better paying jobs in Utah than elsewhere. As a general observation, however, the percentage of the population below the poverty line is about the same in Utah as it is in the United States as a whole.

As already noted, there appears to be a strong relationship between labor force participation and poverty. As the data in Table 14 suggest, 64 percent

TABLE 14.

Percentage of Families Where At Least One Person Worked 35 Hours or More Per Week and Worked 50 to 52 Weeks Per Year

	ALL FAMILIES AT OR ABOVE POVERTY LINE	ALL FAMILIES BELOW POVERTY LINE
U.S.	61	17
Utah	64	23

Source: U.S. Bureau of the Census 1984, vol. 1, Chapter D, Part 1, Table 305; 1983, vol. 1, Chapter D, Part 46, Table 246.

of Utah families and 61 percent of U.S. families at or above the poverty level have at least one family member employed full-time. In families below the poverty level, however, labor force participation drops to around 20 percent. According to Utah and national data, blacks and Indians have the highest levels of poverty and the lowest rates of labor force participation (see Tables 13 and 10). Nationally, whites and Asians have higher employment levels and lower rates of poverty. A full-time job, however, is not the simple solution to poverty, because many family heads in poor families are retired, disabled, single, or inadequately trained or educated.

Data in Table 15 indicate that whites and Asians are more likely to have graduated from high school, which may explain their higher labor force participation rates and lower incidences of poverty. But in the Utah data, these relationships seem to break down. The educational achievement for Asians

TABLE 15.

Percentage of High School Graduates 25 Years and Older

	MALE	FEMALE
White		
U.S.	69.6	68.1
Utah	81.8	80.1
Black		
U.S.	50.8	51.5
Utah	73.2	65.2
Indian		
U.S.	57.0	54.1
Utah	55.6	50.2
Asian		
U.S.	78.8	71.4
Utah	80.4	71.1
Spanish		
U.S.	45.4	42.7
Utah	55.0	49.2

Source: U.S. Bureau of the Census 1983, vol. 1, Chapter C, Part 1, Tables 123, 133; Part 46, Tables 76, 86.

in Utah is above the national level, as are their employment rates (see Table 10), yet their incidence of poverty is also above the national level (see Table 13). From Table 15, it also appears that the high education levels for whites and blacks in Utah are not related to higher labor force participation (Table 10) or to lower poverty figures (Table 13). For Indians, education seems related to poverty, with a smaller percentage graduating from high school in Utah than nationally, a percentage matching their higher levels of poverty in Utah. Spanish Americans have the least amount of education, yet their labor force participation rates are nearly as high as those of whites and Asians, who are much better educated. Their relatively high poverty levels may be partially due to lower levels of education, which keeps them in lower-paying jobs. But educational differences do not in all cases explain ethnic differences in either labor force participation or poverty.

Although the relationships between education, labor force participation, and poverty have not been adequately explained, the data in Table 16 indicate a relationship between education and poverty for whites and blacks. Whereas blacks have a higher incidence of poverty than whites and more women than men are below the poverty line, the relationship between poverty and educational achievement at all educational levels is strong. Ethnic differences exist, but education appears to be a better predictor of poverty. A high percentage

TABLE 16.

Percentage of Individuals at or Below Poverty Line Based on Educational Achievement

	WHITE		BLACK	
	MALE	FEMALE	MALE	FEMALE
No schooling	28	37	50	56
Elementary 1-5	28	37	38	55
6-7	22	30	35	53
8	15	22	33	48
High School 1-3	13	18	34	47
4	7	9	17	30
College 1 or more	4	6	10	17

Source: U.S. Bureau of the Census, Current Population Report 1984, Table 13.

of those with no formal schooling are classified as poor. The percentage of families at or below the poverty line decreases as educational attainment increases for all groups. Such data highlights the importance of education in a labor force that increasingly requires well-trained labor. Unfortunately, discrimination may also be documented in this data, as well. For example, white men with some college are less likely to be poor than black women with some college.

As might be expected, the group with the highest incidence of poverty is families headed by women with minor children (see Table 13). The ages of the children appear to be related to the incidence of poverty. As the data in Table 17 suggest, nearly two-thirds of all families where the oldest child is under six live in poverty. Although Utah figures reflect national percentages, the data are nonetheless high. And while a majority of women in families

TABLE 17.

Poverty Status of Female-Head Families By Age of Children

	UNDER 6	UNDER 18
White		
U.S.	47	23
Utah	50	21
Black		
U.S.	62	44
Utah	58	52
Indian		
U.S.	61	43
Utah	68	41
Asian		
U.S.	47	28
Utah	62	22
Spanish		
U.S.	67	47
Utah	66	40

Source: U.S. Bureau of the Census1983, vol. 1, Chapter C, Part 1, Tables 129, 139; Part 46, Table 104.

with children, but where the husband is absent, are in the labor force (Table 11), few women below the poverty line work full-time (Table 18). The higher full-time employment rates of female family heads with older children seem to contribute to a lower percentage of such families living below the poverty line.

A real challenge faces policy makers who wish to provide a decent level of living for all Americans. In Utah, as elsewhere, there is a high incidence of poverty among families headed by women, especially those with young children. At present, for whatever reason, few female family heads are able to work full-time to earn the income needed to raise family income above the poverty line.

SUMMARY

Economic data for Utah families are not much different from data for families across the country. Utahns have attained slightly more formal education and their labor force participation may be a little above national averages, but the incidence of poverty is similar and median family income is a little lower. Of special importance is the economic plight of female-headed families in Utah and the United States, especially those in which the oldest child is under age 6.

TABLE 18.

Female-Headed Families at or Below the Poverty Line in the United States, Mother Worked Full Time, 50-52 Weeks

	WHITE	BLACK
Children under 6 only	5	4
Children under 6 and 6 to 17 years	6	7
Children 6 to 17 years	7	11

Source: U.S. Bureau of the Census, Current Population Report 1984, Table 19.

REFERENCES

Administrative Office of the United States Courts. *Voluntary and Involuntary Cases Commenced During the Fiscal Year Ending June 30, 1940*. Table f2. Washington, D.C.: Administrative Office of the U.S. Courts, 1941.

_____. *Voluntary and Involuntary Cases Commenced During the Fiscal Year Ending June 30, 1950*. Table f2. Washington, D.C.: Administrative Office of the U.S. Courts, 1951.

_____. *Voluntary and Involuntary Cases Commenced During the Fiscal Year Ending June 30, 1960*. Table f2. Washington, D.C.: Administrative Office of the U.S. Courts, 1961.

_____. *Reports of the Proceedings of the Judicial Conference of the U.S. held in Washington, D.C., March 5, and 6, 1980 and September 24 and 25, 1980*. Annual Report of the Director of the Administrative Office of the United States Courts, pp. 134-38, 547-65.

_____. *Bankruptcy Statistical Tables, Twelve Month Periods Ending June 30, 1970-79*. Washington, D.C.: Administrative Office of the U.S. Courts, 1982.

U.S. Bureau of the Census. *1980 Census of the Population, Vol. 1, Chapter B, General Population Characteristics, Part 1, United States Summary*. Washington, D.C.: Government Printing Office, 1983.

_____. *1980 Census of the Population, Vol. 1, Chapter B, General Population Characteristics, Part 46, Utah*. Washington, D.C.: Government Printing Office, 1983.

_____. *1980 Census of the Population, Vol. 1, Chapter C, General Social and Economic Characteristics, Part 1, United States Summary*. Washington, D.C.: Government Printing Office, 1983.

_____. *1980 Census of the Population, Vol. 1, Chapter D, General Social and Economic Characteristics, Part 46, Utah*. Washington, D.C.: Government Printing Office, 1983.

_____. *1980 Census of the Population, Vol. 1, Chapter D, Detailed Population Characteristics, Part 46, Utah*. Washington, D.C.: Government Printing Office, 1983.

_____. *Current Population Report, Characteristics of the Population Below the Poverty Level, 1982, P-60, No. 144*. Washington, D.C.: Government Printing Office, 1984.

_____. *1980 Census of the Population, Vol. 1, Chapter D, Detailed Population Characteristics, Part 1, United States Summary*. Washington, D.C.: Government Printing Office, 1984.

8.

CHILD CARE

Jean M. Larsen

> Professional child care is a comprehensive service to children and families which functions as a subsystem of the childrearing system and which supplements the care children receive from their families. Professional child care is not a substitute or a competitor for parental care. To some extent, professional child care represents a version of the extended family which has adapted to the social realities of the modern world.
>
> (Caldwell 1984)

The above description of child care as the supervision of children by others than family members highlights the challenges facing families of employed mothers with young children in today's society. This chapter explores the status of child care and its impact on families from national, regional, and state perspectives.

NATIONAL TRENDS

Across the United States, child care today is the object of increased public attention. During 1983 the House of Representatives Select Committee on Children, Youth, and Families conducted a series of preliminary hearings throughout the country regarding issues affecting children and families. The committee singled out child care as a major concern facing all facets of society. Indeed, child care can be viewed as a growing national crisis.

Several factors contribute to the crisis in child care. For example, the demand for professional child care continues to escalate as vast numbers of women with young children enter the work force. Data from the 1980 United States census indicate that over 53 percent of women with children, ages 1 month to 17 years, are in the labor force. According to a recent survey conducted by the

Children's Defense Fund, nearly one-half of mothers with infants and toddlers are currently employed compared to 30 percent in 1970 (Blank 1984). More than 9 million children under the age of six have working mothers. Furthermore, researchers project from the 1984 survey that by the end of the decade about 3.4 million more children of this age will have mothers entering the work force.

A predominant negative factor related to child care concerns the economic ramifications for many women with young children who join the labor force because of financial need. This is particularly evident when families are headed by women, with no husband present. Data on employed parents and their children published in 1982 by the Children's Defense Fund indicate that the average annual earnings of a single mother with children was only $8,951. Researchers estimate from this data that one-third of the income, or $3,000, was used for child care—three times as much as the 10 percent generally thought to be reasonable. While attempts are being made to resolve this apparent inequity at the state level, there is, as yet, no clear indication that the problem is being alleviated.

Sadly, the lack of affordable child care compounds the economic issue of low wages and contributes to the poverty status of many women and children. The financial aspects of child care pose a double-edged dilemma. The majority of mothers with young children work out of economic necessity, yet child care takes a large portion of their earnings. Unfortunately, those who provide child care are themselves trapped in this low income web. Salaries of child care workers nationally are appallingly low with few, if any, benefits. Thus, most center employees are women who, by selecting child care as a profession, have virtually guaranteed themselves a below average standard of living.

The quality and availability of child care are concerns of equal significance relating to the economic dilemma facing working mothers. Professional child care is often not available to meet escalating demand, and the quality of care ranges from excellent to poor with the cost of superior and substandard care being about the same. According to the 1979 final report of the national day care study (Ruopp et al.), there were 18,307 licensed child care centers in the United States, with an enrollment of about 900,000 preschool-age children. Clearly, the available slots for infants and toddlers fell short of accommodating the three million children under three years of age with working mothers. Likewise, there were only 126,000 after-school center openings for some 14.5 million school age children with working mothers. For the most part, working mothers are severely limited in their efforts to find good group programs or family child care homes (i.e., a neighbor who cares for a limited number of children besides her own). The disparity in numbers of licensed facilities and children needing care suggests that many children under six, perhaps a majority, are cared for in unlicensed settings.

The June 1982 population survey on the child care arrangements of working mothers (O'Connell and Rogers) reported a slight increase in the number of licensed child centers and family child care providers—a finding met with some optimism since licensing demonstrates compliance with child care standards. However, a better predictor of program quality is whether or not the child care provider has had training in the area (Ruopp et al. 1979). Low wages provide neither the incentive to pursue a child care career nor motivation to become trained and licensed. The majority of those providing some form of child care have not been trained but function instead under what child development professionals have termed the false assumption that intuitively anyone should be able to care for children.

Recent reports of child abuse in care centers and family care homes have sparked further debate about the adequacy of child care nationally. Licensing practices and standards vary from state to state, leaving much to be desired in terms of quality control. Little, if any, emphasis is placed on either preservice or in-service training. Nor has much attention been given to the content of the program or to the type of learning activities children engage in. Additionally, other problems regarding the specialized care needs of infants, toddlers, and sick children continue to surface without immediate solutions. All of which seems to perpetuate the critical nature of child care in our country.

REGIONAL TRENDS

The current status of child care across the country has been constructed from 1980 census data on maternal employment. As shown in Table 1, the data on working mothers in the eight western states composing the Intermountain Region reflect national trends. Although slightly more than one-half of mothers with dependent children are in the labor force, more with children under age 6 are at home than are working regionally. However, a substantially greater percentage of mothers with school age children (43.1 percent compared to 35.1 percent) are working than are at home.

Although more mothers with young children remain at home than work, the need for child care exceeds available professional child care. The large percentage of school age children with working mothers only adds another

TABLE 1.

Employment Status, Child Age Distribution, and Marital Status of Mothers with Dependent Children, Utah, the Mountain States, and the U.S., 1980

% MOTHERS WITH DEPENDENT CHILDREN	U.S.	MT. STATES REGION*	UTAH
in labor force	53.2	53.1	49.6
not in labor force	46.8	46.9	50.4
with children under age 6 only	19.5	21.6	26.6
with children under age 6 and ages 6 to 17	17.4	19.8	26.9
with children ages 6 to 17 only	63.1	58.4	46.6
married	82.0	84.7	88.6
single	18.0	15.3	11.5
% IN THE LABOR FORCE:			
with children under age 6 only	9.1	10.0	10.3
married	7.4	8.3	8.9
single	1.7	1.7	1.4
with children under age 6 and ages 6 to 17	7.6	8.4	10.3
married	6.4	7.2	9.1
single	1.2	1.2	1.2
with children ages 6 to 17 only	36.6	34.7	29.1
married	28.3	27.1	23.4
single	8.2	7.6	4.7
% NOT IN THE LABOR FORCE:			
with children under age 6 only	10.4	11.8	16.3
married	9.3	10.9	15.5
single	1.1	1.0	0.8
with children under age 6 and ages 6 to 17	9.8	11.4	16.5
married	8.6	10.6	15.8
single	1.3	0.8	0.8
with children ages 6 to 17 only	26.5	23.7	17.5
married	22.0	20.6	15.9
single	4.5	3.0	1.6

*This includes Arizona, Colorado, Idaho, Montana, Nevada, New Mexico, Utah, and Wyoming.

Source: 1980 U.S. Census of the Population

dimension to the child care crisis. Arrangements for before-and-after-school care for seven to thirteen year-olds is fast becoming one of the great challenges of employed women. These youngsters, referred to as ''latchkey'' children, generally go home from school to an empty house rather than to an in-home family care provider or to a child care center. The latchkey child problem exists across the country and is intensified by both increased maternal employment and delayed solutions to inadequate and unavailable child care.

UTAH IN REGIONAL AND NATIONAL PERSPECTIVE

Although the overall percentage of working mothers with dependent children (see Table 1) is slightly lower in Utah than in the region or the nation, there is a more pronounced child care crisis in the state. Two factors intensify this problem in Utah. As shown in Table 2, Utah has a substantially higher percentage (41.4 percent compared to 34.6 percent regionally and 31.4 percent nationally) of employed women with children under age 6. In addition, Utah has a significantly higher percentage of younger children. As noted in Chapter 3, 12.9 percent of Utah's population is under five compared to 7.2 percent nationally. When the increased number of working mothers with children

TABLE 2.

Comparison of Marital Status and Income Level for Employed Mothers with Children Under Age Six, Utah, the Mountain States, and the U.S., 1980

% EMPLOYED MOTHERS WITH CHILDREN UNDER AGE SIX	UTAH	MT. STATES REGION*	U.S.
	41.4	34.6	31.4
married mothers	87.4	84.6	82.7
single mothers	12.6	15.4	17.3
	11.2	10.7	10.8
married mothers below poverty	6.8	5.3	4.1
single mothers below poverty	38.2	36.3	36.6

*This includes Arizona, Colorado, Idaho, Montana, Nevada, New Mexico, Utah, and Wyoming.

Source: 1980 U.S. Census of the Population.

under age 6 is coupled with the state's disproportionately high young child population, the percentage of children needing care becomes much greater in Utah than elsewhere.

A comparison of the data in Table 1 reveals that a higher percentage of Utah mothers with dependent children are married than is the case nationally or regionally. The percentages of married or single employed mothers with children under six, presented in Table 2, are closely correlated to the marital status of all mothers with dependent children. Thus, nearly four times as many married mothers with children under six are employed than single mothers.

A slightly higher percentage of Utah's working mothers fall below the poverty level compared to the region or the nation (see Table 2). This could be influenced by the larger number of dependent children for Utah mothers. A 1984 report by the Utah League of Women Voters found that 23,551 children under age five, the majority of whom are members of two-parent families, live in poverty in Utah. It should also be noted that female headed families run a much higher risk of being among the working poor.

Such is the case, for example, among Utah's working mothers. Only 6.8 percent of married employed mothers compared to 38.2 percent of single employed mothers live in poverty. The league's report goes on to suggest that subsidizing child care for single parents can facilitate work and increase earnings. Some state and federal funds are used to underwrite child care for

TABLE 3.

Comparison of Work Time for Employed Mothers with Children Under Age Six, Utah, the Mountain States, and the U.S., 1980

EMPLOYED MOTHERS WITH CHILDREN UNDER AGE SIX	UTAH	MT. STATES REGION*	U.S.
Mean hours work per week	32.8	34.9	34.3
- married mothers	28.3	31.3	32.6
- single mothers	37.2	38.4	36.0

*This includes Arizona, Colorado, Idaho, Montana, Nevada, New Mexico, Utah, and Wyoming.

Source: 1980 U.S. Census of the Population

low income families, and currently there are between 6,000 and 7,000 Utah children who receive subsidized care each month.

Considering the average number of hours worked per week, the data in Table 3 indicate that more Utah mothers with young children work part time than is the case nationally. The average number of hours worked per week for Utah mothers is 32.8, whereas it is 34.9 for mothers in the region and 34.3 for mothers throughout the nation. In addition, married mothers in Utah work even fewer hours than is true regionally or nationally. The average number of hours worked by single mothers in the state compared to the nation is substantially greater than the average number of hours worked by married mothers.

In terms of the impact of this on the demand for child care, the increased number of married working mothers with young children could very well counterbalance their working fewer hours. This situation is the reverse for single mothers; although there are fewer single than married mothers, they work more hours. Thus, the demand for professional child care continues, with a growing number of children needing care for less than 30 hours a week.

A final factor to consider is the limited number of professional care providers. Although census data do not give a complete picture of child care services, the number of those claiming a career in child care is given. Here, the data indicate a disparity between supply and demand with less than 3.5 percent of employed mothers reporting that they are child care workers. According to the Utah Division of Family Services, there are 150 licensed child care centers and 1,710 licensed family home providers caring for some 16,000 children throughout the state. However, the Utah League of Women Voters estimates that approximately 112,000 Utah children need care because their parents work and they do not have relatives available to care for them.

With such small percentages of the population engaged in professional child care services, one is tempted to ask not only who is caring for the children but also how qualified they are. Presumably, most of this care is being provided by neighborhood babysitters. Unfortunately, it appears difficult to alter the belief that child care is little more than a custodial service with commensurate wages. Thus, there sadly tends to be little commitment to the preparation of child care workers and even some sentiment against those who perform such "menial" tasks. Until recognition is given to the importance and benefit of professional care for the children of employed mothers, little can be accomplished towards addressing a growing crisis that shows no signs of healing.

SUMMARY

Both Utah and the nation are involved in a child care crisis. The impact of this is greater in Utah due to its larger than average family size. Available data support not only this conclusion but the following five points, as well:

1. Of Utah women with dependent children, 49.6 percent are in the labor force compared to 53.2 percent nationally; however, 41.4 percent of Utah's working mothers have children under six compared to 31.4 percent nationally.

2. Utah has a higher birth rate; 12.9 percent of Utah's population, compared to 7.2 percent nationally, is under age 5.

3. A higher percentage of Utah working mothers, particularly single working mothers, live in poverty than is true regionally or nationally.

4. More Utah mothers, with husband present, work part time than elsewhere. However, single mothers both in Utah and elsewhere work more hours per week than married mothers.

5. The number of professional child care providers in Utah does not begin to meet the need. While present licensed child centers and family home providers care for approximately 16,000 children, as many as 95,000 Utah children could be in out-of-home unlicensed care settings.

REFERENCES

Blank, H. *Child Care: The States' Response. A Survey of State Child Care Policies, 1983-84*. Washington, D.C.: Children's Defense Fund, 1984.

Caldwell, B. "What is Quality Child Care?" *Young Children* 39 (1984), 3:3-8.

Children's Defense Fund. *Employed Parents and Their Children: A Data Book*. Washington, D.C.: Children's Defense Fund, 1982.

League of Women Voters of Utah. *The Child Care Challenge*. Salt Lake City, UT: League of Women Voters of Utah, 1984.

O'Connell, M. and C. C. Rogers. *Child Care Arrangements of Working Mothers: June 1982 (Series P-23, No. 129)*. Washington, D.C.: U.S. Department of Congress, 1982.

Ruopp, R., J. Travers, F. Glantz, and C. Coden. *Children at the Center: Final Report of the National Day Care Study.* Contract No. 105-74-1100. Cambridge, MA: Abt Associates Inc., 1979.

Select Committee on Children, Youth, and Families. *U.S. Children and Their Families: Current Conditions and Recent Trends.* 98th Congress, 1st Session, House of Representatives, 20-8300. Washington, D.C.: Government Printing Office, 1983.

9.
DIVORCE

Kristen L. Goodman
Tim B. Heaton

Although the increase in divorce rates beginning in the 1960s slowed somewhat during the late 1970s, the number of men and women experiencing divorce has continued to climb. In 1970, approximately 16,900,000 Americans had divorced. By 1980, the number had increased 16 percent to more than 19,600,000, more than the 11 percent increase in population for the same ten-year period (U.S. Bureau of the Census 1973, 1983).

The increase in divorce over the past decade reflects shifts in social norms and heralds additional changes for the future. More and more children are living in single parent families, and at least half of all poverty households are headed by single women (U.S. Bureau of the Census 1981, 1982). Smaller, disrupted families and individuals living alone also create new and different demands for housing and other consumer goods. These changes can be observed in all parts of the country.

This chapter compares divorce rates and characteristics of divorced persons in Utah, the eight states comprising the Mountain Region, and the United States. We will consider characteristics contributing to divorce and the outcomes of divorce for the men, women, and children involved. Most of the following data comes from the microfiles of the 1980 census.

The number of divorces per 1,000 people (i.e., the crude divorce rates) for Utah, the Mountain Region, and the U.S. are shown in Figure 1 for the years 1970-80 and up through 1983 for Utah and 1984 for the U.S. (Unfortunately, Mountain Region figures are not available after 1980.) In all three areas divorce increased between 1970 and 1975. Each area subsequently experienced both declines and increases during the next five to nine years. Utah's rates were slightly higher than national rates during the 1970s, except in 1976 when Utah's rate of 4.9 was slightly lower than the U.S. rate of 5.0. Between 1981

FIGURE 1.

Divorce Rates Per 1,000 Population for Utah, the Mountain Region, and the United States (All Races)

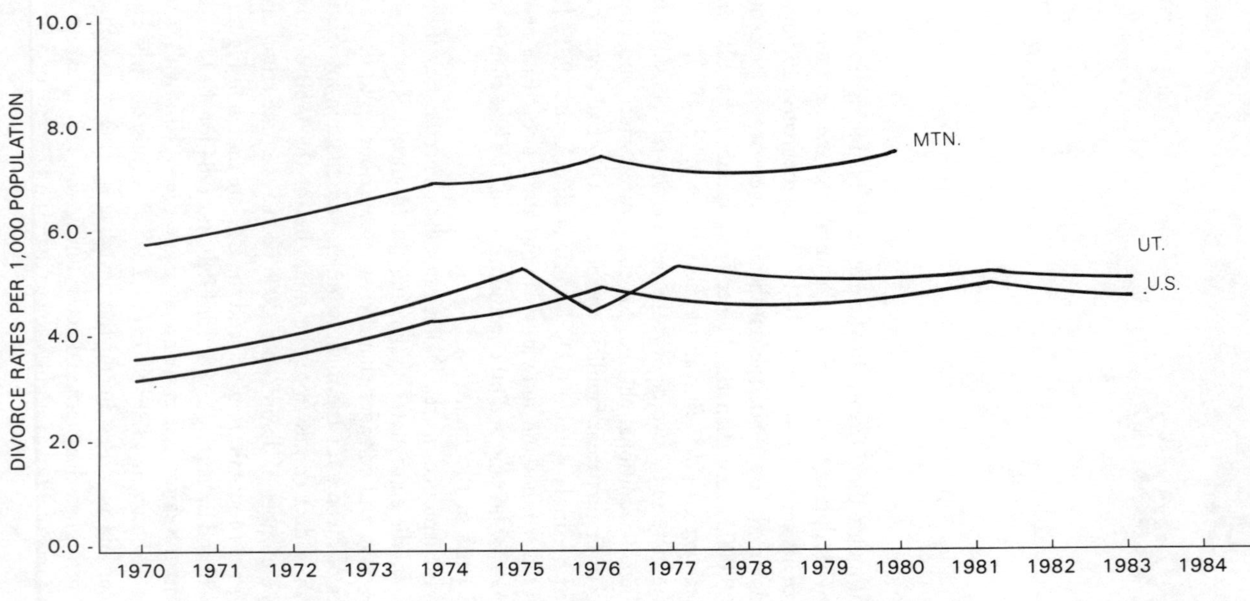

Sources: Vital Statistics of the U.S., 1972, 1977 and 1980, Vol. III Marriage and Divorce. U.S. Monthly Vital Statistics Reports, 1984 and 1985. Utah Quarterly Vital Statistics Report, 1985.

FIGURE 2.

Divorce Rates Per 1,000 Married Women for Utah and the United States—(All Races)

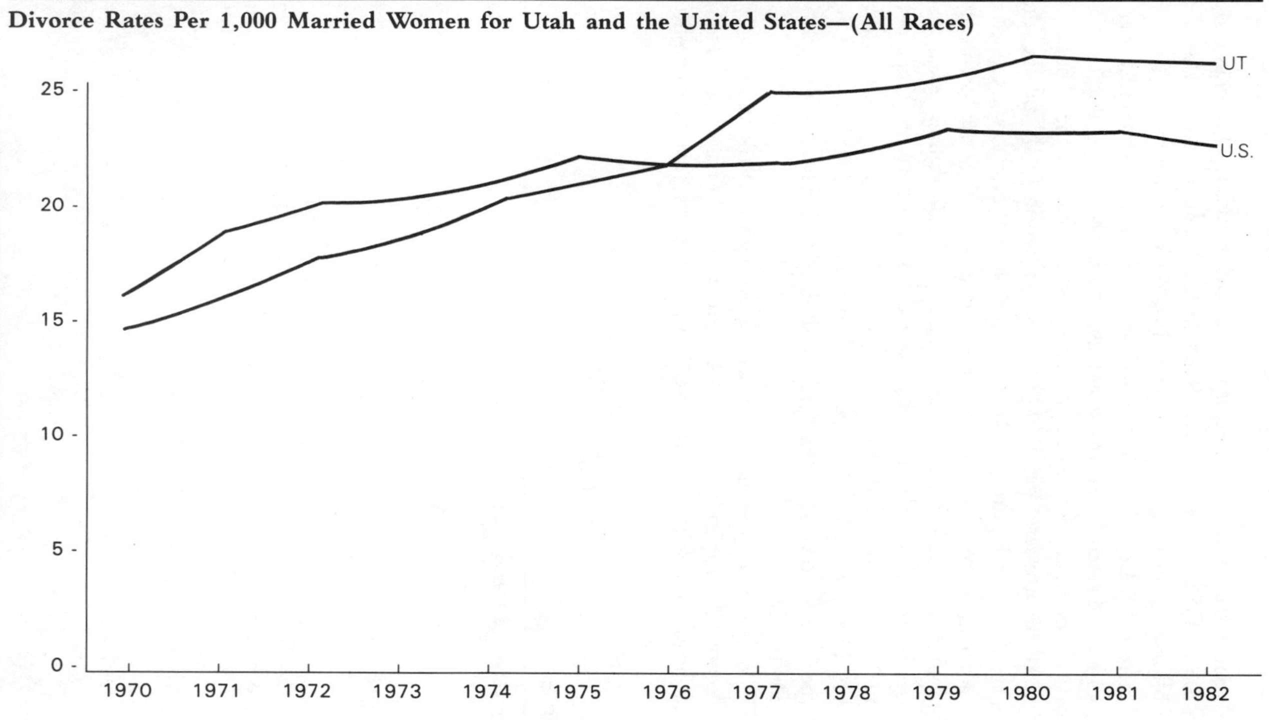

Sources: Monthly Vital Statistics Report, 1974 and 1985. Utah Marriage and Divorce, 1985.

and 1983, Utah's rates increased from 5.3 to 5.4, while U.S. rates dropped from 5.3 in 1981 to 4.9 in 1984. Rates in the Mountain Region were considerably higher than those for Utah and the U.S. during the 1970s, averaging 7.5 from 1974 to 1980, while Utah and U.S. rates averaged just over 5.0. Although more recent rates are not available for the Mountain Region, similar trends have probably continued through the first half of the 1980s.

Refined divorce rates per 1,000 married women in Utah and the United States are shown in Figure 2. (Regional rates are not available.) Refined rates are a better measure of divorce than crude rates since they are based only on the population at risk (i.e., married women). These figures reveal sharper increases in divorce over time and greater differences between Utah and the U.S. In 1970, Utah had 16.6 divorces per 1,000 married women, while the U.S. had 14.9. By 1981, the Utah rate had reached 25.1 and was still higher than the 22.6 nationally. Rates declined slightly in 1982 to 24.9 in Utah and 21.7 for the U.S.

While these rates give an idea of divorce during the 1970s and early 1980s, they do not offer any indication as to the prevalence of divorce or the number of people affected by it. Census data from 1980 show that over one-fifth of

TABLE 1.

Ever-Divorced and Current Marital Status

	UTAH	MOUNTAIN REGION	UNITED STATES
Ever-Married Persons who Have Ever Divorced	21.6%	26.5%	22.8%
Current Marital Status			
Married	65.8	62.3	59.2
Widowed	5.1	5.9	7.8
Divorced	6.0	7.6	6.4
Separated	1.1	1.5	2.3
Never Married	22.3	22.7	24.3
Total			
Men	26,673	40,012	81,265
Women	24,850	41,468	89,362

Source: 1980 U.S. Census of the Population

Americans who have ever been married have also experienced divorce. They also indicate that Utahns are actually less likely to have been divorced than residents of other states: 21.6 percent of all Utahns who have ever been married have also been divorced compared to 26.5 percent regionally and 22.8 percent nationally (see Table 1). When current marital status is considered, Table 1 also shows that Utahns are less likely to be divorced or separated. In Utah, 7.1 percent of adults are divorced or separated compared to 9.1 percent regionally and 8.7 percent nationally. In addition, fewer Utahns are widowed or have never married.

In other words, marital status and divorce figures suggest that even though divorce rates are high in Utah, fewer people have experienced divorce in Utah than nationally. Since more people are currently married (including remarriage after divorce), more risk divorce and consequently contribute to current divorce rates. Another contributing factor is the age of Utahns. There are more young people of marriageable age in the state, and recent marriages more often end in divorce than those contracted a generation or two previously. In short, although crude and refined rates of divorce are above national averages in Utah, fewer Utahns have actually experienced divorce.

CORRELATES OF DIVORCE

Several correlates of divorce have been discussed in the literature (see Kitson and Raschke 1981; Albrecht et al. 1983). This chapter deals only with those that are available in census data such as gender, ethnicity, age at first marriage, educational attainment, marriage cohort, and remarriage.

Typically, women and non-whites are more likely to divorce than others. Table 2 shows that about 1 percent more women than men in Utah and the United States have experienced divorce. But in the Mountain Region, men are slightly more likely to have experienced divorce.

Members of different ethnic groups tend to experience different rates of divorce. For example, blacks in all areas are the most likely to have divorced—about 42 percent in Utah and the Mountain Region and 35 percent in the U.S. Asians are typically the least likely to have divorced—only about 12 percent in Utah and the U.S. and 18.2 percent in the mountain states. Whites fall between these extremes with percentages of 21.3 in Utah, 26.6 regionally, and 21.6 nationally.

Where a particular ethnic group is small—such as blacks in Utah—divorce is often higher than would be expected. Indians are a large minority in both Utah and the Intermountain Region, and their divorce rates are more similar

TABLE 2.

Percent of Ever-Married Persons Who Have Ever Divorced

	UTAH		MOUNTAIN REGION		UNITED STATES	
Gender						
Male	21.1		26.7		22.3	
Female	22.0		26.3		23.3	
Ethnicity						
White	21.3		26.6		21.6	
Spanish	27.5		23.5		24.0	
Black	41.8		42.3		35.0	
Indian	26.1		24.0		31.3	
Asian/Island	12.5		18.2		11.9	
Other	11.8		38.8		25.8	
Age at First Marriage (Whites Only)						
	MALE	FEMALE	MALE	FEMALE	MALE	FEMALE
<17 years	47.6	37.2	52.1	40.5	42.6	35.3
18-19 years	30.6	23.8	36.5	29.2	30.7	26.1
20-21 years	22.1	17.0	29.0	23.7	23.4	19.7
22-24 years	15.4	15.8	22.8	19.6	19.6	15.3
25-29 years	15.7	13.2	21.2	17.5	16.2	13.3
30+ years	20.0	18.2	24.2	18.8	16.1	14.3
Years of Education Completed (Whites Only)						
0-8	27.8	25.5	26.6	23.6	19.9	17.9
9-11	27.5	29.2	30.1	31.7	23.5	26.5
12	23.6	22.8	28.8	26.6	22.8	22.5
13-15	20.5	18.2	28.2	25.9	23.5	22.7
16	12.7	13.6	20.2	18.3	16.5	15.2
17+	12.6	19.1	20.5	25.0	17.1	21.4
Years Since First Marriage (Whites Only)						
<2	7.3	7.5	9.2	9.9	8.3	9.2
3-4	13.2	16.1	18.2	20.1	17.0	18.2
5-7	20.4	22.2	27.3	27.5	23.6	26.9
8-10	25.6	26.2	33.5	32.8	27.7	29.4
11-15	27.9	29.8	34.0	35.3	28.4	31.8
16-20	28.8	32.3	33.9	34.7	28.4	31.5
21+	21.6	21.4	26.2	24.8	21.2	21.1
Percent of Ever-Divorced Now Married						
	64.5	49.3	58.7	48.5	57.9	43.4

Source: 1980 U.S. Census of the Population

to those of whites. Apparently, minorities that differ most in relative size from the dominant group have rates of divorce that vary the most from those of the dominant group.

Because of such differences and in order to eliminate the effects of race on divorce, the rest of this chapter focuses on whites only, comparing them in Utah (where they comprise 93.8 percent of the population) with whites regionally and nationally.

The average age at first marriage for Utah whites married before 1 April 1980 was 21.7 years, lower than the 22.2 years for the Mountain Region or the 22.6 years for the U.S. Women in all areas marry at an average age nearly two years younger than men. About equal proportions of Utah women and women regionally and nationally marry before age 18, but more Utah women marry at 18-21 years. Almost 72 percent of all Utah women are married by age 21, compared to 66.3 percent for the region and 62.5 percent for the U.S. Patterns for Utah men are similar, contributing to the overall lower age at first marriage.

Divorce is correlated with age at first marriage in that people who marry young are more likely to divorce. Table 2 shows the percentage of men and women who have ever married who have also divorced, by age at first marriage. In all areas, those who married young are more likely to divorce than those who delayed marriage. However, delaying too long may also pose problems since those married at age 30 or older are more likely to experience divorce than those married between 25-29 years.

Utahns usually marry between the ages of 20-25 for men and 18-25 for women. Utah men and women who marry at these ages are less likely to divorce than U.S. or Mountain Region residents. But Utahns who marry at either younger or older ages are more likely to divorce. One explanation for this "cross-over effect" (illustrated in Figure 3) is that cultural norms in Utah are less tolerant of deviance in marriage age than is the case nationally.

A second correlate of divorce is education or years of school completed. Education generally has a negative impact on divorce; that is, the more education a person has the less likely he or she is to experience divorce. Patterns of divorce in census data confirm these findings, with one or two exceptions. Men and women with a grade school education have relatively low divorce, probably because many of them are older people who married in an era when divorce was less common (see Table 2 and Figure 4). And people with seventeen or more years of schooling, particularly women, experience more divorce than

FIGURE 3.

Percent of Ever-Divorced Men and Women by Age at First Marriage in Utah, the Mountain Region and the United States (Whites Only)

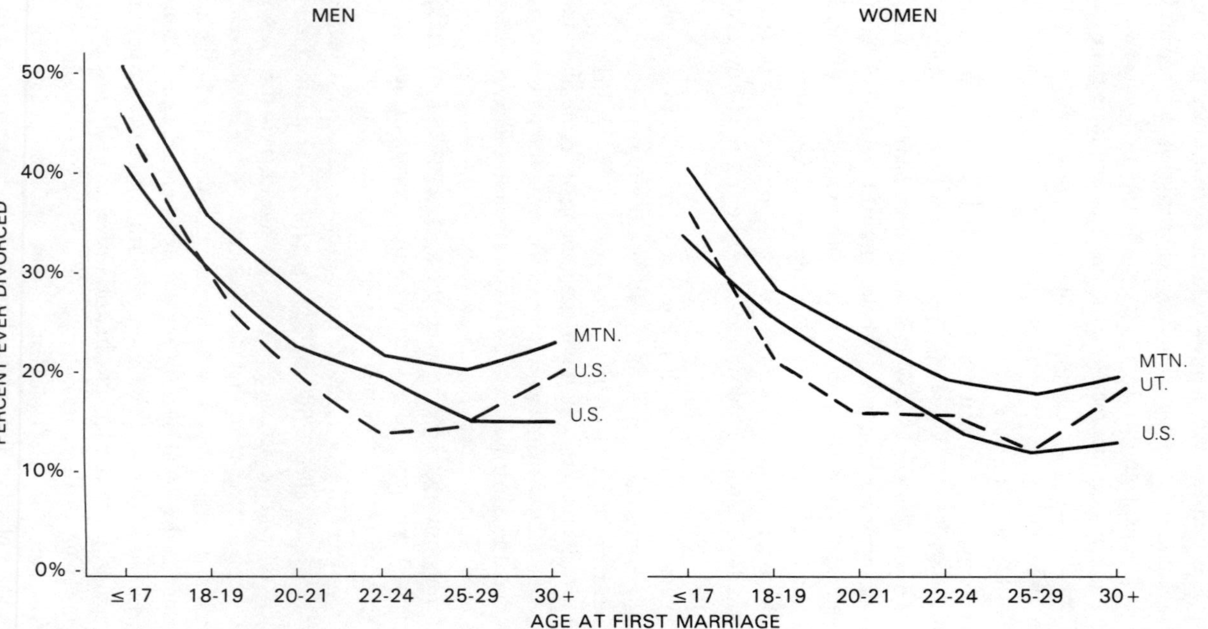

Source: 1980 U.S. Census.

FIGURE 4.

Percent of Ever-Divorced Men and Women by Years of School Completed, for Utah and the United States (Whites Only)

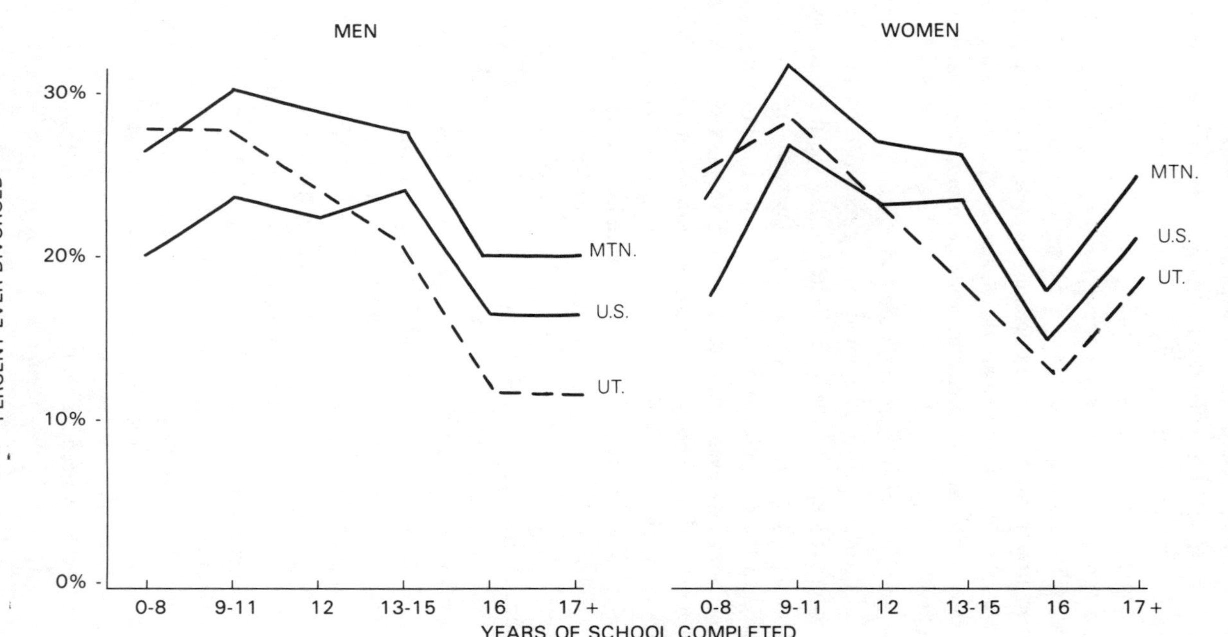

Source: 1980 U.S. Census.

those who stop at sixteen years. It may be that graduate education gives women more economic independence, facilitating divorce, or that women who experience divorce return to school for more education.

A comparison of Utah men and women with couples regionally reveals that Utahns have lower divorce rates for all categories except those with only a grade school education. Among those with college experience, Utahns have a lower proportion of divorced persons than either the region or the nation (see Figure 4). This may be another instance where violating the norm—in this case, scholastic achievement—may be more detrimental in Utah than elsewhere.

Because divorce is more common today than previously, higher proportions of divorced persons are found among recent marriage cohorts who are both young enough to have been affected by the social and economic changes associated with divorce and who have been married long enough to have been exposed to the risk of divorce. Table 2 shows the proportions of men and women who have ever divorced, according to years since first marriage.

Generally, the risk of divorce increases with the number of years since first marriage for the first twenty years of marriage. After this the proportion decreases. Since the census does not provide information about marital duration for divorced persons, the number of years since first marriage serves as the only available measure of time lapsed since marriage. Utah has lower proportions of divorced men and women than the U.S. for all categories except those involving the two oldest cohorts. Here, Utah has slightly more divorced persons. This suggests that the number of Utahns ever divorced has not remained consistently below national averages. Again, Mountain Region proportions are consistently higher than Utah or U.S. figures.

Remarriage is typically less stable than first marriage, and most current remarriages have at least one divorced (as opposed to widowed) spouse (Carter and Glick 1976). Census figures indicate that 18 percent of Utah men who have ever been married and 18.4 percent of Utah women who have ever been married have been married more than once. Comparable national figures are lower with 17.1 percent of men and 17.0 percent of women having been married more than once. Again, Regional percentages are higher: 21.6 for men and 21.4 for women. When current marital status is considered, Utahns who have ever been divorced are more likely to remarry than people in other areas and men are more likely to remarry than women (see Table 2). For example,

TABLE 3.

Fertility and Marital Status (Whites Only) in Percentages

	UTAH			MOUNTAIN REGION			UNITED STATES		
	MARRIED	DIVORCED	SEPARATED	MARRIED	DIVORCED	SEPARATED	MARRIED	DIVORCED	SEPARATED
Number of Children Ever Born									
None	12.4	14.0	17.9	16.9	22.1	19.6	16.6	21.6	19.5
1	13.5	20.0	22.0	16.2	22.0	19.9	17.4	23.0	24.1
2	20.8	22.9	27.5	26.7	24.5	27.8	28.8	23.6	23.7
3	19.0	16.3	12.8	19.1	15.2	15.8	18.9	15.2	14.8
4	15.4	12.0	9.2	10.9	8.2	6.8	9.6	8.6	8.4
5	9.0	7.3	5.5	5.0	4.2	5.6	4.4	4.2	3.4
6	5.2	4.1	1.5	2.5	2.1	2.0	2.3	1.9	2.3
7+	4.9	3.3	3.7	2.7	1.7	2.5	2.1	1.9	3.9
Average Number of Children Ever Born									
	3.83	3.49	3.15	3.34	3.01	3.26	3.22	2.98	3.09
Total		3.32			3.92			2.82	

Source: 1980 U.S. Census of the Population.

almost half of the women in Utah who have ever been divorced have remarried and are currently married compared to about three out of five Utah men who have ever been divorced.

Remarriage helps explain some of the differences between Utah's divorce rates and its proportions of men and women who have ever been divorced. As noted above, remarriage tends to follow divorce rather than widowhood. A remarriage which ends in divorce is counted in the divorce rate, but the population does not gain another person who has ever been divorced. Thus, remarriage in Utah has the potential of increasing divorce rates above national averages while keeping the proportion of men and women who have ever been divorced below national averages. But when Utah is compared with the region, the state is lower on all counts.

OUTCOMES OF DIVORCE

Divorce necessitates many readjustments. It affects family size and often precipitates changes in living arrangements, employment, and income. In this section, divorce-related outcomes such as fertility, housing, living arrangements, employment, and income are compared for currently married and divorced, or separated, persons in Utah, the Mountain Region, and the U.S.

The dissolution of a marriage often interrupts fertility. Thus, divorced women tend to have fewer children than married women. Table 3 shows that divorced, or separated, women are more likely to be childless or to have only one or two children while married women are more likely to have three or more children. When Utah women are compared to women in other parts of the country, they have an average of .4 to .5 children more than other women—a significant difference. The fertility rate of married Utah women is higher than elsewhere, and even divorced women in Utah have more children than married women in other parts of the country. The difference in fertility rates between married and divorced, or separated, women is larger in Utah than in other areas. Also, remarriage is more common and widowhood is less frequent. Thus, even though Utah's divorced, or separated, women have above average fertility rates, fewer of Utah's children live in disrupted households, 14.7 percent in Utah compared to 25.3 percent nationally.

Utahns are slightly more likely to own their own homes than are residents of the region or the nation (see Table 4 and Figure 5). In all areas, men and women who have separated are least likely to own their homes. There are small differences in ownership between divorced and separated men and women

TABLE 4.

Housing and Marital Status (Whites Only)

	UTAH		MOUNTAIN REGION		UNITED STATES	
	MALE	FEMALE	MALE	FEMALE	MALE	FEMALE
Owns Home%						
Married	81.7	81.7	80.5	80.7	80.5	80.7
Divorced	48.5	54.2	50.1	54.7	49.8	48.7
Separated	39.3	46.9	41.5	48.3	46.2	41.8
Value of Home*						
Married	$42,000	$42,000	$32,000	$32,000	$28,500	$28,500
Divorced	19,250	21,750	19,500	21,500	17,500	18,500
Separated	16,000	20,750	18,000	20,500	16,250	17,500
Persons Per Room						
Married	.53	.53	.61	.60	.57	.57
Divorced	.46	.48	.46	.50	.47	.51
Separated	.42	.43	.49	.63	.49	.59
Mortgage Payments						
Married	$322	$323	$333	$333	$295	$295
Divorced	297	259	331	279	287	255
Separated	332	303	371	294	294	261
Rent**						
Married	$187	$187	$203	$203	$193	$192
Divorced	181	182	192	191	191	183
Separated	181	184	188	192	191	183

*Values are approximate because ranges rather than exact numbers were recorded. This does not include the value of group quarters, mobile homes, or non-condominium apartments.

**Values are approximate because ranges rather than exact numbers were recorded.

Source: 1980 U.S. Census of the Population.

FIGURE 5.

Home Values, Home Ownership, and Average Household Size for Married Couples and Divorced Men and Women in Utah, the Mountain Region, and the United Stgates (Whites Only)

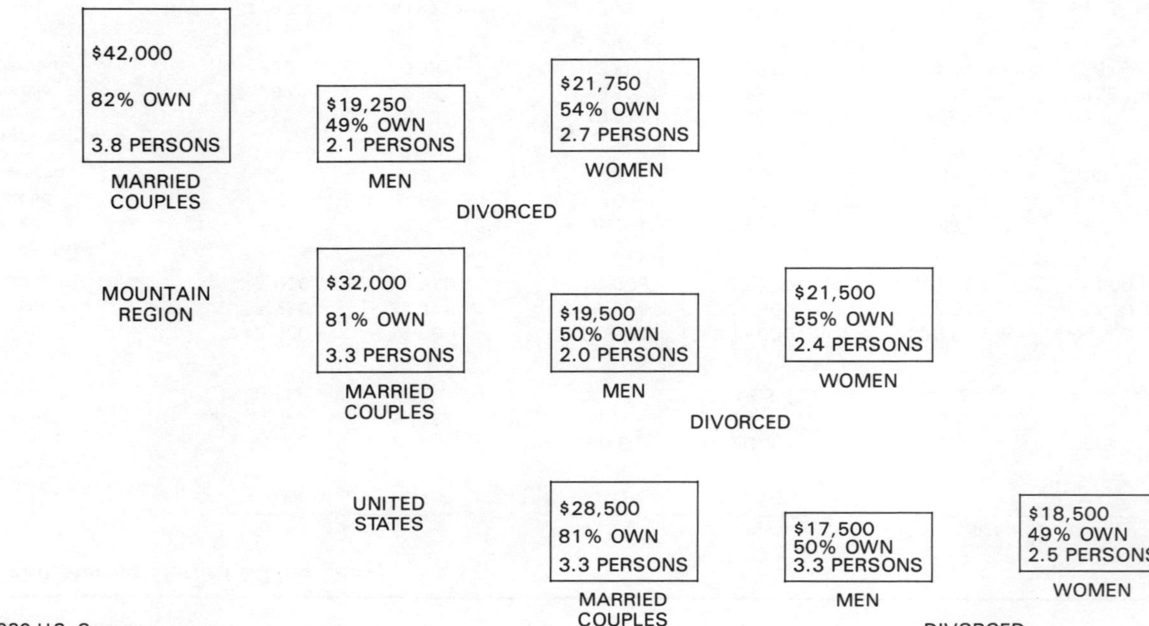

Source: 1980 U.S. Census.

in Utah and the region. But divorced or separated women in Utah and the region are more likely to own their homes than is the case nationally.

Utah homes also tend to be valued higher—$10,000 or more—than homes in other areas. But this is more the result of having larger homes to house larger-than-average families than higher market values. One evidence of this is the number of persons per room, which is lower in Utah (despite larger families) than nationally or regionally (see Table 4).

As one might expect, married couples have more expensive homes than divorced, or separated, men and women, and there is a larger discrepancy in Utah than elsewhere between the home values of married and divorced people. Divorcees in Utah have average home values only half those of married couples; whereas, regionally and nationally the homes of divorcees are valued at almost two-thirds as much as those of married men and women. Nevertheless, the home values of Utah's divorced and separated men and women are not significantly lower than those for the region or the nation. When men and women are compared, divorced and separated women have more valuable homes than do men in all areas. This is understandable because women, not men, are more often responsible for their children and need better housing.

As noted, Utah homes have higher values and house more people than elsewhere. Typically, though, monthly mortgage payments are lower than for homes regionally (see Table 4). Payments average $313 per month in Utah and $336 per month in the region. Still, payments in both areas exceed the average $287 per month for the United States. Divorced and separated men consistently have higher housing costs than do divorced and separated women despite higher home values for women.

Rental costs, as shown in Table 4, follow similar patterns with payments for men and women being close. As with mortgage costs, Utahns also pay lower average monthly rents—$185 per month—than residents of the Mountain Region—$197 per month—or the nation—$190 per month.

In summary, divorced and separated persons in Utah and elsewhere are less likely than married couples to own their homes. Furthermore, based on home values and mortgage and rental payments, Utah does not have excessive housing costs for divorced and separated men and women.

Living arrangements also differ by marital status. (Since all married couples live in family households, their numbers are not shown in Table 5.) Unmarried men are more likely than women to live alone because previously married women often have children with them. About half of all divorced or separated men live alone, compared to less than a third of divorced or separated women.

TABLE 5.

Living Arrangements and Marital Status (Whites Only)

	UTAH		MOUNTAIN REGION		UNITED STATES	
	DIVORCED	SEPARATED	DIVORCED	SEPARATED	DIVORCED	SEPARATED
Living Arrangements%						
Males						
Lives alone	46.8	56.7	47.3	48.6	46.2	47.6
Head of Household						
with children	8.0	5.1	9.3	8.5	8.1	9.3
without children	15.7	6.7	18.3	16.6	17.2	12.2
Not head of household	29.5	31.5	25.2	26.3	28.5	30.9
Females%						
Lives alone	24.8	18.8	29.3	21.7	30.9	21.2
Head of Household						
with children	45.9	48.7	35.5	38.9	35.0	41.6
without children	10.8	7.6	13.1	12.0	13.0	11.0
Not Head of household	18.5	24.9	22.1	27.4	21.7	26.3
Average Household Size						
Males	2.07	1.90	1.97	2.07	2.05	2.11
Females	2.72	3.08	2.44	3.03	2.46	2.94

Source: 1980 U.S. Census of the Population.

Divorced men in Utah are as likely as men regionally or nationally to live alone, while separated Utah men are more likely to live alone. Only 8 percent of divorced and 5.1 percent of separated Utah men head households with dependent children—fewer than is the case regionally or nationally.

Divorced and separated women most often live in female headed households with their own children. Utah women are more often responsible for minor children than are women elsewhere because of their higher fertility and because Utah men have custody of children less often. Approximately 10 percent more Utah women head households with children than is true regionally or nationally. Conversely, divorced or separated Utah women less often live alone or in homes headed by others.

According to Table 5, household sizes are larger among divorced and separated women than men, and are larger in Utah than in the region or the nation. In addition, separated women are more likely than divorced women to have children living with them. This is probably due to the nature of the separation period which is often characterized by some degree of disorganization. Following the divorce, living arrangements typically become more permanent.

In summary, the major difference characterizing the living arrangements of Utah's divorced or separated residents is that because of their high fertility Utah's women bear a greater responsibility for their dependent children than Utah men or than women elsewhere.

Since employment histories are not available, we cannot distinguish between the possible influences of employment either contributing to or resulting from divorce. Thus we are forced to limit our analysis to describing the employment status, occupation, and hours worked for married and divorced or separated persons. Overall, Utah men are more likely to be employed and Utah women less likely to be employed than men and women elsewhere, although the differences are not great. Regionally and nationally, divorced and separated men are almost as likely to be employed as married men. However, in Utah, divorced men are less likely to work than either married or separated men, and separated men are less likely to be unemployed than married men. Marital disruption has little impact on the average hours worked per week by men.

Employment patterns for women are different. Nationally, divorced women are about 30 percent more likely than married women to be in the labor force. According to Table 6, 48 percent of married women regionally and 47.8 percent of married women nationally are employed compared to 44.8 percent of married Utah women. More than three-fourths of divorced women in Utah

TABLE 6.

Labor Force Participation and Marital Status (Whites Only)—in Percentages

	UTAH			MOUNTAIN REGION			UNITED STATES		
	MARRIED	DIVORCED	SEPARATED	MARRIED	DIVORCED	SEPARATED	MARRIED	DIVORCED	SEPARATED
Employment Status									
Males									
employed	82.4	73.6	77.0	78.8	73.8	72.8	77.4	72.5	74.1
unemployed	2.5	7.3	8.4	2.5	6.4	7.7	3.1	6.9	6.2
Females									
employed	43.0	72.3	63.8	45.9	74.4	64.4	45.6	69.5	61.2
unemployed	1.8	4.4	5.9	2.1	3.6	6.3	2.2	4.0	5.9
Mean Hours Worked Per Week									
Males	44.4	44.0	44.3	45.4	43.3	44.4	44.3	43.5	44.0
Females	32.8	39.3	37.7	34.7	39.5	37.8	34.7	38.9	37.4
Occupation—males									
Executive, Administrative, & Managerial	15.6	10.5	10.8	15.7	11.5	8.7	14.8	12.3	13.4
Professional	12.8	8.5	9.0	12.1	10.0	8.7	11.4	9.3	10.0
Technical, Sales & Administrative Support	19.1	17.9	13.8	19.0	18.2	14.9	18.2	18.5	16.3
Service	5.9	7.0	8.4	6.9	12.3	13.9	6.3	10.0	11.4
Farming, Forestry, and Fishing	3.3	2.7	1.8	6.0	4.0	6.8	4.6	3.3	3.4

TABLE 6. CONTINUED

Precision Production, Craft & Repair	24.8	27.7	29.9	23.3	24.2	28.5	23.4	22.6	19.0
Operators, Fabricators, and Laborers	18.4	25.3	26.3	16.9	19.3	18.2	21.1	23.7	25.6
Armed Forces and Retired Armed Forces	.2	.3	—	.2	.5	.3	.1	.3	1.0
Occupation—females									
Executive, Administrative, & Managerial	7.4	9.7	7.0	8.0	9.3	4.8	6.9	9.9	6.7
Professional	13.1	9.9	7.8	14.0	11.7	9.7	14.3	11.9	10.4
Technical, Sales & Administrative Support	47.3	46.8	47.1	47.9	45.7	41.4	46.4	43.3	43.0
Service	17.8	16.0	22.5	18.2	21.5	27.6	15.9	17.7	20.2
Farming, Forestry, and Fishing	.7	.4	.8	1.5	.6	1.5	1.3	.5	1.0
Precision Production, Craft & Repair	2.8	3.5	1.6	2.4	2.8	3.1	2.3	3.2	2.3
Operators, Fabricators, and Laborers	10.7	13.4	13.1	7.7	8.1	11.6	12.6	13.3	15.9
Armed Forces and Retired Armed Forces	.3	.4	—	.3	.2	.2	.4	.3	.6

Source: 1980 U.S. Census of the Population.

are employed, slightly less than is the case regionally but more than in the U.S. Figures for separated women are lower. Although there are fewer women than men who are unemployed (i.e., between jobs), divorced and separated women are two to three times more likely than married women to be unemployed.

Women are more apt than men to work part time, averaging fewer hours worked per week. Divorced women are not only the most likely to be employed, but, when they are employed they work more hours than other women, averaging about 39 hours per week. Finally, employed married women in Utah are more likely than married women or divorced or separated women elsewhere to be working part time, averaging only 32.8 hours per week.

Gender differences in occupations are greater than geographic differences between Utahns and the region or the U.S. In general, more than 40 percent of women are concentrated in technical, sales, administrative support (e.g., secretarial) occupations, and other white collar jobs (including executive, administrative, and managerial professions). Men also hold white collar jobs, but they are more likely to have occupations in precision production, crafts, and repair businesses or as operators, fabricators, and laborers.

Divorced or separated men tend to have more blue collar jobs than do married men; this is true not only in Utah but in the region and the nation as well. Divorced and separated women are less likely than married women to be in professional occupations (e.g., law, medicine, etc.) but are more likely to have executive, administrative, or management positions. In general, their occupational status is similar to married women in Utah, the region, and the nation.

Wage and salary incomes reflect differences in employment patterns. Overall, Utahns earn less than residents of the region or the nation. Wages average $10,910 per year for Utah, $11,274 for the region, and $11,800 for the U.S. The fact that Utah's men and women earn less on the average than men and women regionally or nationally evidences Utah's disadvantaged economy.

Discrepancies between wages for men and women are greater than differences arising from marital status or geography (see Table 7). Typically, women have incomes about half those of men. Some of this is due to part-time work and lower paying occupations among women, but considerable differences still remain among full-time workers in the same occupations, placing divorced and separated women in a particularly disadvantaged status.

TABLE 7.

Income, Poverty and Marital Status (Whites Only)

	UTAH		MOUNTAIN REGION		UNITED STATES	
	MALE	FEMALE	MALE	FEMALE	MALE	FEMALE
Mean Wage and Salary Income*						
Married	$17,832	$ 6,162	$17,978	$ 6,963	$18,654	$ 7,313
Divorced	14,135	8,459	15,085	9,142	15,542	9,574
Separated	13,409	6,802	13,687	6,857	16,366	7,459
Mean Household Income						
Married	$23,430	$23,367	$25,607	$25,201	$24,770	$24,770
Divorced	19,768	14,002	21,315	15,740	20,491	15,223
Separated	18,372	12,523	20,756	12,799	20,989	13,435
Percent Below 125% of Poverty Level						
Married	8.0	8.3	7.6	7.9	7.6	7.9
Divorced	11.8	30.3	13.1	25.2	13.5	25.4
Separated	10.6	43.6	16.1	41.7	13.3	37.5
Percent Receiving Public Assistance						
Married	1.3	1.2	1.4	1.3	1.7	1.7
Divorced	2.7	14.9	1.9	9.1	3.2	13.1
Separated	.5	17.8	3.2	15.3	3.7	20.5
Mean Public Assistance Income**						
Married	$2,552	$2,040	$2,310	$1,961	$2,373	$2,021
Divorced	1,802	2,402	1,928	1,986	1,953	2,492
Separated	2,805	2,211	2,463	1,947	1,858	2,508

*For those with income.
**For those with Public Assistance income.

Source: 1980 U.S. Census of the Population

Household income is different from wage and salary income in that it includes income from all sources for all members of the household and is a better indicator of available resources. For example, household income for a divorced woman may include not only her wages but child support and public assistance payments. Like wage and salary income, household income is lower in Utah than in the region or the nation, and women report lower household incomes than men (see Table 7).

Married couples have the highest household incomes because in almost one-half of all marriages both the husband and wife are employed. Separated men and women have the lowest household incomes; these are lower in Utah than in the region or the nation. Finally, separated women in Utah have household incomes averaging only about half those of married couples in the state.

Because of their lower household incomes and larger families, Utahns are more likely to live in poverty (see Table 7). Single women are more than twice as likely as men to live in poverty and are overly represented among poverty households. Separated women, in particular, suffer severe economic problems. In Utah, 43.6 percent of separated women live in poverty compared to 41.7 percent regionally and 37.5 percent nationally. All are about five times more likely to live in poverty than married women in the same areas. Again, single women in Utah often occupy extremely disadvantaged positions.

One avenue of financial help for men and women with low incomes is public assistance, but both the availability and the amount of aid differs. For example, even though a higher proportion of Utah families live in poverty, only 2.3 percent receive public assistance. This compares to 2.4 percent for the region and to 3.2 percent for the U.S. In all areas, separated women are most likely to receive assistance. At least five times as many separated women as men receive public assistance, but this still is not enough to raise them out of poverty. Average payments to recipients are higher in Utah ($2,230 per year) than in the region ($2,012 per year) or the nation ($2,150 per year). More women than men receive public assistance, but amounts are higher for married and separated men than women (Table 7). Typically, divorced women receive higher payments than divorced men or other women, but, again, even with this assistance, 25 to 30 percent live in poverty.

SUMMARY

While Utah's divorce rates are higher than national averages, they are lower than regional rates. There are also fewer men and women who have ever been divorced in the state than is true either regionally or nationally. These differences are attributed to Utah's younger population and to its higher rates of marriage and remarriage.

Non-whites, those who marry young, and those with lower education tend to have higher rates of divorce. Because of Utah's homogeneity, those who vary from the state's cultural norms—being an ethnic minority, marrying too early or too late, having too little education, for example—are more likely to experience divorce compared to the rest of the region or the nation.

Distinct differences in housing, living arrangements, employment, and income exist between married and divorced or separated persons. These characteristics present challenges for divorced and separated women. In many ways, separated women are more disadvantaged than divorcees. Low incomes coupled with responsibility for children create high rates of poverty. These and related problems are particularly severe in Utah where families are larger and incomes are lower than regionally or nationally.

These results suggest two areas of concern for Utahns. First, more attention should be devoted to the causes of divorce among minorities or among those who do not conform to norms regarding age at marriage and educational attainment. Second, policies need to be developed to help begin alleviating the growing economic plight of divorced and separated women.

REFERENCES

Albrecht, Stan L., Howard M. Bahr, and Kristen L. Goodman. *Divorce and Remarriage: Problems, Adaptations and Adjustments*. Westport, CT: Greenwood Press, 1983.

Carter, Hugh and Paul C. Glick. *Marriage and Divorce: A Social and Economic Study*. Cambridge, MA: Harvard University Press, 1976.

Kitson, Gay C. and Helen J. Raschke. "Divorce Research: What We Know; What We Need to Know." *Journal of Divorce* 4 (Spring 1981): 1-37.

National Center for Health Statistics. *Vital Statistics of the United States, 1972, Vol. 3, Marriage and Divorce*. Washington, D.C.: U.S. Government Printing Office, 1977.

_____. *Vital Statistics of the United States, 1977, Vol. 3, Marriage and Divorce*. Washington, D.C.: U.S. Government Printing Office, 1981.

_____. *Annual Summary of Births, Deaths, Marriages, and Divorces: United States, 1983*. Monthly Vital Statistics Report, Vol. 32, No. 13. Hyattsville, MD: Public Health Service, 1984.

_____. *Advance Report of Final Divorce Statistics, 1982*. Monthly Vital Statistics Report, Vol. 33, No. 11. Hyattsville, MD: Public Heath Service, 1985.

_____. *Births, Marriages, Divorces, and Deaths for 1984*. Monthly Vital Statistics Report, Vol. 33, No. 12. Hyattsville, MD: Public Health Service, 1985.

_____. *Vital Statistics of the United States, 1980, Vol. 3, Marriage and Divorce.* Washington, D. C.: U.S. Government Printing Office, 1985.

U.S. Department of Commerce, Bureau of the Census. *1970 Census of the Population, Vol. 1, Characteristics of the Population, Part I, U.S. Summary.* Washington, D.C.: U.S. Government Printing Office, 1973.

_____. "Households, Families, Marital Status, and Living Arrangements: March 1980." *Current Population Reports*. Series P-20, No. 366. Washington, D.C.: U.S. Government Printing Office, 1981.

_____. "Money Income and Poverty Status of Families and Persons in the United States: 1981." *Current Population Reports*. Series P-60, No. 134. Washington, D.C.: U.S. Government Printing Office, 1982.

_____. *1980 Census of the Population, Vol. 1, Characteristics of the Population, Detailed Population Characteristics, Part 46, Utah*. Washington, D.C.: U.S. Government Printing Office, 1983.

Utah Bureau of Health Statistics. *Utah Marriage and Divorce: 1980-1982*. Salt Lake City, Utah: Utah Department of Health, 1985.

_____. *Utah Quarterly Vital Statistics Report, 1983*. Vol. 6, No. 1. Salt Lake City, Utah: Utah Department of Health, 1985.

10.
NONTRADITIONAL FAMILIES

Stephen J. Bahr
Rita Edmonds
Jinnah Kelson

The traditional concept of a family is that of a man and woman who marry and have children, who raise and nurture those children, and who remain together until one partner dies. However, a growing number of families no longer conform to this pattern. Unmarried couples, childless couples, single-parent families, and blended families are four alternative types that have become more common during the past twenty-five years. This chapter examines these nontraditional families in Utah and offers comparisons with the United States.

Before discussing different family types, however, we should define what a family is. For our purposes, a family can be a married couple (with or without children), a parent and a child or children, or an unmarried couple living in the same household. According to the Census Bureau unmarried couples are not considered a family. But because of recent social and legal changes regarding cohabitation, we have decided to include unmarried couples in our definition. An unmarried couple is composed of two unrelated adults of the opposite sex who share a housing unit (U.S. Bureau of the Census, *Census of the Population,* 1980, 1983). Throughout the following discussion, the terms unmarried couple and cohabitation are used interchangeably.

UNMARRIED COUPLES

There has been a significant increase in the number of unmarried couples in the United States—almost four times as many in 1984 as in 1970 (U.S. Bureau of the Census, *Statistical Abstract*, 1984). In 1980, Utah's nearly 7,000 unmarried couples comprised 1.9 percent of all families in the state. By comparison, the nation's 1.8 million unmarried couples comprised 2.9 percent of all families (see Table 1). Thus, unmarried couples are a more common family type in the United States than in Utah.

Table 2 shows the marital status of unmarried couples who are living together. In Utah cohabitants are more likely to be never married or divorced and are less likely to be separated or widowed than they are nationally. About 49 percent of Utah's cohabitants have never been married compared to 46 percent nationally. Forty-three percent of Utah cohabitants are divorced compared to 35 percent in the United States. Over 10 percent of cohabitants nationally are married but separated from their spouses compared to 5 percent in Utah. The percentage of cohabitants who are widowed is 8 percent nationally compared to 3 percent in Utah.

Unmarried couples in Utah are more likely to have children than unmarried couples in the United States. Thirty-four percent of unmarried couples in Utah have at least one child under the age of 15 compared to 29 percent of unmarried couples nationally (U.S. Bureau of the Census, *Census of the Population,* 1983, 1984). This is consistent with Utah's high fertility.

Data from 1970 on unmarried couples in Utah are not available, and therefore we can only speculate about changes in cohabitation during the past decade. Given the increases in nonmarital cohabitation in the United States, one can assume that similar increases occurred in Utah. Between 1970 and 1980 there was a 300 percent jump in the number of unmarried couples in the United States from half a million to 1.5 million (U. S. Bureau of the Census, *Statistical Abstract*, 1984). By 1984 this number had increased to almost 2 million. Local

TABLE 1.

Family Types in Utah and the United States—1980 (in Percent)

FAMILY TYPES	UTAH	UNITED STATES
Married Couples	86.7	80.4
Unmarried Couples	1.9	2.9
Single-Parent Families	11.4	16.7
Total %	100.0	100.0
Total Number of Families	361,122	60,954,113

Source: 1980 U.S. Census of the Population.

policy makers will no doubt find it important to examine trends in unmarried couples during the coming decade.

CHILDLESS COUPLES

In American society married couples ideally have children. Indeed, one of the traditional purposes of marriage has been to bear and raise children, and couples who do not, for whatever reason, deviate from a strong societal norm. Such marriages are nontraditional, particularly if they are childless by choice (Veevers 1980). The following analysis compares childlessness in Utah, the Intermountain Region, and the United States. To adequately study childlessness we need information on whether or not it is voluntary. Since no such data exist, we are limited to an examination of childlessness generally.

Table 3 shows the percentage of women who have ever been married who are also childless. Clearly, married couples without children form a minority. In the United States less than 20 percent of couples who have ever been married are childless.

Not unexpectedly, given its emphasis on family life, Utah has considerably less childlessness than either the Intermountain Region or the United States. Only 12 percent of Utah women who have ever been married are childless compared to 16 percent regionally and 17 percent nationally.

These figures include women who, though currently childless, may yet bear a child. Perhaps it is more accurate to examine only women who have reached the end of their childbearing years (age 45 and over). Among this

TABLE 2.

Marital Status of Unmarried Couples in Utah and the United States—1980 (in Percent)

MARITAL STATUS	UTAH	UNITED STATES
Never Married	48.7	46.2
Divorced	42.6	35.0
Married, Spouse Absent	5.4	10.5
Widowed	3.2	8.3

Source: 1980 U.S. Census of the Population.

group, only 7 percent of Utah women who have ever been married are childless compared to 12 percent regionally and 13 percent nationally.

Table 3 also shows some interesting differences between whites and non-whites. In Utah and the United States non-whites are more likely to be childless. However, in the Intermountain Region whites are more likely to be childless.

Being a parent is the norm for the majority of married women. Over 93 percent of Utah women over 45 who have ever been married have had at least one child compared to almost 87 percent nationally.

SINGLE-PARENT FAMILIES

The number of single-parent families in the United States has increased dramatically. During the late 1960s and early 1970s the divorce rate grew steadily, and since 1975 there have been more than one million divorces each year. Furthermore, recent estimates indicate that over 40 percent of current marriages will eventually end in divorce (Norton and Glick 1979; Preston 1975; Schoen et al. 1985). Indeed, more than half of all children will live in a single-parent family before they reach age 18 (Furstenburg and Nord 1982; Glick 1979; Norton and Glick 1986). Single-parent homes are also formed by the death of a parent or by the birth of a child outside of marriage. However, the increase in single-parent families in the United States is due largely to the rise in divorce rates.

A summary of family types in Utah and the United States is provided in Table 1. It shows that single-parent families are less common in Utah, that 87 percent of all Utah families are married couple families while 11 percent

TABLE 3.

Percent of Ever Married Women Who Are Childless—1980

	ALL AGES			AGE 45 AND OVER		
	WHITE	NON-WHITE	TOTAL	WHITE	NON-WHITE	TOTAL
Utah	12.1	16.3	12.3	6.9	8.9	6.9
Intermountain Region	17.2	11.7	16.2	12.1	9.1	11.7
United States	17.2	15.7	16.8	12.9	16.7	13.4

Source: 1980 U.S. Census of the Population and Housing.

are single-parent families. By comparison, 80 percent of all families nationally are married couple families and 17 percent are single-parent families. There is little difference between the western region and the United States in the proportion of single-parent families.

A comparison of the changes in the proportion of single-parent families in Utah and in the United States is given in Table 4. Here the percentages differ slightly from those presented in Table 1 because unmarried couples were not included. In 1970 single-parent families comprised 9.9 percent of all Utah families. By 1980, this had risen to 11.6 percent, an increase of 1.7 percent. In the United States these figures were 14 percent in 1970 and 17.2 percent in 1980, an increase of 3.2 percent. Thus, although the proportion of Utah families headed by single persons increased during the past decade, the national increase was greater.

A detailed comparison of single-parent families is shown in Table 5. In both Utah and the United States over 80 percent of single-parent families are headed by women, and from 1970 to 1980 the proportion of single-parent families headed by women increased 1.7 percent in Utah and 3 percent nationally. These data challenge the popular view that more men are becoming heads of single-parent families.

TABLE 4.

Family Types in Utah and United States, 1970 and 1980 (in Percent)

	UTAH			UNITED STATES		
FAMILY TYPES	1970	1980	PER-CENT INC.	1970	1980	PER-CENT INC.
Married Couples	90.1	88.4		86.0	82.8	
Single-Parent Families	9.9	11.6	1.7	14.0	17.2	3.2
Total Percent	100.0	100.0		100.0	100.0	
Total Number of Families	249,741	354,171		51,168,599	59,190,133	

The percentages are slightly different from Table 1 because unmarried couples are not included here.

Source: 1970 U.S. Census of the Population 1980 U.S. Census of the Population.

The most common marital status of single persons heading families is "divorced." During the past decade the proportion of divorced single-parent families has greatly increased, while the proportion that have never married has only risen moderately. For example, in 1970, 37 percent of divorced women headed families in Utah compared to 52 percent in 1980. A similar increase occurred for Utah men and for men and women nationally. During the same time, the proportion of men and women who are separated decreased, while the proportion who are widowed decreased substantially (see Table 5).

Divorce is more common among female heads of families, while never having been married is more common among men. For example, 31 percent of single male heads of family in Utah have never been married compared to 11 percent

TABLE 5.

Single-Parent Families by Sex and Marital Status of Head, Utah and United States, 1970 and 1980

	UTAH		UNITED STATES	
	1970	1980	1970	1980
Female Headed				
Married, Spouse Absent	15.8	13.1	22.8	18.4
Divorced	37.2	51.9	23.9	36.1
Widowed	40.2	24.4	41.1	29.3
Never Married	6.8	10.5	12.3	16.3
Total	100.0	99.9	100.1	100.1
Male Headed				
Married, Spouse Absent	31.6	15.5	29.2	17.1
Divorced	19.1	37.1	13.9	30.2
Widowed	26.0	15.9	27.7	19.8
Never Married	23.4	31.4	29.2	32.9
+3.7				
Total	100.1	99.9	100.0	100.0
All Single-Parent Families				
Female Headed	79.8	81.5	77.4	80.4
Male Headed	20.2	18.5	22.6	19.6
Total	100.0	100.0	100.0	100.0

Source: 1970 U.S. Census of the Population; 1980 U.S. Census of the Population.

among women. Similar patterns exist for single-parent families in the United States (see Table 5).

Divorce is also more common among single parents in Utah than in the United States. For example, 52 percent of Utah female heads of families are divorced compared to 36 percent nationally. Female heads of families are more likely to be separated or never married in the United States than in Utah. Among males similar patterns occur but the differences are much smaller. Thirty-seven percent of single-parent men in Utah are divorced compared to 30 percent among men in the United States. On the other hand, male heads of single-parent families are more likely to be separated, widowed, or never married in the United States than in Utah (see Table 5).

In summary, single-parent families are less common in Utah than in the United States. During the past decade the number of single-parent families has increased, but this has been less in Utah than in the United States. A large majority of single-parent families in Utah and the United States are headed by women. The proportion of divorced single parents has increased during the past decade. Divorce is currently the most common marital status of singles heading families and is more common among women than men. There are more divorced single heads of families in Utah than in the United States.

REMARRIAGE

The fourth type of nontraditional family examined is the so-called "blended family," or step-family, created by remarriage. As the divorce rate has risen in the United States, blended families have become common. About 80 percent of divorced persons eventually remarry, and over 40 percent of all marriages involve the remarriage of one or both spouses (Glick 1980). In addition, at least one spouse has been divorced in 20 percent of all current marriages, and one-sixth of all children under the age of 18 live in remarried-couple households (Cherlin and McCarthy 1985).

Table 6 shows the proportion of ever-married men and women in Utah and the United States who have been married two or more times. Remarriage is slightly more frequent in Utah than in the United States. In Utah 18 percent of all men and women who have married have done so more than once compared to 17 percent nationally and 22 percent regionally.

During the past ten years remarriage has increased in Utah. In 1970 15.4 percent of women who had ever been married had married more than once. This rose to 18.1 percent by 1980, an increase of 2.7 percent. For men, the comparable increase was from 15.1 percent to 17.8 percent, again a rise of 2.7 percent. In the United States similar trends were evident with an increase of 2.3 percent among women and 2.8 percent among men.

Research has found that men tend to remarry more often than women (Glick 1980). The data in Table 6 also show that in the United States more men than women are remarried. However, in Utah slightly more women than men are remarried.

SUMMARY

Even though nontraditional family types have increased in recent years, the vast majority of American families are still composed of married couples. In Utah 87 percent of all families are married couples compared to 80 percent nationally.

TABLE 6.

Percent of Ever Married Persons Who Have Married Two Or More Times, Utah and United States, 1970 and 1980

	FEMALES			MALES		
	1970	1980	PERCENT INCREASE	1970	1980	PERCENT INCREASE
Utah						
Married, Spouse Present	11.2	12.7		13.1	15.0	
Other	4.2	5.4		2.0	2.8	
Total	15.4	18.1	2.7	15.1	17.8	2.7
Western Region						
Married, Spouse Present	–	14.2		–	17.1	
Other	–	7.8		–	4.3	
Total	–	22.0		–	21.4	
United States						
Married, Spouse Present	10.1	11.2		12.2	14.1	
Other	4.7	5.9		2.3	3.2	
Total	14.8	17.1	2.3	14.5	17.3	2.8

Source: 1970 U.S. Census of the Population; 1980 U.S. Census of the Population.

The four most common types of nontraditional families are unmarried couples, childless couples, single-parent families, and remarried families. Unmarried couples, childless couples, and single-parent families are less common in Utah than in the United States, but remarriage is more frequent in Utah than in the United States. In Utah 2 percent of all families involve unmarried couples compared to 3 percent nationally. Among evermarried Utah women over age 45, 7 percent are childless compared to 13 percent in the United States. Eleven percent of Utah families are headed by single parents compared to 17 percent nationally. Eighteen percent of Utah men and women who have ever been married have remarried compared to 17 percent for the United States.

Almost half of all cohabiting couples have never been married, and a sizable minority are divorced. Cohabitants in Utah are more likely to be divorced than in the United States.

Although single parenthood increased during the past decade, the increase in Utah was less than in the United States. In both Utah and the United States over 80 percent of all single-parent families are headed by women. The most common way single-parent families are formed is through divorce. A greater proportion of single-parent families are created by divorce in Utah than in the United States and among females than males.

While we have studied only four types of nontraditional families, a number of other types exist. Unfortunately, adequate data on their prevalence are not available. For example, same sex couples appear to be more common than in the past, but there are no data on their prevalence or stability. Because homosexuality is still sharply proscribed by society, men and women involved in same-sex couples tend to keep their relationships private. Utah's polygamous population also deserves greater attention.

Family life for nontraditional families can be unstable, probably because of social pressure to move towards a more traditional type of family. Many unmarried couples marry, most childless couples have a child, and a large majority of persons in single-parent families remarry. Thus, more people experience nontraditional family status at some time in their lives than may be reflected in the data. For example, over 40 percent of current marriages will end in divorce (Schoen et al. 1985), even though in 1980 only 17 percent of all families were headed by single parents.

During the past decade these and other nontraditional families have increased in Utah and the United States. It is important that we learn how and why they change.

REFERENCES

Cherlin, Andrew and James McCarthy. "Remarried Couple Households: Data from the June 1980 Current Population Survey." *Journal of Marriage and the Family* 47 (1985): 23-38.

Furstenberg, Frank F., Jr. and Christine W. Nord. "The Life Course of Children of Divorce: Marital Disruption and Parental Contact." *Family Planning Perspectives* 14 (1982): 211-12.

Glick, Paul C. "Children of Divorced Parents in Demographic Perspective." *Journal of Social Issues* 35 (1979): 170-82.

_____. "Remarriage: Some Recent Changes and Variations." *Journal of Family Issues* 1 (1980): 455-78.

Norton, Arthur J. and Paul C. Glick. "Marital Instability in America: Past, Present, and Future." In G. Levinger and O. C. Moles, eds., *Divorce and Separation: Context, Censes, and Consequences*, New York: Basic Books, 1979, pp. 6-19.

_____. "One Parent Families: A Social and Economic Profile." *Family Relations* 35 (1986): 9-17.

Preston, Samuel H. "Estimating the Proportion of American Marriages that End in Divorce." *Sociological Methods and Research* 3 (1975): 435-60.

Schoen, Robert, William Urton, Karen Woodrow, and John Baj. "Marriage and Divorce in Twentieth Century American Cohorts." *Demography* 22 (1985): 101-14.

U.S. Bureau of the Census. *Census of the Population: 1970, Vol. 1, Characteristics of the Population, Part 1, United States Summary, Section Z*. Washington, D.C.: Government Printing Office, 1973.

_____. *Census of the Population: 1970, Vol. 1, Characteristics of the Population, Part 46, Utah*. Washington, D.C.: Government Printing Office, 1973.

_____. *Census of the Population: 1980, Vol. 1, Characteristics of the Population, Chapter D, Detailed Population Characteristics, Part 46, Utah, PC80-1-B46*. Washington, D.C.: Government Printing Office, 1983.

_____. *Census of the Population and Housing, 1980: Public-Use Microdata Samples Technical Documentation*. Washington, D.C.: Bureau of the Census, 1983.

_____. *Census of the Population: 1980, Vol. 1, Characteristics of the Population, Chapter D, Detailed opulation Characteristics, Part 1, United States Summary, Section A: United States, PC80-1-D1-A*. Washington, D.C.: Governmen' Printing Office, 1984.

_____. *Census of the Population: 1980, Vol. 1, Characteristics of the Population, Chapter D, Detailed Population Characteristics, Part 1, United States Summary, Section B: Regions, PC80-1-D1-B.* Washington, D.C.: Government Printing Office, 1984.

_____. *Statistical Abstract of the United States: 1985.* 105th Edition. Washington, D.C.: Government Printing Office, 1984.

Veevers, Jean E. *Childless by Choice.* Toronto: Butterworths, 1980.

11.
FAMILY VIOLENCE IN UTAH

Boyd C. Rollins
Craig K. Manscill

The past decade witnessed increased public attention on violence, especially physical violence, in the American family. This awareness was most visibly expressed in the establishment of child abuse and neglect registries in various states, child and women protection shelters, sexual abuse sensitivity training for young children in public schools, annual professional conferences on family violence, and feature articles on family violence in the media. This has been happening across the United States, including Utah. What is the basis for this increased awareness? Has family violence increased in frequency and severity? If so, to what might one attribute the changes?

In Utah, the 1978 state legislature passed a ''Reporting of Child Abuse or Neglect Act,'' requiring that any person having reason to believe that a child had been abused or neglected must report such to the nearest peace officer, law enforcement agency, or office of the State Division of Family Services. This act also established the Utah Central Registry for Child Abuse and Neglect as a repository for information on all cases of suspected child abuse or neglect. Five years later, a Spouse Abuse Procedures Act, outlining procedures for identifying and investigating domestic violence, was presented to state legislators. These efforts are additional evidence of the increasing awareness of family violence, providing an added incentive to recognize, report, and cope with incidences of family violence.

It is difficult to verify the number and severity of acts of family violence. Most estimates are viewed with suspicion by professionals and laymen alike. Students of family physical violence in the U.S. (Gil 1970; Straus et al. 1980; Pagelow 1984) conclude that the lack of uniform definitions regarding acts of violence such as child physical abuse and child sexual abuse hinder accurate reporting. Also, they indicate that it is difficult to obtain accurate information regardless of definitions. Cross-country comparisons are suspect since different regions use different criteria to report and confirm an incidence of abuse. Comparisons across time probably suffer from changing criteria also. What is defined as abuse today might not have been a decade ago, or might depend on the social identification of the reporter or the perpetrator.

Differences in estimates of family violence can be substantial. For example, Straus et al. (1980) estimated from a 1975 survey that approximately 1.7 million dependent children (about 3 percent of all U.S. children ages 3 to 17) were severely physically abused by their parents. Severe physical abuse was defined as kicking, biting, punching, beating up, threatening with a knife or gun, or using a knife or gun. From the same survey it was estimated that 6 percent of all married persons were severely physically abused by their spouse. In contrast, the U.S. National Center on Child Abuse and Neglect (Corfman 1979) reported 250,000 cases of child physical abuse in 1975 in the U.S. based on "confirmed" cases through state social agencies. The Strauss study, however, obtained self reports from a random sample of U.S. households. The discrepancy between the two estimates is revealing. One is seven times greater than the other. Thus any attempt to answer questions about incidence, trends, and correlates of family physical violence in Utah and comparisons between Utah and other states must be done cautiously.

To describe family violence in Utah, three sources of data are used: the 1978-84 records in the Utah Central Register for Child Abuse and Neglect, a survey of incidences of child abuse reported through social services agencies in all counties in the United States, 1967-68 (Gil 1970), and Uniform Federal Bureau of Investigation Crime Reports.

The following findings consist of the frequency of the physical abuse of Utah children, 1979-84; the rate of abuse per 1,000 children as well as the frequency and rate of the sexual abuse of Utah children during the same period; comparisons of child abuse in Utah, the Mountain Region, and the U.S., 1967-68; and comparisons of family homicide in Utah and the U.S., 1978-83.

CHILD PHYSICAL ABUSE

Confirmed cases of child physical abuse in Utah, 1967-68, are meager compared to those in 1984. In 1967 some twenty-one cases were reported, while in 1968 eighteen cases were reported. This contrasts with 1,042 cases in 1984. Such a dramatic increase is astounding unless one suspects changes in reporting procedures or in confirming procedures. Nevertheless, the reports for the earlier period are consistent with other states. The rates in Utah per 100,000 children 18 years old and younger were 4.8 in 1967 and 3.9 in 1968—substantially less than the national rates of 8.4 and 9.3 for these same years (Gil 1970). In fact, Utah during these two years ranked 29th and 27th nationally. Of the eight states in the Mountain Region, Utah tied for fifth place in 1967 and was third in 1968. These data, however limited, suggest that Utah was neither unusually high nor low in confirmed child abuse cases in the late 1960s. From 1979 to 1984 both the number of confirmed child abuse cases and the rate of abuse per 1,000 children increased (Table 1). In 1984, the year with the highest rate, .16 percent of Utah children experienced some form of physical abuse, the perpetrator typically being either the father or the mother or both.

CHILD SEXUAL ABUSE

Reports of the sexual abuse of Utah children, 1979-84, also come from the Utah Central Registry for Child Abuse or Neglect. Again, the increase from 1979 to 1984 was substantial. In 1979 there were 149 confirmed reports—out of a population of 548,438 dependent children—compared to 941—out of a population of 644,220 dependent children—five years later (Table 2). The rate per 1,000 increased from 0.272 in 1979 to 1.461 in 1984. If the 1984

TABLE 1.

Child Physical Abuse in Utah: Incidence and Rates Per 1,000 Children Ages 18 Years or Less

YEAR	INCIDENCE	RATE/1,000
1979	563	1.027
1980	771	1.366
1981	835	1.419
1982	681*	1.122
1983	994	1.589
1984	1,042	1.617

*The data here include only those cases where physical abuse was the primary cause of investigation. The other years included all incidence of physical abuse regardless of the primary cause of investigation.

rate continued for the next seventeen years, approximately 1 out every 35 Utah children would be sexually abused by the time they reach age 18. Obviously, such an estimate is liberal and assumes that a child is confirmed as sexually abused only once. Nevertheless, our estimate is substantially less than current newspaper reports (see the *Daily Herald*, 15 April 1986) that 1 out of every 3 or 4 Utah women is sexually abused by the time she reaches age 18.

Based on confirmed sexual abuse cases in Utah in 1984, we estimate that 1 out of 35 children will be sexually abused by age 18. If we were to include only females, this figure would be, at most, 1 out of 17.5—a rate substantially less than the 1 in 3 or 4 cited in newspapers. While the same 1984 data were used as a basis for estimation, the newspaper accounts were based on a liberal estimate suggested by Sarafino (1979). This procedure assumes four things: there are 3.5 unreported cases for every confirmed reported case of abuse, the rate continues for eighteen years with no repeated victims (that is, each reported and confirmed case is a victim only once), 9 out of 10 confirmed reported cases are women, and there are an equal number of dependent males and females in the population.

With 941 confirmed reported cases of child sexual abuse out of a population of 644,220 children ages one month to 18 years in Utah in 1984, the rate is 1 out of 685. However, if 3.5 cases are unreported for each reported

TABLE 2.

Child Sexual Abuse in Utah: Incidence and Rates Per 1,000 Children Ages 18 Years or Less

YEAR	INCIDENCE	RATE
1979	149	0.272
1980	216	0.383
1981	237	0.403
1982	264*	0.435
1983	611	0.977
1984	941	1.461

*The data here include only those cases where sexual abuse was reported as the primary cause of investigation. Other years include all evidence of sexual abuse regardless of the primary cause of investigation.

case, the real number of cases rises to 4,234 out of 644,220, or 1 in 152. Furthermore, if, for eighteen consecutive years there are 4,234 new cases each year and the population remains constant, the incidence increases to 76,212 out of 644,220, or 1 in 8.5. Finally, if 9 out of 10 sexual abuse cases involve dependent female children and 1 out of 2 dependent children is female, the incidence for females over 18 years of age is 68,590 out of 322,110, or 1 in 4.7. To change a rate from 1 in 685 to 1 in 4 on the basis of questionable assumptions is obviously a hazardous procedure. We do not claim that confirmed cases of child physical abuse or sexual abuse in the Utah Central Registry of Child Abuse and Neglect accurately represent what happens to Utah's children. Most likely there are many unobserved or unreported cases. Still, these data, whatever their limitations, are the best we have at present.

While data from the Utah Central Registry for Child Abuse and Neglect indicate a steady increase in the number and rate of confirmed child abuse reports during the past decade, the Associated Press recently reported that a national survey of two-parent households found that the percentage of U.S. children abused by their parents decreased from 3.6 in 1972 to 1.9 in 1985. From these two sources one might conclude that the trend in Utah is opposite the national trend. However, Utah data come from cases that are confirmed by the investigations of social workers and police. The national survey was based on the self reports of members of households on what happened in their own homes. While the past decade witnessed considerable media exposure to child abuse, it may have contributed to the increase in the observation and reporting of child abuse, resulting in an increase of confirmed cases. At the same time, the increased publicity may have decreased the likelihood that adults would voluntarily report their own acts of physical violence toward children. As stated at the beginning of this chapter, the accuracy of reporting the incidence of child abuse and the lack of consistent definitions make it difficult to offer chronological or regional comparisons.

MURDER

Sadly, murder, the most extreme form of physical violence, can be a part of family life. It is shocking to realize that homicide occurs between people who are related. From 1978 to 1983, according to FBI statistics, 14.1 percent of all murders reported in the United States involved husbands, wives, and children (see Table 3). In Utah during the same six years only 7.5 percent of murders were family homicides (see Table 4).

Family homicide is a gruesome reality, involving spouses, parents, children, or siblings. Spouse killings nationally accounted for 8.9 percent of all murders during this five-year period, while in Utah 3.8 percent of all murders were spouse killings. Nationally, the killing of children by parents accounted for 2.5 percent of all murders. In Utah, it comprised 2.4 percent. The percentage of murders in which children killed parents was 1.6 nationally and 0.5 for Utah. Murder between siblings accounted for 1.3 percent of all murders nationally and for 0.8 percent in Utah. Thus the difference between family murder locally and nationally is seen in the smaller percentage of spouse murders in Utah.

In each of the four combinations of family homicide, Utah figures, as percentages of the state's family population, were less than or equal to national percentages. This fact takes on additional significance when one remembers that Utah is noted for its large families. Clearly, a larger nuclear family provides a greater opportunity for the occurrence of family violence; the probability that parents will kill children, that children will kill parents, and that siblings will kill other siblings increases as the number of children in a family grows.

The most substantial difference between Utah and national figures was in the category of spouse killings. The percentage of murders in which husbands kill wives or in which wives kill husbands was more than double in the U.S. than in Utah. The same holds true for children killing parents. The differences between Utah and national percentages for parents killing children and sibling murder were negligible.

TABLE 3.

Nuclear Family Murder: Incidence and Percent of U.S. Homicides, 1978-1983

		NUCLEAR FAMILY MURDERS (% OF ALL MURDERS)				
YEAR	TOTAL MURDERS IN U.S.	SPOUSE KILLING SPOUSE	PARENT KILLING CHILD	CHILD KILLING PARENT	SIBLING KILLING SIBLING	TOTAL
1978	19,555	9.9	2.6	1.6	1.1	15.2
1979	20,591	9.0	2.2	1.4	1.1	13.7
1980	21,860	8.3	2.1	1.4	1.3	13.1
1981	20,053	8.6	2.3	1.5	1.5	13.9
1982	21,012	8.2	2.7	1.6	1.3	13.8
1983	19,308	9.4	2.2	1.9	1.4	14.9
Total	122,379	8.9	2.4	1.6	1.3	14.1

When examining trends from 1978 to 1983, a different perspective can be gained by comparing Utah and the United States. Nationally, the total number of all varieties of murder peaked in 1980 at 21,860 and then declined over the next three years to 19,308. Even so, the percentage of family murders rose from 13.1 to 14.9. In 1983 percentage totals for each of the four types of family murder were higher than averages for the previous five years. Utah's total number of murders has not changed with the national trends nor has the percentage of family murders. The total number of murders in Utah was similar in 1980 and 1983, fifty-five and fifty-four respectively. There was no consistent pattern of change in the percentage of Utah family murders except for spouse killing spouse, which increased from 3.2 in 1981 to 4.3 in 1983. Thus, extreme family violence as a percentage of all homicide is substantially less in Utah than in the U.S. Likewise, the family murder rate is substantially lower in Utah than in the U.S. In addition, the 1983 Utah murder rate per 100,000 residents was one-half that of the U.S. rate.

SUMMARY

The data in this chapter suggest that substantiated cases of child sexual and physical abuse in Utah increased during the past decade. However, such an increase more probably indicates a greater tendency to report and confirm cases

TABLE 4.

Nuclear Family Murder: Percent of Utah Homicides, 1978-1983

		NUCLEAR FAMILY MURDERS (% OF ALL MURDERS)				
YEAR	TOTAL MURDERS IN UTAH	SPOUSE KILLING SPOUSE	PARENT KILLING CHILD	CHILD KILLING PARENT	SIBLING KILLING SIBLING	TOTAL
1978	50	3.0	0.5	0.0	0.0	3.5
1979	68	5.4	4.1	0.7	0.0	10.2
1980	55	*	2.2	1.1	1.1	8.2
1981	53	3.2	2.7	0.4	1.6	7.9
1982	53	3.2	1.6	0.0	1.1	5.9
1983	54	4.3	3.2	0.5	1.0	9.0
Total	333	3.8	2.4	0.5	0.8	7.5

*Not reported in 1980.

than an actual increase in the proportion of abused children. There is no evidence that the situation in Utah is much different from the U.S. Regarding family homicide, where the evidence of severe physical abuse is more difficult to conceal, the percentage of all murders that are family-related is less in Utah than nationally, and the trend towards an increasing percentage of family homicides in the U.S. over the past decade is not evident in Utah. A clearer description of the actual frequency, trends, and correlates of family violence in Utah requires more accurate procedures than those presently available.

REFERENCES

Corfman, E. *Families Today.* Vol. 2. Washington, D.C.: U.S. Government Printing Office, 1979.

Gil, D. G. *Violence Against Children: Physical Child Abuse in the United States.* Cambridge, MA: Harvard University Press, 1970.

Pagelow, M. D. *Family Violence.* New York: Praeger, 1984.

Sarafino, E. P. "Estimates of Sexual Offences Against Children." *Child Welfare* 58 (1979), 2:127-33.

Straus, M. A., R. J. Gelles, and S. K. Steinmetz. *Behind Closed Doors: Violence in the American Family.* New York: Doubleday, 1980.

12. ETHNIC GROUPS IN UTAH

Cardell Jacobson

''Why can't they be more like us'' has probably been heard whenever culturally or physically different groups have come together. Despite pressures for assimilation, racial and ethnic identities have been surprisingly persistent and resilient in Utah as well as in the nation as a whole. Early settlers of Utah made distinctions between the British, the Swedes, the Danes, the Welsh, and the Germans as did Americans generally. And like Americans, Utahns continue to pay particular attention to Black Americans, Mexican Americans, Native Americans, and other groups. This chapter provides a demographic description of the major ethnic groups in Utah today and offers some national and regional comparisons.

Important ethnic groups in Utah today include Black Americans, Native Americans, Japanese Americans, Chinese Americans, other Asian Americans, Mexican Americans, and other Spanish Americans. Because of their small numbers, several groups were combined for the following analysis. Japanese and Chinese Americans were combined because both were early immigrant groups compared to other Asian Americans such as Filipinos, Koreans, Indians, Pakistanis, Indonesians, Fiji Islanders, Cambodians, Indochinese, Vietnamese, or Hawaiians. Other Spanish Americans include Cubans, Puerto Ricans, and anyone listing Central or South America as his or her place of origin.

A HISTORICAL NOTE

American Indians, of course, were the first inhabitants of Utah. According to estimates, approximately 6,000 Native Americans occupied the territory comprising Utah during the mid-1800s (Gurgel, ''Ethnic Minorities,'' 1981). The Navajo in the isolated southern part of the state were not influenced as much by whites as were more northern tribes. The Utes of Central Utah, however, were resettled to the Uintah valley in 1865 as a result of the Black

Hawk War (O'Neil 1976). Fourteen years later, the Utes of the White River Band in Colorado's San Juan Mountains were also forced to resettle in what has become known as the Uintah-Ouray reservation. Other tribes in the state included the Southern Paiutes, a migratory tribe, and the Gosiutes (O'Neil 1976).

Despite the influx of Colorado Utes, the number of Indians in Utah declined during the late 1800s, reaching a low of 2,623 at the turn of the century before growing to 19,256 in 1980. Most of this growth occurred from 1950 to 1980, as the 1950 census listed only 2,729 Indians in Utah. Gurgel ("Ethnic Minorities," 1981, 122) states that most of this increase resulted from immigration to Utah, though he acknowledges that Indians also have had high birth rates. Growing self-identification as an Indian for those of mixed ancestry may also account for some of the increase.

Three blacks reportedly accompanied the Mormon pioneers into the Great Salt Lake Valley in 1847, but they were not the first to arrive in the area. James Beckwourth and other black trappers and hunters preceded them by some twenty years (Coleman 1976). Coleman estimates that by the mid-1970s there were 150 descendants of the three blacks who entered the Salt Lake Valley with Brigham Young. Nevertheless, the size and growth of the black population in Utah have always been negligible. The 1850 census listed fifty blacks, about half of whom were slaves, while the 1860 census listed fifty-nine blacks. In the late nineteenth century several blacks spent time with the military in the state; some chose to remain or later to return to Utah. Six hundred and seventy-two blacks were identified by the Census Bureau at the turn of the century. During World War II a number of black soldiers were again stationed in Utah, while others migrated to take advantage of the high labor needs in newly established government facilities. By 1980 the black population in Utah had grown to 9,225 but constituted only two-thirds of 1 percent of the total population (Gurgel, "Ethnic Minorities," 1981). Though blacks comprise a small proportion of Utah's population, their importance nationally justifies their inclusion in any discussion of minorities in Utah.

Chinese railroad workers were the first Asians to arrive in Utah. More than 12,000 helped build the Central Pacific Railroad as it entered the territory in the late 1860s (Conley 1976). Large numbers of laborers remained, primarily in Box Elder County, as section hands maintaining the railroad. The passage of Chinese exclusion laws, beginning in 1882, reduced the population. Some returned to China. Others moved to Salt Lake City, and by 1890 there were more Chinese in Salt Lake City than in Box Elder County.

Japanese workers also arrived in the late nineteenth century, working primarily in agriculture and on railroad section gangs. The numbers of both Chinese and Japanese were small at the turn of the century with only 417 Asians listed in the 1900 census. By 1910, 2,110 Japanese were listed, and the number increased to 2,936 by 1920 (Papanikolas and Kasai 1976). Additional increases in the Japanese population occurred during World War II when a number were "interned" at Topaz near Delta, Utah. Most returned to the West Coast following their internment, but some remained and established permanent homes in Utah. By 1980, approximately 2,700 Chinese and 5,500 Japanese lived in the state. In the late 1970s and early 1980s several refugee groups, such as the Hmong, Vietnamese, Cambodians, and Indo-Chinese, resettled in Utah, contributing to the growth of the total Asian population from 6,386 in 1970 to 15,076 in 1980.

Despite their proximity, Spanish Americans were one of the last groups to come to Utah. The 1900 census listed a mere 40 Hispanics in the state, and the 1910 census listed only 166. A large influx occurred during the next decade, the result, in part, of the revolutionary war in Mexico. Others were attracted by job opportunities in mining, railroads, and agriculture. Mexican Americans were used as strikebreakers by Kennecott Copper in 1912, while others found their way to the coal mines of Carbon County (Mayer 1976).

Utah's Spanish population declined during the 1930s due to the mass deportations of Mexicans and some Mexican Americans. Those of Mexican ancestry in Utah decreased from over 2,300 in 1920 to 1,069 in 1930 (Gurgel, "Postscript," 1981). With the advent of World War II, a second influx of Mexican American laborers took advantage of new jobs at government facilities and in mines and agriculture. The Mexican American population has continued to grow; 60,302 Spanish Utahns were counted in the 1980 census.

The proportions of each of these groups listed in the 1980 census for Utah, the Mountain Region, and the United States are listed in Table 1. In addition, the number and percentage of each group in the Utah microdata sample of the 1980 census are listed. The majority of information presented in the remainder of this chapter comes from these two samples.

Taken together, minorities in Utah are a small proportion of the population. The major difference between Utah and the nation lies in the small number of blacks. Nationally blacks constitute 11.7 percent of the population, while they number less than 1 percent in Utah.

When combined, Mexican Americans and others of Spanish origin comprise the largest minority group in Utah. Yet they, too, form a smaller proportion of Utah residents than is the case nationally. This is surprising considering Utah's proximity to other states with large Mexican American populations. Compared to a number of eastern states, Utah also has relatively few Cubans or Puerto Ricans. Furthermore, Mexican Americans are immigrants to Utah, whereas they are indigenous to most southwestern states.

Utah's 1.32 percent Indian population is roughly double the national average but smaller than the 3.2 percent in the Mountain Region. Utah's Asian population, however, is approximately the same proportion as in the United States as a whole.

The minority groups are not evenly distributed throughout the state. Nearly two-thirds of Utah's Indians are located in the five counties of San Juan, Salt Lake, Uintah, Utah, and Box Elder, though they constitute a large proportion in only San Juan County. San Juan and Uintah counties have reservations located within their boundaries, while Box Elder has been home to an Indian school. Utah County has a number of Indians in attendance at Brigham Young University. Salt Lake County is the largest metropolitan area in the state, and a number of Indians have been drawn to economic opportunities

TABLE 1.

Percentage of Racial/Ethnic Groups in U.S., Region and Utah, 1980

	1980 CENSUS			UTAH SAMPLE	
	U.S.	REGION	UTAH	NUMBER	PERCENT
Whites	83.15	87.58	94.66	42753	94.65
Blacks	11.70	2.37	0.62	312	0.69
Indians	0.63	3.20	1.32	488	0.86
Japanese/Chinese	0.67	0.41	0.56	341	0.75
Other Asians	3.86	6.44	2.85	362	0.80
Mexican American				496	1.10
and Other Spanish	6.45	12.69	4.11	416	0.92

While the census treats Mexican American and other Spanish as two separate racial and ethnic designations, they have been treated as one ethnic group for the Utah sample.

Source: Statistical Abstract of the U.S., 104th Edition, Washington, D. C.: Government Printing Office, 1984, p. 36. The Utah sample is the 5 percent microfile for Utah from the 1980 U.S. census.

there. Along with the other two metropolitan counties in the state, Davis and Weber, 72.5 percent of the state's total Indian population can be found in seven counties (Gurgel, "Postscript," 1981).

Blacks, Spanish, and Asian groups are concentrated in Utah's urban areas. Slightly over 92 percent of Utah blacks live in the three counties of Salt Lake, Davis, and Weber. Likewise, 74.4 percent of Spanish residents and 73.9 percent of Asians live in these three counties. If Utah County is added, the percentage of Spanish and Asians increases to 82.7 and 87.1 percent, respectively. By comparison, 61.9 percent of Utah whites live in Salt Lake, Davis, and Weber counties. If Utah County is added, the white percentage rises to 77.1.

A DEMOGRAPHIC PROFILE

Two goals are pursued in the remainder of this chapter: the first, to provide a profile of Utah's ethnic groups on a variety of demographic and social variables; the second, to provide a comparison of Utah's ethnic groups to their larger national populations. These profiles are based on the Utah microsample and the corresponding national microsample. The demographic variables in this section are average age, number of children born to each female, number of persons per household, percentage of households in which a married couple lives, and average age at marriage. The relevant figures for each ethnic group appear in Table 2, and following this section are discussions of housing and income.

Note that the average age of Utahns is lower than the national average. This is true for each ethnic group as well as for the state as a whole. Indians in Utah have the lowest average age, followed closely by Mexican Americans, other Asians and other Spanish. The average age of other Spanish residents is deceptive. The average for Cuban Americans is 37.5, inflating the average, otherwise the average age would be lower. As is true nationally, Chinese and Japanese comprise the oldest population, followed by whites. The average age of Utah whites, however, is nearly seven years below the national average.

These differences reflect a number of variables such as the death rate and health care. The most important factor is the birth rate. Those groups with a high birth rate have a lower average age.

One other factor affecting the age of a population is immigration. Immigrant groups are usually composed of young adults. Utah's other Asians are young, in part, because of the resettlement of several groups of "Boat Peoples" from Vietnam.

TABLE 2.

Comparison of Ethnic Groups in the State of Utah and the U.S. on Selected Demographic Variables*

VARIABLE	WHITES	BLACKS	INDIANS	CHINESE/ JAPANESE	OTHER ASIANS	MEXICAN AMERICANS	OTHER SPANISH
Average Age**							
Utah	24.4	22.2	18.2	28.8	20.5	19.8	20.9
U.S.	31.3	24.9	23.4	31.4	26.6	21.8	25.3
Number of Children born per woman							
Utah	3.5	3.2	3.6	2.8	3.5	3.6	3.4
U.S.	2.9	3.3	3.5	2.8	3.0	3.7	3.0
Average Age at First Marriage							
Utah	21.7	22.4	21.8	24.1	22.6	21.2	21.4
U.S.	22.6	23.1	22.1	25.1	24.7	22.3	23.5
Number of Persons in Household							
Utah	3.8	3.4	5.2	3.6	5.7	4.0	3.8
U.S.	3.3	4.1	4.2	3.6	4.4	4.5	3.8
Married Couple Household (%)							
Utah	78.9	56.4	67.5	74.7	79.2	73.7	74.7
U.S.	74.5	51.9	65.5	73.6	75.7	74.6	68.4

*Based on the 5 percent microfile for Utah from the 1980 U.S. Census, ages 18 and older, except where noted.
**Calculated from the 1980 U.S. Census.

The number of children born to Utah women in the 5 percent sample varies less among ethnic groups than might be expected, primarily because of the high birth rate of Utah whites. Most minorities have birth rates above the national average. But white Utahns also have higher rates than the national average, as discussed in other chapters. Only Utah's Japanese and Chinese populations have the same rate as nationally. Blacks fall slightly below the state average at 3.2, though they are close to the national figure of 3.3. The number of children per woman for other Asians is higher in Utah than nationally. Again this probably reflects the high number of recent Asian immigrants to Utah. The rate for other Spanish Utahns is also higher than nationally.

Utahns consistently marry about one year younger than Americans generally. Each of Utah's ethnic groups shows this pattern. Nationally, blacks, other Asians, and especially Japanese and Chinese marry older than whites (see Table 2). These groups in Utah also marry older but still about a year younger than nationally.

The number of persons per household is a function of both the birth rate and the extent to which other relatives (e.g., grandparents, uncles, aunts, etc.), live with the family. Nationally, the extended family exists more often among ethnic groups than among whites. The picture in Utah is considerably different. Utah whites have a higher number of persons per household—3.8 percent compared to 3.3 percent nationally—because of their higher birth rates. Utah blacks have a smaller number of individuals per household than whites, and both blacks and Mexican Americans have smaller numbers than is the case nationally. Two other groups in Utah, Indians and other Asians, have higher rates. Indians average 5.2 persons per household compared to 4.2 nationally, and other Asians average 5.7 compared to 4.4. Both groups tend to have extended family members living with them—Indians because of poverty and other Asians because of poverty and recent immigration.

The percentage of Utah families living in married households varies to some extent among groups. The two major differences are for blacks and Indians where only 56.4 percent and 67.5 percent live in married households. Slightly more than three-fourths of the other groups live in married households. With the exception of Mexican Americans, more Utah families in each of the groups live in married households than is true nationally. The difference, however, is only a few percentage points.

The differences among Utah's ethnic groups are similar to those among minorities nationally. Chinese and Japanese comprise the oldest population, because they marry later and have lower birth rates. Conversely, Indians and Mexican Americans are the youngest, because they marry earlier and have more children. Utahns in general are younger, have higher birth rates, marry younger, and are more likely to live in married households than Americans generally. This is true for almost all ethnic groups. The one variable on which Utahns differ is the number of persons per household. Here, Utah's Mexican Americans and blacks are lower than national averages, while whites, Indians, and other Asians are higher.

HOUSING DATA

Despite the larger average number of persons per household among most minority groups in Utah, houses in the state typically have fewer rooms. While Indians and other Asians have the largest number of persons per household, they occupy the smallest average number of rooms. Mexican and other Spanish Americans have 4.0 and 3.8 persons per household but have a slightly larger number of rooms, 5.4. Chinese and Japanese and whites have the largest number of rooms but only 3.6 and 3.8 persons per household. Blacks have an average of 5.0 rooms but the smallest number of persons per household, 3.4.

The cost of housing in Utah is higher than the national average. The average for Utah whites is nearly $9,000 more than nationally. And, though still less than housing for whites, the cost of housing for Utah blacks is roughly twice the national average for blacks. As might be expected, the cost of housing correlates with the average number of rooms. White and Japanese/Chinese housing is the most expensive, with Indian housing the least expensive (see Table 3). The one exception is for other Asians. They live in more expensive housing than might be expected and pay the highest rent of any group, including whites. The large number of persons per household probably accounts for some of this discrepancy, but their recent immigration may also be a factor. There may be discrimination against them, or they may not have become astute consumers in their new country. These recent immigrants tend not to locate in ghetto areas where blacks, Mexican Americans, and other groups are located. Rather, they are interspersed throughout the population where rental costs are sometimes moderately high.

As might be expected, those groups with the lowest incomes tend to own their homes less often than those with higher incomes. Thus, only 23.9 percent of Utah whites and 25.0 percent of the Japanese/Chinese rent, while 58.7 percent of other Asians and 56.7 percent of blacks rent. Mexican and other Spanish Americans have intermediate levels of home ownership. Indians

TABLE 3.

Housing and Rental Data for Utah and U.S. Minorities

VARIABLE	WHITES	BLACKS	INDIANS	CHINESE/ JAPANESE	OTHER ASIANS	MEXICAN AMERICANS	OTHER SPANISH
Rooms in Home							
Utah	6.0	5.0	4.5	5.8	4.9	5.4	5.4
Value of Housing (in $)							
Utah	58,810	52,326	31,746	58,611	54,350	48,972	52,350
U.S.	49,317	26,250	31,842	74,388	68,039	35,895	58,630
% Renters							
Utah	23.9	56.7	44.4	25.0	58.7	38.8	37.6
U.S.	25.8	47.0	42.2	38.0	48.3	40.6	51.5
Rental Cost (in $)							
Utah	181	175	163	164	191	170	176
U.S.	185	147	160	207	202	174	188

*Based on the 5 percent microfile for Utah from the 1980 U.S. Census, ages 18 years and older.

also have intermediate levels, despite having the lowest incomes of all groups (see Table 4). Their small homes, their reservation status, and the provision of some housing by the Bureau of Indian Affairs, no doubt, account for this anomaly.

In summary, the lowest income groups tend to have the smallest housing, rent more often, and pay less for housing than other groups. There are two exceptions: Indians and other Asians. Peculiar circumstances help explain these variations.

SOCIO-ECONOMIC VARIABLES

Ethnic groups vary on a variety of social variables. Several are presented in Table 4, including family and personal income which account for some of the results presented earlier. Personal and family income in turn are explained in part by the other two variables in Table 4, education and type of occupation.

Income figures reflect a variety of variables: age, seniority, type of occupation, educational training, spouse's employment status, as well as discrimination and prejudice. For example, the average family income of Japanese and Chinese in Utah exceeds that of whites by 12 percent. The average *individual* income of Chinese and Japanese, however, is slightly lower than white income in Utah despite their higher educational levels. The higher family income probably results from a higher proportion of Japanese and Chinese wives working. Other minority groups in Utah earn less than whites with Indians having the lowest family and individual incomes. Spanish groups have family incomes closest to whites, with other Asians and blacks following. Other Asians have relatively good family income because of the large number of working relatives in the home. Their individual income levels, however, are below all other ethnic groups in Utah, except Indians.

The individual income of several groups in Utah is lower than in the United States. Utah whites make about $500 less than Americans generally, while Japanese and Chinese about $800 less. Indians make $1,000 less, and other Asians about $3,400 less. A slightly lower wage scale in Utah accounts for some of these differences. In addition, the rural nature of Utah's Indians and the recent immigration to Utah of a number of other Asians may account for the differences for those groups (see Table 4). Other groups, however, do relatively well in Utah. Individual Utah blacks average slightly more than blacks nationally, while Mexican and other Spanish Americans in Utah make $600 and $450 more, respectively, than nationally.

TABLE 4.

Comparison of Ethnic Groups in Utah and the U.S. on Selected Social Variables

VARIABLE	WHITES	BLACKS	INDIANS	CHINESE/ JAPANESE	OTHER ASIANS	MEXICAN AMERICANS	OTHER SPANISH
Family Income (in $)							
Utah	23,812	17,966	14,990	26,663	19,524	18,719	21,366
U.S.	25,011	18,003	16,691	28,137	26,789	18,887	20,286
Individual Income (in $)							
Utah	9,944	7,078	5,753	9,662	6,188	8,009	9,114
U.S.	10,435	6,947	6,669	10,497	9,630	7,387	8,660
Individual Minority Income as a % of White Income							
Utah		71.2	57.9	97.2	62.2	80.5	91.7
U.S.		66.6	63.9	100.6	92.3	70.8	83.0
% High School Graduates							
Utah	85.1	72.6	60.6	89.7	65.9	55.6	63.1
U.S.	74.5	59.0	60.3	79.3	78.5	44.7	57.8
% with 4 or more years of College							
Utah	19.7	13.0	7.5	29.9	16.4	7.1	9.7
U.S.	17.4	8.6	8.5	33.2	34.9	4.9	11.7
Number Years of Schooling (for those 25-34 years of age)							
Utah	15.9	15.7	14.4	17.4	14.6	14.4	15.1
U.S.	15.6	14.4	14.3	16.8	16.2	12.7	14.2
% Working in White-Collar Occupations*							
Utah	53.3	36.8	29.4	61.7	34.6	38.8	41.2
U.S.	53.2	35.6	33.9	58.9	56.6	29.7	44.9

*Percent engaged in managerial, professional, technical, sales, or administrative occupations.

Education, of course, is an important factor in determining individual and family income. Utah has long had higher levels of education than the nation as a whole (see Table 4). Most of Utah's minorities have higher educational levels than is true nationally. The exception is in the area of other Asians, who in Utah have a disproportionate number of recent immigrants. But each Utah group has a higher proportion of high school graduates than the same group does nationally.

Nevertheless, Utah does not do as well in graduating some minority students from college as it does in graduating them from high school. A higher percentage of Indians, Chinese and Japanese, other Asians, and other Spanish graduate from college nationally than in Utah. Blacks and Mexican Americans do better in Utah than nationally in college, however.

Overall, Japanese and Chinese have the highest percentage graduating from high school and from college. The percentage of Japanese/Chinese graduating from college is 29.9 percent compared to 19.7 percent among whites. More Chinese and Japanese also graduate from high school than whites, 89.7 compared to 85.1 percent.

Mexican Americans in Utah, with only 55.6 percent graduating from high school and 7.1 percent graduating from college, have the lowest educational level of any group. Their educational levels are followed first slightly by Indians, then by other Spanish, other Asians, and blacks. This highlights an irony that is evident nationally, as well. Blacks have higher educational levels than these other groups yet have significantly lower incomes. Many researchers attribute this to discrimination, though other variables such as southern origins, job career patterns, and type of occupation must also be considered.

Attributing differences in income to discrimination is difficult, in part, because the differences may reflect past rather than present discrimination. One method to separate past from present discrimination is to examine the education and income levels of that generation most recently completing its education, those 25-34 years old. As can be seen in Table 4, the rankings on education do not change for this age group. Chinese and Japanese still have the highest number of years attended with whites a distant second. Indians still have the lowest. Blacks are close to whites and are considerably higher than all the other groups, except whites and Japanese and Chinese.

Clearly the recent generation of blacks and Mexican Americans has done well educationally in Utah. Blacks are only two-tenths of a year behind whites, while Mexican Americans are 1.5 years behind. Furthermore, both groups are substantially ahead of figures nationally. Blacks in Utah, aged 25-34, have an average of 1.3 more years of education than blacks nationally. Mexican Americans in Utah have an average of 1.7 more years of education than Mexican Americans nationally.

Individual income for blacks and Mexican Americans and Chinese and Japanese, aged 25-34, also approaches white income in Utah. Individual black incomes in Utah are 92 percent of those of whites. The percentage among Mexican Americans is 90. Other groups of the same age lag further behind; the percentage for other Asians and for Indians is 72, and for other Spanish, 85 percent.

Part of the explanation for low income among blacks, despite their education, may lie in the kinds of jobs they hold. The percentage of each ethnic group engaged in white collar jobs is listed in Table 4. Indians have the lowest percentage in these occupations followed by Mexican Americans and blacks. These differences are probably insignificant, but the percentages are all lower than the percentage of whites and Chinese/Japanese engaged in white collar occupations.

Nevertheless, compared to national figures several of Utah's groups do well occupationally. Nine percent more Mexican Americans in Utah are engaged in white collar jobs than nationally, a significant difference. And blacks and Chinese/Japanese are slightly above national figures, though the differences are probably not as significant. Other Spanish Utahns are below the national average, while Indians are only slightly below national averages—despite being isolated and rural. The only minority group in Utah that is significantly below the national average is other Asians. Again this low percentage reflects the high proportion of recent immigrants to Utah.

In summary, minorities in Utah, with the exception of Chinese and Japanese, do not do as well economically as whites. Even then, Chinese and Japanese should do better than whites considering their significantly higher levels of education. Overall, Utah has a lower wage scale than the United States, which is reflected in the income of the state's minorities. There are two important exceptions: Utah blacks and Mexican Americans have higher incomes than they do nationally. Utah's lower incomes are surprising considering that the educational levels of Utahns and Utah minorities, in particular, are higher than is the case nationally. Utah appears to do a good job in educating its minority populations through high school but falters at the college level. Again, blacks and Mexican Americans are exceptions; they have higher levels of college education in Utah than they do nationally. Finally, these same two groups plus Chinese and Japanese are more likely to be engaged in white collar occupations than the same groups nationally. Utah's other minorities, however, are less likely to be engaged in white collar occupations.

SUMMARY

The relative success of Utah's blacks and Mexican Americans is partly attributable to their small numbers. Historically, minority groups fare well when their numbers are small and when there is not a large influx. No doubt there was greater hostility to Chinese and Japanese during the late nineteenth century when these groups arrived in large numbers. Even then, however, they were viewed as temporary workers. Hostility was no doubt again provoked when Japanese were interned at Topaz. But they were relatively isolated and most returned to the West Coast after internment. Other minorities were tolerated and accepted in Utah's mining industries because of their isolation. Utah has not been free from ethnic and racial hostility, however. The KKK was active in the state during parts of the nineteenth and twentieth centuries, and there are still considerable disparities between whites and most ethnic groups in Utah on virtually all of the variables examined. Nevertheless, their smaller-than-average numbers appear to have resulted in slightly better intergroup cooperation in Utah than has occurred elsewhere in the United States.

REFERENCES

Coleman, Ronald G. "Blacks in Utah History: An Unknown Legacy." In H. Z. Papanikolas, ed., *The People of Utah*, Salt Lake City, Utah: Utah State Historical Society, 1976, pp. 115-40.

Conley, Don C. "The Pioneer Chinese of Utah." In H. Z. Papanikolas, ed., *The Peoples of Utah*, Salt Lake City, Utah: Utah State Historical Society, 1976, pp. 251-79.

Gurgel, Klaus D. "Ethnic Minorities." In W. L. Wahlquist, ed., *Atlas of Utah*, Provo, Utah: Brigham Young University Press, 1981, pp. 121-22.

_____. "Postscript." In W. L. Wahlquist, ed., *Atlas of Utah*, Provo, Utah: Brigham Young University Press, 1981, pp. 273-74.

O'Neil, Floyd A. "The Utes, Southern Paiutes, and Gosiutes." In H. Z. Papanikolas, ed., *The Peoples of Utah*, Salt Lake City, Utah: Utah State Historical Society, 1976, pp. 27-60.

Mayer, Vincente V. "After Escalante: The Spanish-Speaking People of Utah." In H. Z. Papanikolas, ed., *The Peoples of Utah*, Salt Lake City, Utah: Utah State Historical Society, 1976, pp. 437-68.

Papanikolas, Helen Z. and Alice Kasai. "Japanese Life in Utah." In H. Z. Papanikolas, ed., *The Peoples of Utah*, Salt Lake City, Utah: Utah State Historical Society, 1976, pp. 333-62.

13.

THE DEMOGRAPHY OF UTAH MORMONS

Tim B. Heaton

Utah may be the most "churched" state in the nation (Wahlquist 1981). In large measure, the state's religious orientation can be attributed to the dominance of the Church of Jesus Christ of Latter-day Saints, or Mormon. In 1980 Mormons constituted 70 percent of Utah's population (Deseret News 1982). Although this represents a modest decline from the 73.4 percent of a decade earlier, it is still a substantial majority of the total population. In fact, the cultural traditions and organizational effectiveness of the Mormon church may yield an influence even greater than that suggested by population figures alone.

As a consequence, no other religious group has a sizable minority. Only the Roman Catholics, with just over 4 percent, can claim more than 1 percent of Utah's population. Clearly, one of the major religious distinctions in Utah is that between Mormons and non-Mormons. The first question addressed in this chapter concerns the similarity or dissimilarity between these two groups. The second derives from regional and national comparisons: Since Mormons dominate in the state, how do Utah Mormons compare demographically with Mormons who form a minority in other states?

SOURCES OF DATA

Demographic information for Utah's population is taken from the U.S. census. However, this does not contain information on religious affiliation. Demographic data for the state's Mormon population has therefore been drawn from a survey recently sponsored by the Mormon church. Unfortunately, these data have the disadvantage of not being directly comparable to census data. Nonetheless, they are the best source of demographic information on the Mormons available.

Data collection for the Mormon survey was initiated in spring 1981. In the first stage, questionnaires were mailed to a random sample of 7,446 adults aged 19 and over from a computerized list of all Mormons in the United States and Canada. A reminder post card was sent out two weeks later. These two mailings generated a response rate of 54 percent. Additional follow-up efforts, including telephone or personal interviews, yielded a total response rate of 81 percent. Only 4 percent of the original sample refused to respond. One percent had died or were no longer members of the church. The final 14 percent were unknown to local church leaders and unavailable to telephone or mailing approaches.

Each respondent was asked to fill out a questionnaire loosely resembling the 1980 U.S. census form in content. All responses were kept confidential. The information which follows includes responses gathered from all members of a respondent's household ages 16 and over. Weighting was used to correct a sampling bias favoring households with more adults.

We suspect some bias in terms of the religious participation of respondents since those who refused and those who were not located are probably less involved in the Mormon church. This makes it impossible to establish a one-to-one correspondence between survey results and characteristics of all Mormons. The variables analyzed, however, do not involve religious attitudes or opinions. Thus we believe that response bias due to the church's official sponsorship of the survey or to patterns of the religious involvement of the respondents is minimal.

UTAH MORMONS COMPARED TO THE STATE POPULATION

Table 1 contains information on the demographic characteristics of the Utah population from the U.S. census and of Utah Mormons from the Church Membership Survey. Comparisons are made separately for males and females for the population aged 16 and over. The computation of sex ratios at the end of the table indicates a predominance of females in both populations. There are 95 men for every 100 women in the state and 94 men for every 100 women in the Mormon population.

With the exception of the 16-19 age group, both groups are similar with respect to age structure. The Mormon sample, however, shows a smaller percentage in this first age category. This discrepancy is probably a result of methodological differences. The census was collected on a single day, but the Mormon survey took several months, possibly causing some differences in the age criterion.

Utah is a racially homogeneous state with over 92 percent of the population identifying themselves as white non-Hispanic. The Utah Mormon population is even more homogeneous with over 98 percent white non-Hispanic. In the state, Hispanics constitute nearly 4 percent of the population, while

TABLE 1.

Comparison of the Utah Census with a Utah Mormon Sample—Demographic Characteristics (in Percentages)

	UTAH CENSUS		UTAH MORMON SAMPLE	
CHARACTERISTIC	MALES	FEMALES	MALES	FEMALES
Age				
16-19	11.7	11.1	8.1	6.9
20-24	15.8	16.1	15.6	17.8
25-29	14.7	13.6	16.1	13.5
30-34	11.6	10.7	12.9	11.4
35-44	14.7	14.2	15.0	14.0
45-54	11.6	11.4	11.0	11.8
55-64	10.3	10.1	10.2	10.5
65-74	6.4	7.7	7.3	8.1
75+	3.2	5.2	3.8	5.9
Total	100.0	100.0	100.0	100.0
Race				
White	92.6	93.1	98.2	97.9
Black	.9	.5	.1	.0
Hispanic	3.9	3.6	.5	.6
American Indian	1.1	1.2	.4	.6
Other	1.6	1.6	.8	.8
Total	100.0	100.0	100.0	100.0
Marital Status				
Currently Married	67.4	64.2	70.7	67.5
Divorced/Separated	5.6	8.1	3.1	6.2
Widowed	1.6	8.4	1.2	7.7
Never Married	25.4	19.3	25.0	18.7
Total	100.0	100.0	100.0	100.0
Ever Divorced (Ever Married Population)				
No	78.9	78.0	86.0	83.8
Yes	21.1	22.0	14.0	16.2
Total	100.0	100.0	100.0	100.0

TABLE 1. CONTINUED

CHARACTERISTIC	UTAH CENSUS MALES	UTAH CENSUS FEMALES	UTAH MORMON SAMPLE MALES	UTAH MORMON SAMPLE FEMALES
Age at First Marriage				
14-17	3.9	16.2	11.3	11.0
18-19	14.9	29.8	11.1	25.7
20-21	22.8	24.9	20.4	27.6
22-24	32.5	17.3	38.9	21.9
25-29	18.7	8.0	10.4	8.4
30+	7.2	3.7	7.8	5.5
Total	100.0	100.0	100.0	100.0
Children Ever Born				
0		28.4		16.9
1		11.8		11.7
2		16.8		17.8
3		15.2		17.6
4		12.0		13.6
5		7.2		11.0
6		4.2		5.1
7+		4.5		6.3
Total		100.0		100.0
Education				
0-8	5.7	5.8	3.9	4.4
9-11	18.4	18.3	11.2	12.6
12	31.8	39.4	32.9	38.9
13-15	24.7	24.6	27.5	29.7
16	9.2	8.0	11.7	9.9
17+	10.2	3.9	12.8	4.4
Total	100.0	100.0	100.0	100.0
Employment Status				
Employed	75.6	46.7	80.0	45.0
Unemployed	4.3	2.6	4.4	4.4
Not in Labor Force	20.2	50.7	15.6	50.7
Total	100.0	100.0	100.0	100.0

TABLE 1. CONTINUED

CHARACTERISTIC	UTAH CENSUS		UTAH MORMON SAMPLE	
	MALES	FEMALES	MALES	FEMALES
Hours Worked				
1-19	6.4	16.6	5.0	18.7
20-34	9.2	21.6	8.3	20.9
35-44	51.7	53.0	50.2	51.4
45+	32.7	8.7	36.5	9.0
Total	100.0	100.0	100.0	100.0
Occupation				
White Collar	41.6	65.0	48.2	69.2
Blue Collar	54.4	34.0	50.8	30.5
Farm	3.9	.9	1.0	.3
Total	100.0	100.0	100.0	100.0
Income				
$ 0- 1999	7.5	24.6	5.7	20.9
2000- 4999	12.5	28.9	9.1	26.9
5000- 9999	18.3	27.0	14.4	26.5
10000-14999	17.4	12.6	16.1	14.9
15000-19999	16.8	4.4	16.0	6.6
20000-29999	18.8	1.8	23.9	3.1
30000-49999	6.8	.5	11.7	.3
50000+	2.0	.2	3.1	.9
Total	100.0	100.0	100.0	100.0
Mobility (Residence 5 years ago):				
Same House	44.8	46.5	50.1	49.5
Different House, same county	27.9	27.3	22.6	25.6
Different county, same state	8.1	8.5	9.4	10.6
Different State	19.1	17.7	17.8	14.4
Total	100.0	100.0	100.0	100.0

Sample size may vary across variables because of missing values and differences in the relevant population base.

American Indians and others (mostly Asian) make up over 1 percent. No minority contains over 1 percent of the Mormon group. Blacks are a small minority in either case.

Mormons are more likely to be married than is true for the state as a whole. For men, about 67 percent of Utahns compared to 71 percent of Mormons are currently married. For women the figures are 64 percent and 68 percent, respectively. Correspondingly, Mormons have smaller percentages in the divorced/separated, widowed, and never married categories. Differences in divorce are even more pronounced when one looks at the proportion of men and women who have ever been divorced. For men, the Mormon sample is 7.1 points lower, and for women the difference is 5.8 points. These discrepancies suggest a substantially higher divorce rate for the non-Mormon population.

Age and marriage distributions indicate that Mormons marry older than the population as a whole. Only 32.8 percent of Mormon men marry before age 22 compared to 41.6 percent of Utahns. Likewise, 36.7 percent of Mormon women compared to 46 percent of Utah women marry before age 20.

The distribution of children suggests that Mormons have higher fertility rates than the state as a whole. In part, this could be due to the higher percentage of Mormons who marry. Mormons are less likely to be childless and have noticeably higher percentages reporting 3-5 children, as well as a slightly higher percentage reporting families of seven or more children.

It bears repeating that differences in the two data sets belie strict comparisons between the two groups. For example, a childless rate of 16.9 percent for Mormons and 28.4 percent for the Utahns generally would require a rate of 55 percent for non-Mormons (assuming that the state is 70 percent LDS). The magnitude of this figure indicates that comparisons between rates can only suggest possible differences, not indicate the magnitude of those differences.

Educational distributions suggest a slightly more educated Mormon population. For men, 52 percent of Mormons report posthigh school education compared to 44.1 percent for the state. For women the values are 43.2 percent compared to 36.5 percent.

Employment figures indicate that Mormon men are more likely to be employed and less likely to be unemployed compared to the Utah data. Mormon women are just as likely to be employed but more likely to be unemployed than is the case for Utahns generally. The distribution of hours worked indicates that the amount of time devoted to the job for the employed population is approximately equal, except that Mormon men are more likely to work more than forty-five hours per week.

In the Mormon sample, both men and women are more likely to be found in white collar occupations than is true in the census data. Most of the difference is made up in blue collar occupations since farming is rare as a principle occupation.

Consistent with their higher occupational status and educational achievement, Mormons also tend to do better financially. Nearly 40 percent of Mormon men report an income of over $20,000 per year compared to less than 30 percent of the Utah sample. For women the figures are much lower. Still, 25.8 percent of Mormon women compared to 19.5 percent of all Utah women make over $10,000.

Finally, we consider residential mobility. Utah Mormons are more likely to report living in the same residence as they did five years earlier by about 5 percentage points. They are more likely to have moved across county boundaries but less likely to have made local moves within county boundaries. Consistent with the state's declining percentage of Mormons, a larger percentage of Utahns report living in a different state five years earlier than is true for Mormons.

In sum, these data suggest differences between Utah Mormons and the entire population of the state. These differences are consistent with the ideology of the Mormon church, which stresses family and socio-economic achievement, as well as with the historical Mormon role in populating the state and establishing its economy. In comparison with state census data, Mormons are characterized by higher rates of marriage, lower divorce, larger families, and higher levels of educational, occupational, and financial success.

UTAH MORMONS AND OTHER MORMONS

For comparative purposes, the U.S. sample of Mormons is divided into three groups. Utah, the core of Mormon culture, is the first. Characteristics for this group have already been reported but bear repeating for comparison. The second group includes Mormons in the western states where they constitute an important minority. Outside the West Mormons are a small minority, so all non-western states are included in the third category. Characteristics for these three groups are presented in Table 2.

The three groups are similar with respect to age structure, but regions outside Utah have a lower sex ratio. There are 94 males per 100 females in Utah compared to 89 in the West and 85 elsewhere.

TABLE 2.

Comparisons of Utah Mormons With Mormons in the Western and Other U.S.—Demographic Characteristics (in Percentages)

	REGION					
	UTAH		WEST		OTHER	
CHARACTERISTIC	MALE	FEMALE	MALE	FEMALE	MALE	FEMALE
Age						
16-19	8.1	6.9	7.0	7.1	7.7	5.5
20-24	15.6	17.8	14.0	15.1	14.4	14.5
25-29	16.1	13.5	15.1	13.9	19.0	17.1
30-34	12.9	11.4	13.5	12.8	14.5	14.7
35-44	15.0	14.0	18.0	15.8	19.7	18.9
45-54	11.0	11.8	12.1	13.4	10.7	12.5
55-64	10.2	10.5	10.2	9.9	8.2	9.2
65-74	7.3	8.1	6.0	7.3	4.0	4.5
75+	3.8	5.9	4.1	4.7	1.7	3.1
Total	100.0	100.0	100.0	100.0	100.0	100.0
Race						
White	98.2	97.9	96.4	94.3	93.4	92.4
Black	.1	.0	.1	.1	.5	.3
Hispanic	.5	.6	1.4	3.0	2.0	2.6
American Indian	.4	.6	1.2	1.2	.7	1.2
Other	.8	.8	1.0	1.4	3.4	3.4
Total	100.0	100.0	100.0	100.0	100.0	100.0

TABLE 2. CONTINUED

Marital Status						
Currently Married	70.7	67.5	66.8	66.8	64.5	64.9
Divorced/Separated	3.1	6.2	5.3	8.2	5.4	10.8
Widowed	1.2	7.7	1.4	6.5	.2	4.8
Never Married	25.0	18.7	26.5	18.6	30.0	19.6
Total	100.0	100.0	100.0	100.0	100.0	100.0
Ever Divorced (Ever Married Population)						
No	86.0	83.8	80.7	77.5	81.6	75.8
Yes	14.0	16.2	19.3	22.5	18.4	24.2
Total	100.0	100.0	100.0	100.0	100.0	100.0
Age at First Marriage						
14-17	1.3	11.0	1.3	12.6	2.0	15.4
15-19	11.1	25.7	11.6	28.6	11.9	30.6
20-21	20.4	27.6	21.9	25.3	22.3	24.0
22-24	38.9	21.9	35.0	18.2	34.3	15.4
25-29	20.4	8.4	20.3	9.0	19.4	9.6
30 +	7.8	5.5	10.0	6.2	10.3	5.1
Total	100.0	100.0	100.0	100.0	100.0	100.0
Children Ever Born						
0		16.9		24.4		23.6
1		11.7		12.1		13.5
2		17.8		18.5		18.5
3		17.6		16.7		18.5
4		13.6		12.0		11.6
5		11.0		7.2		7.0
6		5.1		4.7		3.6
7 +		6.3		4.4		3.7
Total		100.0		100.0		100.0

TABLE 2. CONTINUED

Education						
0-8	3.9	4.4	5.7	4.4	5.9	6.4
9-11	11.2	12.6	11.2	13.4	13.3	14.1
12	32.9	38.9	32.8	38.3	34.5	37.2
13-15	27.5	29.7	27.5	32.5	19.0	28.6
16	11.7	9.9	9.6	6.8	11.0	8.0
17+	12.8	4.4	13.2	4.6	16.2	5.8
Total	100.0	100.0	100.0	100.0	100.0	100.0
Employment Status						
Employed	80.0	45.0	79.8	45.0	79.8	45.6
Unemployed	4.4	4.4	4.7	6.3	6.2	6.4
Not in Labor Force	15.6	50.7	15.6	48.7	13.9	47.9
Total	100.0	100.0	100.0	100.0	100.0	100.0
Hours Worked						
1-19	5.0	18.7	4.6	16.1	3.5	13.8
20-34	8.3	20.9	5.9	20.2	4.9	19.0
35-44	50.2	51.4	49.2	52.0	48.9	54.8
45+	36.5	9.0	40.4	11.8	42.7	12.3
Total	100.0	100.0	100.0	100.0	100.0	100.0
Occupation						
White Collar	48.2	69.2	47.6	66.5	48.4	62.3
Blue Collar	50.8	30.5	51.1	33.0	50.9	37.3
Farm	1.0	.3	1.3	.5	.7	.4
Total	100.0	100.0	100.0	100.0	100.0	100.0

TABLE 2. CONTINUED

Income						
$ 0- 1999	5.7	20.9	5.5	21.1	3.7	17.7
2000- 4999	9.1	26.9	8.0	26.5	6.3	20.8
5000- 9999	14.4	26.5	13.3	23.8	13.1	31.6
10000-14999	16.1	14.9	14.6	15.5	16.5	16.2
15000-19999	16.0	6.6	15.7	7.6	14.3	8.8
20000-29999	23.9	3.1	25.5	4.5	24.9	3.8
30000-49999	11.7	.3	13.6	.5	15.2	.9
50000+	3.1	.9	3.8	.4	6.1	.2
Total	100.0	100.0	100.0	100.0	100.0	100.0
Mobility (Residence 5 years ago):						
Same House	50.1	49.5	44.1	44.8	40.2	42.3
Different House, same county	22.6	25.6	25.4	25.2	18.7	21.4
Different County, same state	9.4	10.6	10.7	11.7	9.6	9.9
Different State	17.8	14.4	19.7	18.3	31.5	26.4
Total	100.0	100.0	100.0	100.0	100.0	100.0
N[a]	2091	2229	2554	2867	1182	1392

Sample size may vary across variables because of missing values and differences in the relevant population base.

Mormons outside Utah are less likely to be white non-Hispanic. Each of the other minority groups considered (i.e., blacks, American Indians, Hispanics, and others) are more common outside Utah. Still, whites constitute over 90 percent of the Mormon population in each region.

In terms of marital status, the main difference is that Utah Mormons are less likely to be currently divorced or separated. The differences are even greater when one looks at the percentage of men and women who have ever divorced. For men, the values are 14.0 for Utah, 19.3 for the West, and 18.4 elsewhere. For women, they are 16.2, 22.5, and 24.2, respectively.

Early marriage does not appear to be any more common among Utahns than among other Mormons. In comparison with other regions, fewer Utah Mormon men marry after age 30, but marriage before age 20 is most common among Mormon women who live outside the West—46 percent compared to 36.7 percent in Utah and 31.2 in the West. Utah Mormons also have larger families than other Mormons. They are less likely to be childless and more likely to have four or more children.

In terms of education, Utah and the West are roughly equal; about the same percentages report some college experience. Mormons outside the West are less likely to enter college, but the percentage with post-graduate education is just as high or higher than in Utah or the West.

Employment status is comparable in the three regions, but part-time employment may be more common in Utah. Also, there is a slight tendency for more white collar work among women in Utah compared to the other two regions.

Income appears to be slightly lower in Utah. Of men in the Utah group, 36.7 report incomes greater than $20,000 compared to 42.9 in the West and 46.2 elsewhere. Likewise, 25.8 percent of Utah women report incomes above $10,000 compared to 28.5 in the West and 29.9 elsewhere.

Finally, Utah Mormons are less mobile than other Mormons. A higher percentage report having lived in the same house for at least five years and are less likely to have moved across state lines.

Most of the differences we find between Utah Mormons and Mormons living elsewhere in the U.S. are probably not significant. There does appear to be more of an emphasis on traditional family values in Utah with less divorce and larger families. Since Utah is at the core of Mormon culture these results are not surprising. In terms of socio-economic achievement, Utah Mormons may do better in schooling and occupation but not when it comes to actual income. Simply put, Utah Mormons are not distinctive compared to Mormons elsewhere.

SUMMARY

The Church of Jesus Christ of Latter-day Saints is the dominant religion in Utah. Its local membership accounts for about 70 percent of the population. Comparing Mormons with state census data suggests that the church has a traditionalizing influence on family life (i.e., lower divorce and larger families) and a positive influence on socio-economic achievement. Mormons appear to be fairly homogeneous. Utah Mormons do not differ greatly in terms of demographic characteristics, at least, from Mormons in other western states or throughout the United States.

REFERENCES

Deseret News. *The 1983 Church Almanac.* Salt Lake City: Deseret News Press, 1982.

Wahlquist, Wayne L., ed. *Atlas of Utah.* Provo, Utah: Brigham Young University Press, 1981.

14.
EDUCATION

Adrian Van Mondrans
Ralph B. Smith
with Vanessa Moss

Educational and civic leaders alike are finding themselves increasingly confronted with challenges regarding the future of public education in the United States. Yet few states face the overwhelming dilemmas confronting Utah. Utah teachers struggle with minimal salaries and large classes, while the state searches for ways to finance dramatic increases in enrollments with only a slowly increasing tax base. While the outlook is bleak, there is also a brighter side. Utah teachers have remained committed to their occupation when less dedicated teachers would have withdrawn from public education. This chapter reports on various factors affecting education, with national and regional comparisons, thereby affording readers a perspective from which to assess the quality of education in Utah.

ENROLLMENTS AND SCHOOLS

Utah's population in 1983 stood at 1,619,000, of which 23 percent (or 378,208) were enrolled in public elementary and secondary schools. By comparison, 19 percent of the U.S. population was enrolled in public elementary and secondary schools (*Utah Education Association Research Bulletin* 1984).

Nationally, there are 83,688 public elementary, secondary, and kindergarten-through-grade 12 schools. Of this, 59,325 (or 70 percent) are elementary, 22,619 (or 27 percent) are secondary, and 1,743 (or 2 percent) include both elementary and secondary grades. In Utah there are 621 schools, of which 429 (or 69 percent) are elementary, 188 (or 30 percent) are secondary, and four (or 1 percent) combine both elementary and secondary grades. In addition, there are 24 private schools, 15 of which are elementary, five are secondary, and four combine both elementary and secondary grades.

Utah has nine public institutions of higher education. Of this number, four are four-year colleges or universities, three are community colleges, and two are technical colleges. There are also five private institutions of higher learning, including one major university, a four-year college, and three business schools (U.S. Department of Education, *Digest of Education Statistics*, 1984).

DISTRICTS

In 1982, there were 15,840 school districts in the United States. Of this number, 15,517 were operating districts and 323 were non-operating districts. Utah has forty school districts, all operating. Only Hawaii, with one district, and Nevada, with seventeen, have fewer districts than Utah. Rhode Island also has forty districts. The range in the number of districts runs from one in Hawaii to 1,075 in Texas. Other states with over a thousand districts include, besides Texas, California with 1,033, Nebraska with 1,014, and Illinois with 1,010.

Generally, the consolidation of school districts into fewer entities lessens administrative costs and increases the opportunity to promote specialized and advanced classes. Thus, Utah's few districts may be an advantage.

TABLE 1.

Elementary School Enrollments (1970-82)

	1970	1981	1982	1970-82 INC./DEC.	PERCENT INC./DEC.
U.S.	32,577,000	27,269,119	27,142,803	−5,434,197	−16.7
Utah	213,000	261,722	275,145	+62,145	+29.2
HIGH SCHOOL ENROLLMENTS (1970-82)					
U.S.	13,332,000	12,879,254	12,500,673	−831,327	−6.2
Utah	91,000	93,832	95,038	+4,038	+4.4
PUBLIC ELEMENTARY AND SECONDARY SCHOOL ENROLLMENTS					
U.S.	44,791,000	40,984,000	39,540,000	−5,251,000	−11.7
Utah	310,000	344,000	366,000	+56,000	+18.1

Source: U.S. Department of Education, The Condition of Education, 1984, Table 1.2; U.S. Bureau of the Census 1984, Table 211.

The average number of schools per school district nationally is 5.3. In Utah it is 15.5. Within in the region, the ratios are 15.9 in Nevada, 7.7 in Wyoming, 7.0 in Colorado, 6.9 in New Mexico, 4.8 in Idaho, 3.6 in Arizona, and 1.4 in Montana. To the extent consolidation is effective, the provision for specialized staff occurs at higher rates in Utah than regionally, even though the burden on taxpayers and teachers is higher in Utah than elsewhere (U.S. Department of Education, *Digest of Education Statistics*, 1984).

PUBLIC SCHOOL ENROLLMENTS

Public elementary and secondary school enrollments nationally have changed over the past twelve years from 1970 to 1982, with a general trend that reflects declining enrollments. Thirty-seven states have experienced a decrease in total enrollments ranging from 3.1 percent in Louisiana to 26.9 percent in South Dakota. Three states reported no change, while ten saw increases ranging from 4.4 percent (in Utah's high school enrollments) to 54.3 percent (in Nevada). Among elementary and secondary schools, the former typically experienced greater decreases.

TABLE 2.

Public Elementary and Secondary Schools — Enrollment as Percentage of all Persons Aged 5-17

	1960	1970	1978	1980	1982
United States	82.2	86.9	89.2	86.5	87.1
Mountain States	(NA)	90.9	96.2	92.6	92.8
Montana	81.8	89.3	94.4	92.9	93.2
Idaho	87.7	90.09	98.5	95.4	96.3
Wyoming	93.7	93.5	97.9	97.3	95.2
Colorado	89.5	91.5	95.1	92.2	93.1
New Mexico	84.6	89.0	93.4	89.5	89.9
Arizona	96.5	86.0	93.4	89.5	89.9
Utah	92.2	96.8	99.4	98.2	97.6*
Nevada	99.9	98.4	97.3	93.4	93.3

*Utah ranks first nationally with the highest percentage of enrollments among 5-17 year-olds.

Source: U.S. Bureau of the Census 1974, Tables 196; 1984, Table 230; 1979, Table 240.

Though declining enrollments would seem to be the rule nationwide, statistics for Utah reflect substantial increases in elementary school enrollments. While elementary enrollments declined 16.7 percent nationally, they increased 29.2 percent in Utah (see Table 1).

Nationwide, secondary school enrollments declined 6.2 percent, while statistics for Utah reflected an increase (see Table 1). When elementary and secondary school enrollments are combined, enrollments nationally show a decline of 11.7 percent, whereas Utah enrollments increased 18.1 percent (see Table 1).

Not only has Utah experienced substantial increases in public school enrollments, which, in turn, increase the burden on school resources, the percentage of its students in public schools is the highest in the nation. According to Table 2, 87.1 percent of all children, ages 5 to 17, nationally are enrolled in public schools. For Utah this figure is 97.6 percent, the highest in the nation. Among the mountain states, 92.8 percent are enrolled in public schools, with the range being 89.9 to 97.6 percent (U.S. Department of Education, *The Condition of Education*, 1984).

Table 3 reports the percentage of Utah's population ever having attended school. In all categories, Utah ranks above national averages, placing it among the highest in the nation.

In 1980, Utah ranked first nationally regarding the percentage of the population (93 percent) completing one to three years of high school. Utah ranked

TABLE 3.

Years of School Completed 1980
Percentage of Population Completing at Least:

	8 YEARS OR LESS ELEMENTARY	1-3 YEARS HIGH SCHOOL	4 YEARS HIGH SCHOOL	1-3 YEARS COLLEGE	4 YEARS COLLEGE
United States	100.0	81.7	66.5	31.9	16.2
Utah	100.0	93.0	80.0	44.1	19.9
Utah Rank	–	1	2	1	7
Range	–	72.0-93.0	53.1-82.5	20.4-44.1	10.4-23.0

Source: U.S. Bureau of the Census 1984, Table 224.

second as to the percentage of the population (80 percent) completing four years of high school. Regarding college, Utah ranked first nationally with 44.1 percent of its population completing one to three years of college, and seventh nationally with 19.9 percent completing four years of college (see Table 6).

TABLE 4.

Percentage of Population over 25 with High School Diploma

	1970	1976	1980
Utah Rank	1	1	1
Utah Percentage	67.3	78.9	80.0
U.S. Percentage	52.3	63.8	66.3

Source: Nelson 1983, Exhibit 38.

TABLE 5.

Persons 25 Years Old and Over with Less Than 9 and Less Than 12 Years of School Completed, April 1970 and April 1980

	1970	1976
Less Than 9 Years		
United States	28.3	18.3
Utah	13.4*	7.1*
Range	13.4-44.8	7.2-31.3
Less Than 12 Years		
United States	47.7	33.5
Utah	32.5*	20.2*
Range	32.5-62.2	20.2-46.9

*Lowest percentage in nation.

Source: U.S. Department of Education, The Condition of Education, 1984, Table 4.1.

As to the percentage over 25 years of age with a high school diploma, Utah ranked second nationwide in 1980 with 80 percent completing high school. This compares to 66.3 percent nationally (see Tables 4 and 5).

The percentage of the population over 25 years of age in Utah with less than nine years of school is a remarkably low 7.1 percent, a figure placing the state first nationally. Similarly, the percentage over 25 with less than twelve years of school in Utah is 20.2, the lowest in the nation. Utah's record makes it clear that the state has a literate population. The dramatic improvement from 1970 to 1980 reflects Utah's enviable educational attainment.

TABLE 6.

Utah Elementary Class Size, 1983-84

GRADE	AVE. CLASS SIZE	TOTAL CLASSES	NO. CLASSES 0-24	NO. CLASSES 25-29	NO. CLASSES 30-39	NO. CLASSES 40+
K	26.5	1068	274	625	168	1
1	25.3	1056	414	573	68	1
2	25.9	1072	328	631	113	0
3	26.9	946	205	553	188	0
4	28.4	811	132	340	339	0
5	29.0	719	85	273	350	1
6	29.6	446	47	157	262	0
Comb Class	26.6	331	97	149	78	7
Totals	27.0	6469	1582	3301	1576	10
	UTAH MIDDLE/JUNIOR HIGH CLASS SIZE					
All	29.1	11,884	1,138	5,092	4,826	828*
	UTAH HIGH SCHOOL CLASS SIZE					
All	26.8	11,869	2,783	4,703	4,383	754**

*240 classes had over 50 students.
**193 classes had over 50 students.

Source: Utah Education Association Research Bulletin 1984, 2, 6-17.

MINORITY, PRIVATE SCHOOL, AND HIGHER EDUCATION ENROLLMENTS

Minority enrollments in Utah's public schools constitute 7.3 percent of the total public school enrollment. In 1980, 343,987 students were enrolled in the state's public schools. Of this, 12,014 (3.5 percent) were Hispanics, 6,124 (1.8 percent) were American Indians, 5,241 (1.5 percent) were Asians, and 1,708 (0.5 percent) were blacks. Data for the United States indicate that 26.7 percent of all students in public schools are minorities, of which 16.1 percent are blacks, 8 percent are Hispanics, 1.9 percent are Asians, and 0.8 percent are American Indians.

National statistics note an increase of 6 percent in minority enrollments from 1970 to 1980. During the same time, minority enrollments in Utah increased only 1.1 percent (U.S. Department of Education, *Digest of Education Statistics*, 1984).

Total enrollments in private schools in the United States numbered 4,961,755 in 1980. Of this, 795,260 were enrolled in non-denominational institutions, while 4,166,495 were enrolled in church-related schools. Figures for Utah showed 5,555 students enrolled in private elementary and secondary schools, 1,862 enrolled in non-denominational schools, and 3,693 enrolled in church-related schools. For Utah, enrollments in Catholic institutions were greatest at 3,055, with the remaining students distributed among Lutheran, Seventh-Day Adventist, and other church-related schools (U.S. Department of Education, *Digest of Education Statistics*, 1984).

Whereas public school enrollments in the United States declined from 1970 to 1982, higher education enrollments rose dramatically from 8,580,900 to 12,426,000, an increase of 45 percent. For Utah, the state's 81,700 higher education enrollment in 1970 increased only 21 percent to 99,000 in 1982 (U.S. Bureau of the Census 1984). It is to be noted that 34,400 students (34.7 percent) were enrolled in Utah's private colleges and universities.

CLASS SIZE AND PUPIL-TEACHER RATIOS

Statistics on class size in Utah reflect the heavy student loads borne by teachers. At the elementary level the average class size is 27, with 1,576 (24.4 percent) classes having enrollments between 30 and 39. At the junior high school level, the average class size is 29.1. However, 4,826 (40.6 percent) of all junior high school classes enroll between 30 and 39 students, and 828 (7 percent) enroll in excess of 40 students (see Table 6). The average high school

TABLE 7.

Pupil-Teacher Ratio in Enrollment in Elementary and Secondary Day Schools, U.S., Mountain States, and Utah, 1969-81

	1969	1970	1971[a]	1972[a]	1973	1974	1975	1976[b]	1977[b]	1978[b]	1981
United States	22.7	22.3	21.3	21.8	21.4	20.9	29.4	20.2	19.9	19.7	18.9
Mountain States											
Arizona	23.4	23.4	24.0	23.8	24.4	23.0	21.5	21.4	21.2	21.0	19.8
Colorado	22.8	23.3	23.6	23.1	21.7	20.9	21.3	20.0	19.4	19.2	18.7
Idaho	22.6	22.7	23.1	24.1	22.9	21.9	21.8	21.6	21.1	20.8	20.9
Montana	20.7	21.0	—	—	19.9	19.1	19.0	17.8	17.5	15.3	16.5
Nevada	24.9	25.7	24.0	24.3	24.3	24.0	24.3	23.7	22.4	22.4	21.1
New Mexico	23.5	24.2	23.2	23.1	22.6	22.3	21.3	22.1	20.4	20.2	18.8
Utah	26.6	26.8	26.6	25.3	24.7	24.5	26.0	24.3	24.5	24.3	27.4
Wyoming	19.4	19.0	18.5	18.2	17.6	17.4	16.9	18.2	18.4	18.2	15.0

[a]No data available for Montana.
[b]Ratio figured from number of full-time and part-time teachers divided by number of students enrolled.

Source: U.S. Department of Health, Education, and Welfare 1970, Table 8; 1973, Table 7; 1976, Table 7; U.S. Department of Health, Education, and Welfare, Digest of Education Statistics, 1979, Tables 29, 48; U.S. Department of Health, Education, and Welfare, Digest of Education Statistics, 1984, Table 36.

class size in Utah is 26.8, the lowest of all. Yet, 4,383 (36.9 percent) of all high school classes enroll between 30 and 39 students, and 754 (6.4 percent) enroll in excess of 40 students (see Table 6).

Many researchers believe that young children who are acquiring basic reading, writing, mathematics, and other skills need the greatest amount of teacher time. Thus, the substantial elementary enrollments is a concern warranting the attention of Utah's educators. The junior high school years are also critical. Here again, enrollments should concern those responsible for the state's educational needs.

The pupil-teacher ratio is an important measure of a teacher's responsibility and work load. Utah has long had the highest pupil-teacher ratio in the nation. By whatever measure, be it total enrollment or average daily attendance, Utah's teachers carry the heaviest student load of any state in the nation.

Data from the *1983-84 Digest of Education Statistics* set the average pupil-per-teacher ratio based on enrollment for the United States at 18.9 (see Table 7), while the same figure for Utah is 27.4. The lowest pupil-teacher ratio nationally is 15.0 in Colorado and Wyoming. Similar statistics, based on average daily attendance, report the average for the United States at 17.5, while for Utah it is 25.7. The lowest is 13.9 in Wyoming and Kansas. Table 7 provides pupil-teacher ratios for the United States and for the states surrounding Utah. In private elementary schools the average number of pupils per teacher is 17.9, ranging from 11.3 in Vermont to 21.1 in Michigan. For Utah it is 18.0, well under that found in public schools.

TABLE 8.

Utah and National ACT Standard Score Averages 1983 and 1984

	UTAH		NATION	
TEST	1983	1984	1983	1984
English	17.9	18.3	17.8	18.1
Mathematics	16.4	17.1	16.9	17.3
Social Studies	17.3	17.8	17.1	17.3
Natural Science	21.4	21.4	20.9	21.0
Composite	18.4	18.8	18.3	18.5

Source: Utah State Office of Education, "Utah ACT Performance."

PERFORMANCE OF UTAH HIGH SCHOOL STUDENTS

The performance of high school students on nationally administered standardized tests allows one to make some general observations as to the quality of instruction and the preparation of students. Two recognized examinations, the American College Test (ACT) and the Scholastic Aptitude Test (SAT), are administered to high school students yearly. In Utah, most high school students take the ACT, while relatively few take the SAT.

ACT scores for 1982 placed Utah students at the national average (*Education Week*, 18 Jan. 1984, 12-13). Two years later, a comparison of Utah with national groups revealed some improvement in English, social studies, natural science, and the composite score, but the state still trailed in mathematics.

Table 8 shows the performance of Utah students on the various portions of the ACT. While the state's young women did better than the young men in English, the men outperformed the women in all other areas of the test.

Overall, Utah high school students, whether college-bound or vocationally-oriented, rated their high school experience more positively than was true nationally. Students indicated that they were "most satisfied" with the number and variety of courses, classroom instruction, and provisions for outstanding students. On the other hand, students expressed "least satisfaction" with grading practices and policies; school rules, regulations and policies; laboratory facilities; and provision for special help in reading, mathematics, and other subjects.

Comparing the performance of Utah high school students with students in other states, *Education USA* (16 Jan. 1984) listed the composite score for twenty-eight states where the ACT was administered. Among these, Utah ranked 17th with a composite score for all students of 18.4 out of 36, the average for the nation.

Data are also available on the performance of Utah high school students on the SAT for the years 1982-84, including performance averages, the range of scores, and the rank of Utah compared to other states (see Table 9). Scores are encouraging on both the verbal and math sections, with Utah students ranking third and eighth, respectively. However, a caution should be noted. The percentage of Utah's college-bound students taking the SAT is low, only 4 percent, compared, for example, to 69 percent in Connecticut. Comparisons are thus "delicate," since it is generally accepted that the greater the number of students taking a test the lower the scores. In Utah, with only 4 percent of college-bound students taking the test, scores tend to be high.

On the other hand, over 70 percent of Utah high school seniors took the ACT. A state report indicates that "this high percentage of Utah students taking the ACT means that the Utah group of test-takers likely includes many lower-scoring students who would not elect to take the ACT in other states (Utah State Office of Education 1984). The report goes on to note that the high percentage of students taking the test "depress[es] the average scores for the state in comparison with other states in the nation."

Education Week (18 Jan. 1984) reported comparative data on ACT scores for the years 1972 and 1982. In 1972, the composite score for Utah was 19.7, ranking the state 14th out of twenty-eight. But by 1982, Utah's composite scores had fallen 1.3 points, placing the state 17th.

The performance of Utah students to be gleaned from comparisons with other states is probably somewhere between their performance on the ACT and on the SAT. In other words, Utah high school graduates are at or above national averages on college entrance examinations.

TEACHERS

The number of full-time equivalent (FTE) teachers in the United States increased by 61,446 (3 percent) from 1970 to 1981. Nationally, thirty-three states experienced increases ranging from 1 to 48.3 percent, while seventeen

TABLE 9.

SAT Verbal and Math Scores

	1982	1983	1984
Verbal	494	508	503
Range	378-522	383-520	384-520
Utah Rank	5	3	3
National Average	426	425	426
Math	528	545	542
Range	412-572	415-573	419-570
Utah Rank	10	5	8
National Average	467	468	471

Sources: Educational USA, 4 Oct. 1982, 26 Sept. 1983; Biemiller 1984.

states noted decreases ranging from 0.2 to 31.4 percent. Utah teachers increased by 1,633, or 14.4 percent (U.S. Department of Education, *The Condition of Education*, 1984).

Instructional staff in Utah's public schools numbered 16,190, of which 12,983 were teachers. There were 3,207 other professionals in elementary and secondary schools, including 566 principals, 161 assistant principals, two curriculum specialists, 332 library/media specialists, 330 guidance and counseling personnel, 109 school psychologists, and 1,707 "others." In addition, there were forty superintendents and 192 district staff personnel. Supporting the professional staff were 8,590 non-professionals, including teacher aides, office and clerical staff, and others.

As noted, Utah's student/teacher ratio is highest in the nation. Professional and support staff serve approximately 378,000 students, a ratio of approximately twenty-three students per professional. Some Utahns view with concern the number of educators who are not teachers. Taxpayers and legislators sometimes ask if the number of non-teaching professionals could be reduced without harming the quality of education, reassigning them instead to the classroom where they would help reduce the student/teacher ratio. The ratio of classroom teachers to other professional educators in Utah is 4.0. This compares to 5.9 nationally. Utah's schools have more professional educators assigned to duties other than teaching than is true nationally. If Utah's ratio were brought into line with national figures approximately 1,000 professionals would be available for teaching activities. Assuming vacancies could be made available, the result would reduce the student/teacher ratio by 2.2 students to 25.2 students per teacher (U.S. Department of Education, *Digest of Education Statistics*, 1984).

SALARIES AND TEACHING ASSIGNMENTS

Teacher salaries in the United States differ from state to state due to varying degrees of emphasis placed on educational preparation, available funding (e.g., taxable property), regional differences in the cost of living, and other factors. Salary information is available from several sources, such as the National Educational Association, Utah Department of Education, the *Statistical Abstract of the United States*, and others. Table 10 provides some information on salaries in Utah. Data for 1982-83 rank Utah 26th, with an average salary of $19,667 compared to $20,531 nationally. Teacher salaries in Utah have remained at or near the national average.

Table 11 notes the number and percentage of teachers in Utah who have assignments in major subject areas. The numbers and percentages are divided into three categories indicating whether or not the subject to which the teacher is assigned relates to his or her college major or minor. The first set of figures represents the major teaching assignment, the second represents a minor teaching assignment, and the third indicates whether the teacher has had either a major or a minor in the subject field.

TABLE 10.

10-Year Salary Trend for Teachers Only in the United States

AVERAGE ANNUAL SALARIES AND PERCENT INCREASE, 1972-73 to 1982-83

SCHOOL YEAR	ELEMEN-TARY	PERCENT INCREASE	SECOND-ARY	PERCENT INCREASE	TOTAL	PERCENT INCREASE
1972-73	$ 9,893	—	$10,057	—	$10,176	—
1973-74	10,507	6.2	11,077	5.4	10,778	5.9
1974-75	11,334	7.4	12,000	8.3	11,690	8.5
1975-76	12,282	8.4	12,947	7.9	12,591	7.7
1976-77	12,988	5.7	13,776	6.4	13,352	6.0
1977-78	13,860	6.7	14,611	6.1	14,207	6.4
1978-79	14,665	5.8	15,441	5.7	15,002	5.7
1979-80	15,556	6.1	16,434	6.4	15,951	6.2
1980-81	17,204	10.6	18,071	10.0	17,597	10.3
1981-82	18,670	8.6	19,712	9.1	19,142	8.8
1982-83	20,042	7.3	21,100	7.0	20,531	7.3

ANNUAL AVERAGE TEACHER SALARIES, 1981/82 - 1982/82

	1981/82	1982/83	PERCENT INCREASE
United States	$19,142	$20,531	7.3
Utah	18,152	19,667	8.4
Utah Rank	30	26	18

Source: Education Week, 23 March 1983, 15.

TABLE 11.

Teacher Assignments—Number of Teachers in Utah
Assignment by Subject Area

(Bold represents a major teaching assignment, plain represents a minor teaching assignment)

SUBJECT	COLLEGIATE MAJOR	COLLEGIATE MINOR	NEITHER MAJOR NOR MINOR	TOTAL
Agriculture	**62**	**0**	**2**	**64**
% Total	**96.9**	**0**	**3.1**	**100**
Number	16	0	0	16
% Total	100	0	0	100
Art	**216**	**19**	**17**	**252**
% Total	**85.7**	**7.5**	**6.8**	**100**
Number	15	7	23	45
% Total	33.3	15.6	51.1	100
Business Ed.	**203**	**23**	**23**	**252**
% Total	**80.6**	**9.1**	**10.3**	**100**
Number	90	12	23	125
% Total	72.0	9.6	18.4	100
Driver Education	**0**	**43**	**39**	**82**
% Total	**0**	**52.4**	**47.6**	**100**
Number	0	17	28	45
% Total	0	37.8	62.2	100
Foreign Language	**152**	**43**	**34**	**229**
% Total	**66.4**	**18.8**	**14.8**	**100**
Number	39	50	30	119
% Total	32.8	42.0	25.2	100
Health and Physical Ed.	**656**	**29**	**22**	**707**
% Total	**92.8**	**4.1**	**3.1**	**100**
Number	376	57	82	515
% Total	73.0	11.1	15.9	100
Homemaking	**336**	**4**	**13**	**353**
% Total	**95.2**	**1.1**	**3.7**	**100**
Number	47	1	6	54
% Total	61.2	3.2	35.4	100
Industrial Arts	**293**	**7**	**17**	**317**
% Total	**92.4**	**2.2**	**5.4**	**100**
Number	19	1	11	31
% Total	61.21	3.2	35.4	100

TABLE 11. CONTINUED

SUBJECT	COLLEGIATE MAJOR	COLLEGIATE MINOR	NEITHER MAJOR NOR MINOR	TOTAL
Language Arts	**833**	**230**	**130**	**1103**
% Total	**69.8**	**19.3**	**10.9**	**100**
Number	205	114	136	455
% Total	45.1	25.1	29.8	100
Mathematics	**352**	**190**	**214**	**756**
% Total	**46.6**	**25.1**	**28.3**	**100**
Number	205	36	183	259
% Total	15.4	13.9	70.7	100
Music	**357**	**17**	**17**	**391**
% Total	**91.4**	**4.3**	**4.3**	**100**
Number	60	8	10	78
% Total	76.9	10.3	12.8	100
Science	**198**	**63**	**323**	**584**
% Total	**33.9**	**10.8**	**55.3**	**100**
Number	51	42	201	292
% Total	17.3	14.3	68.4	100
(Biological)	**117**	**1 7**	**45**	**179**
% Total	**65.4**	**9.5**	**25.1**	**100**
(Number)	29	17	35	71
% Total	40.8	9.9	49.3	100
(Earth Space)	**3**	**2**	**23**	**28**
% Total	**10.7**	**7.1**	**82.2**	**100**
(Number)	3	0	24	27
% Total	11.1	0	88.9	100
(General)	**43**	**25**	**214**	**282**
% Total	**15.2**	**8.9**	**75.9**	**100**
(Number)	12	13	89	114
% Total	10.5	11.4	78.1	100
(Physical)	**35**	**19**	**41**	**95**
% Total	**36.8**	**20.0**	**43.2**	**100**
(Number)	7	22	53	82
% Total	8.6	26.8	64.6	100
Social Sciences	**557**	**107**	**57**	**721**
% Total	**77.3**	**14.8**	**7.9**	**100**
Number	167	91	82	340
% Total	4.1	26.8	24.1	100

Source: Utah State Office of Education, Status of Teacher Personnel 42-73.

In areas such as agriculture, art, business education, health, physical education, homemaking, industrial arts, and music, 80 to 90 percent of the teachers had majored in these areas in college. Of those teachers whose minor teaching assignments included any of the above, except art and industrial arts, 70 to 80 percent had majored in these fields. Fifty-one percent of all teachers whose minor assignment was art had neither majored nor minored in art, while 36 percent whose minor assignment was industrial arts had neither majored nor minored in industrial arts.

In foreign language, language arts, and social studies the statistics are similar, with approximately 70 percent of the teachers with major assignments teaching in the area of their college major. The majority of teachers whose minor assignments were in foreign languages or social studies had majored or minored in foreign language, language arts, or social studies. However, 7 to 30 percent of teachers in one of these two fields taught without having majored or minored in the subject.

The most surprising statistics are those related to mathematics and science. Only 46.6 percent of teachers providing instruction in mathematics had completed a college major in the field, while 25 percent had college minors. Twenty-eight percent of teachers teaching math had neither a major nor a minor in the area. For those with a minor assignment in math, 15.4 percent had majored in math and 13.9 percent had minored in it. However, 70.7 percent of teachers with a minor assignment in math had neither majored nor minored in the field. Clearly, a majority of mathematics teachers in Utah have not been adequately trained in their field.

The picture for science is even more surprising, with only 33.9 percent of those with major assignments in the area having majored in science in college and only 10.8 percent of those having minored in science in college currently teaching in the field. The majority of science teachers, 55.3 percent, neither majored nor minored in science in college. For those with minor assignments in science, 68.4 percent had neither a science major or minor. Indeed, only 17.3 percent had majored in science.

The majority of teachers in earth, space, general, and physical science had neither a college major nor minor in the particular subject area he or she taught.

APPROPRIATIONS FOR HIGHER EDUCATION

The *Chronicle of Higher Education* (31 Oct. 1984) reported state appropriations for higher education, making possible some general state-by-state comparisons. Total 1984-85 appropriations for higher education in the United

States slightly exceeded $28 billion, while appropriations for Utah totaled $226,207,000, ranking the state 34th nationally. Per capita appropriations for higher education in Utah were $120.88, ranking the state 13th, while appropriations per $1,000 of personal income for higher education ranked Utah sixth. Here, the state's appropriation was $15.54 per capita compared to $10.28 nationally.

These figures reflect a two-year change of 18 percent, bringing Utah from a national ranking of 13th in appropriations per $1,000 of personal income, while a ten-year change of 199 percent raised Utah from a national ranking of 11th. In all, the data place Utah above the national average and in the top quarter among states in regards to the burden on taxpayers in supporting higher education.

Utah's four-year institutions and three community colleges all experienced two-year increases in appropriations ranging from 17 to 19 percent. A significant two-year change in appropriations also affected the state's two technical colleges, where the reported increase was 25 percent.

Regarding appropriations per student, Utah ranked 16th nationally in 1983-84. This is in sharp contrast to the average annual tuition (i.e., $964) required to attend college, which ranked Utah 30th among the fifty states. (Tuition across the country ranged from $515 to $3,520.)

MINIMUM COMPETENCY TESTING

Utah is numbered among those states having adopted minimum competency testing programs designed to assess the performance of teachers. In Utah, such testing is determined by local school districts. Teachers hired in 1980 were the first to be assessed through competency tests. In other states, competency tests are also required of students to determine grade promotion, early exit, remediation, and "other" issues. Utah is among nineteen states requiring competency tests for high school graduation. Three states defer to local school districts as to whether such tests are needed, fifteen states require competency tests to determine the need for remediation, seventeen states use them in "other" ways, and five states allow for local options (U.S. Department of Education, *The Condition of Education*, 1984).

The motivation for teachers and students alike to prepare themselves better through competency tests could benefit all concerned. However, this benefit may be offset by the burden on local and state educational systems to direct resources from other areas to develop, implement, and use competency tests.

Early indications suggest that the benefits may be slower in coming than originally thought because of the difficulty inherent in creating a comprehensive, fair, and representative competency testing program.

STATE HOME-INSTRUCTION LAWS

Instruction at home is permitted in states throughout the country, some by statutory provision and some under the authority of the courts, the attorney general's office, or state board of education regulations. In only two states, New Mexico and North Carolina, is it difficult, if not impossible, to conduct home-school instruction. Thirty-five states have statutory provisions permitting home instruction.

Other provisions require that home-school teachers be certified, that the program, including the curriculum, be approved by local or state officials. Eight states require teachers to be certified, twenty-four require approval of the home-instruction program, and sixteen specify the curriculum. Like other states, however, Utah has no provisions in any of these areas. Fourteen states specify "other" requirements, including regular reports, tests, evidence of attendance, some supervision, and competency in teaching. Again, there are no such additional provisions regarding home instruction in Utah.

Table 12 summarizes the status of home-instruction in the United States. An asterisk indicates Utah's position regarding these provisions.

TABLE 12.

Status of Home-Instruction in The United States 1983-84

	HOME-INSTRUCTION PERMITTED	TEACHER CERTIFIED	PROGRAM APPROVED	CURRICULUM SPECIFIED	OTHER REQUIRE-MENTS
Yes	35*	8	24	16	–
No	1	11*	1*	–*	–*
No statutory provision	14	19	12	19	–
Not applicable	–	10	10	10	–
Others	–	2	3	5	14

Source: Education Week, 30 Jan. 1985, 14-15.

USE OF MICROCOMPUTERS

New technology, in the form of microcomputers, has found its way into the public schools. A report in *Education Week* (18 April 1984) notes the percentage of public schools using microcomputers and the number of students per computer in elementary, junior high, senior high, and K-12 schools in the state.

Regarding the use of new technology in the classroom, Utah ranks fourth nationally with 85.7 percent of its schools using microcomputers for instructional purposes. This compares to 68.4 percent elsewhere, ranging from 36.6 percent in Hawaii to 92.8 percent in Minnesota.

With reference to the number of students per computer, Utah reported 130.9 in elementary schools compared to 112.4 nationally. At the junior high school level Utah reported 103.1 students per computer, while the national average was 102.4. The report on high schools placed Utah high among states with 41 students for every microcomputer. This compares favorably to 76.6 students per computer nationally, placing Utah fourth among all states. The K-12 report found that Utah reported 34.3 students per computer compared to 69.3 elsewhere. Here, Utah ranked sixth.

SUMMARY

The future of Utah's education presents educators with difficult but hopefully surmountable challenges. There is little doubt that the state's resources are already severely taxed and that teachers are working under difficult circumstances. The decisions facing school administrators, state policy makers, and Utah tax payers will not be easy ones.

REFERENCES

Biemiller, Lawrence. "SAT Scores Rise 3 Points in Math, 1 on Verbal Test." *Chronicle of Higher Education*, 26 Sept. 1984.

Educational USA, 4 Oct. 1982, 26 Sept. 1983.

"Foreign Students in U.S. Institutions, 1983-84." *Chronicle of Higher Education*, 5 Sept. 1984.

"How the States Rank on 7 Scales." *Chronicle of Higher Education*, 31 Oct. 1984.

Nelson, David E. *Utah Educational Quality Indicators*. Salt Lake City: Utah State Office of Education, 1983.

"Percent of Public Schools Using Microcomputers and Number of Students Per Computer In Schools With Computers, Fall 1983." *Education Week*, 18 April 1984.

"State Education Statistics." *Education Week*, 18 Jan. 1984.

"State Home-Instruction Laws As of August 1984." *Education Week*, 30 Jan. 1985.

"State Policies on 'Master Teachers.' " *Education Week*, 17 Aug. 1983.

U.S. Bureau of the Census. *16th Census of the United States*. Vol. 2. Washington, D.C.: U.S. Government Printing Office, 1940.

_____. *17th Biennial Census of the United States*. Vol. 2. Washington, D.C.: U.S. Government Printing Office, 1950.

_____. *Characteristics of the Population*. Vol. 1. Washington, D.C.: U.S. Government Printing Office, 1960.

_____. *Census of the Population, General Social and Economic Characteristics, United States Summary*. Washington, D.C.: U.S. Government Printing Office, 1970.

_____. *Statistical Abstract of the United States*. 95th Edition. Washington, D.C.: U.S. Government Printing Office, 1974.

_____. *Statistical Abstract of the United States*. 100th Edition. Washington, D.C.: U.S. Government Printing Office, 1979.

_____. *Census of the Population, General Social and Economic Characteristics, Arizona*. Washington, D.C.: U.S. Government Printing Office, 1980.

_____. *Census of the Population, General Social and Economic Characteristics, Colorado*. Washington, D.C.: U.S. Government Printing Office, 1980.

_____. *Census of the Population, General Social and Economic Characteristics, Idaho*. Washington, D.C.: U.S. Government Printing Office, 1980.

_____. *Census of the Population, General Social and Economic Characteristics, Montana*. Washington, D.C.: U.S. Government Printing Office, 1980.

_____. *Census of the Population, General Social and Economic Characteristics, Nevada*. Washington, D.C.: U.S. Government Printing Office, 1980.

_____. *Census of the Population, General Social and Economic Characteristics, New Mexico*. Washington, D.C.: U.S. Government Printing Office, 1980.

_____. *Census of the Population, General Social and Economic Characteristics, United States Summary*. Washington, D.C.: U.S. Government Printing Office, 1980.

_____. *Census of the Population, General Social and Economic Characteristics, Wyoming*. Washington, D.C.: U.S. Government Printing Office, 1980.

_____. *Statistical Abstract of the United States*. 104th Edition. Washington, D.C.: U.S. Government Printing Office, 1984.

U.S. Department of Education. *Digest of Education Statistics*. Washington, D.C.: U.S. Government Printing Office, 1984.

_____. *The Condition of Education*. Washington, D.C.: U.S. Government Printing Office, 1984.

U.S. Department of Health, Education, and Welfare. *Elementary and Secondary Education: Statistics of Public Schools.* Washington, D.C.: U.S. Government Printing Office, 1970.

_____. *Elementary and Secondary Education: Statistics of Public Schools.* Washington, D.C.: U.S. Government Printing Office, 1973.

_____. *Elementary and Secondary Education: Statistics of Public Elementary and Secondary Day Schools.* Washington, D.C.: U.S. Government Printing Office, 1976.

_____. *Digest of Education Statistics.* Washington, D.C.: U.S. Government Printing Office, 1979.

Utah Education Association *Research Bulletin.* "Class Size Survey." Vol. 30, 1985.

_____. "How Utah Ranks." Vol. 29, 1984.

Utah State Office of Education. *Status of Teacher Personnel in Utah, 1983-84.* Salt Lake City, 1984.

_____. *Utah ACT Performance for 1983-84.* Salt Lake City, 1984.

15.

THE MONETARY EFFECTS OF EDUCATION

Thomas K. Martin

Utah spends nearly half of its annual budget on education. Based on figures from the *Deseret News* (Webb and Costanzo 1983; Webb 1985), Utah allocated 45 percent of its $2 billion 1983 budget for primary, secondary, and higher education. The next year, legislators allocated 47 percent of a $2.4 billion budget to education. In 1985, 49 percent of Utah's $2.5 billion budget was earmarked for education. Unpublished figures from the Utah State Office of Education show more than a 100 percent increase in school budgets from 1976 to 1983. During the same eight years, the United States Consumer Price Index (CPI) increased 65 percent (U.S. Bureau of the Census 1983, Table 797).

Returns on expenditures for education are usually divided into two categories, monetary and nonmonetary. The latter refers to things like cognitive and personal development, greater sensitivity to and awareness of the environment, and improved quality of social, political, and community life. Monetary effects include individual earnings, productivity, high levels of demand for goods and services, and the availability of a well-trained labor force. While the importance of education's nonmonetary effects is generally acknowledged, when people consider returns to education they often think in terms of individual earnings (Belanger and Lavallee 1980; Hossler 1982). This chapter addresses such question as: How does education in Utah affect a person's ability to earn money? And how does the monetary return to education in Utah compare to that in neighboring states or to the rest of the nation?

One insight into these and other questions appeared in an article published over a decade ago. In that article, Edward F. Renshaw (1972) asked, "Are we overestimating the returns from a college education?" To illustrate the sometimes questionable economic value of higher education, Renshaw cited the example of England and Scotland, observing that although nearly twice as many Scots received university training as English and Welsh, Scottish salaries were lower. He then went on to observe,

> The example of England and Scotland might be considered unique: yet one does not have to look very hard to find a close parallel in the United States. In 1950 Utah had the largest percentage of college educated adults and the next to smallest percentage of the functionally illiterate, but it ranked in the lower half of all states with regard to per capita income.

Thus we have an early indication that monetary returns to education in Utah may be less than those in other states. Table 1 verifies Renshaw's claim in regards to Utah's standing in per capita income. Based on two different indicators, Utah in 1950 did indeed rank in the lower half of all states in per capita income. More discouraging is the fact that since 1950 Utah's position fell steadily until, in 1980, Utah ranked 45th and 37th as measured by the two indicators. Even among its neighboring seven states Utah ranked at or near the bottom in per capita income for each year shown in Table 1.

TABLE 1.

Utah's Rank Among States, Per Capita Income, 1950-80

	U.S. BUREAU OF ECONOMIC ANALYSIS*		U.S. BUREAU OF THE CENSUS**	
	YEAR	RANK	YEAR	RANK
U.S.	1950	30		
	1960	30	1959	28
	1970	39	1969	33
	1980	45	1979	37
Mountain States***	1950	6		
	1960	6	1959	5
	1970	7	1969	5
	1980	8	1979	6

*Estimates derived from projections and adjustments based on income tax returns.
**Estimates derived from U.S. Census reported money income.
***Includes Arizona, Colorado, Idaho, Montana, Nevada, New Mexico, Utah, and Wyoming.

Source: U.S. Bureau of the Census 1974, Table 611; 1983, Tables 751, 772.

Some have criticized the use of per capita income as a basis for comparisons of income. Since Utah has larger families than other states, per capita income tends to be low. However, because per capita income fails to take into account economies of scale associated with family life, some researchers suggest that median family income is a more reasonable basis for comparing Utahns' incomes to those in other states. Median family income also has problems as a measure of average income in Utah. Since median family income does not control for family size, it tends to make incomes appear high since Utah's large families presumably require incomes to be distributed across more people. The most accurate picture probably lies somewhere between these two estimates of average income.

Utah's ranking among the fifty states and the mountain states in terms of median family income is shown in Table 2. Using median family income does raise Utah's ranking relative to income in other states. While Utah ranked consistently among the bottom half of states in terms of per capita income, Table 2 indicates that Utah ranked in the second quartile in terms of median family income.

Every United States census conducted during the last forty years has ranked Utah first both nationally and regionally regarding the percentage of residents attaining 1-3 years of high school (see Table 3). Except for 1980 when the state ranked a close second behind Alaska, Utah ranked first in the nation and in the mountain states in the percentage of high school graduates. The

TABLE 2.

Utah's Rank Among States for Median Family Income, 1959-71

	YEAR	RANK
U.S.	1959	16
	1969	23
	1979	22
Mountain States	1959	2
	1969	3
	1979	4

*Includes Arizona, Colorado, Idaho, Montana, Nevada, New Mexico, Utah, and Wyoming.

Source: U.S. Bureau of the Census 1983, Table 770.

last four censuses also ranked Utah first nationally and regionally in the percentage of residents attaining 1-3 years of college. In terms of the percentage of residents with four or more years of college, Utah tied with Colorado for first nationally and regionally in 1950. In 1960 and again in 1970 Utah tied for second, but the 1980 census showed that Utah had fallen to eighth place. Although Utah's ranking dropped six positions from 1970 to 1980, the state still ranked in the top quartile of all states in terms of the percentage of residents attaining four or more years of college.

While Utah ranked solidly in the top quartile nationally in educational attainment during the last thirty-five years, it ranked in the bottom half in per capita income and only in the second quartile in median family income. This may be an additional indication that education in Utah has not provided the same monetary returns as in other states.

This comparatively low monetary return to education may not be a unique Utah phenomenon. In Table 4 a similar pattern emerges when we compare the Mountain Region to the other eight geographical regions across the country.

TABLE 3.

Utah's Rank Among States for Percentage of Residents Attaining Given Levels of Education, 25 Years and Older, 1950-80

YEAR	1-3 YEARS HIGH SCHOOL	4 YEARS HIGH SCHOOL	1-3 YEARS COLLEGE	4 OR MORE YEARS COLLEGE
U.S.				
1950	1	1	1	1 (tie)
1960	1	1	1	2 (tie)
1970	1	1 (tie)	1	2 (tie)
1980	1	2	1 (tie)	8
Mountain States				
1950	1	1	1	1 (tie)
1960	1	1	1	2 (tie)
1970	1	1	1	2
1980	1	1	1 (tie)	2

*Includes Arizona, Colorado, Idaho, Montana, Nevada, New Mexico, Utah, and Wyoming.

Source: U.S. Bureau of the Census 1954, Table 136; 1964, Table 148; 1974, Table 193; 1983, Table 224.

The eight mountain states ranked either first or second among all regions in educational attainment during each of the last four census years. At the same time, the mountain states ranked fifth, sixth, or seventh in terms of per capita income. Still, Utah appears to be an extreme case, even regionally, since it ranked first or second in educational attainment while ranking at or near the bottom in per capita income. Although using median family income improved Utah's position regionally, the state's average income ranking was still below its ranking in educational attainment during each year shown.

In order to estimate more precisely the effect of education on income, data from the 1980 U.S. Census were used to regress 1979 income on education while controlling for age, employment status, race, and gender. Two different models were estimated: one, a linear model, assumed that each year of education had equal income producing effects; the other, a credential model, assumed that the income effects of education depended upon whether or not a given level of education was completed and a credential obtained, such as a high school diploma or a college degree. Separate analyses were performed for males and females using data from Utah, the mountain states, and the United States. Estimates were made for full-time employed white adults only. The results are shown in Table 5, which represents actual dollar effects of education on income.

TABLE 4.

Mountain States Region's* Rank for Per Capita Income and Educational Attainment, 1950-80

		EDUCATIONAL ATTAINMENT			
YEAR	INCOME	1-3 YEARS HIGH SCHOOL	4 YEARS HIGH SCHOOL	1-3 YEARS COLLEGE	4 OR MORE YEARS COLLEGE
1950	6	2	2	2	2
1960	5	2	2	1 (tie)	2
1970	6	2	1	2	1 (tie)
1980	7	1	1	2	2

*Includes Arizona, Colorado, Idaho, Montana, Nevada, New Mexico, Utah, and Wyoming, and compares them to the nine other census divisions.

Source: U.S. Bureau of the Census 1954, Table 136; 1964, Table 148; 1974, Table 193; 1983, Table 224.

TABLE 5.

Effects of Education (in $) on Income While Controlling for Age (Full-Time Employed Whites, 25 Year of Age and Older Only) for Utah, The Mountain States, and the U.S., Males and Females, 1979.

	LINEAR MODEL		CREDENTIAL MODEL					
	EFFECT	R^2	SOME HS EFFECT	HS GRAD EFFECT	SOME COL EFFECT	COL GRAD EFFECT	POSTGRAD EFFECT	R^2
UTAH*								
Males (n=12,860)	795	.05	2,886	4,593	5,753	7,848	9,600	.05
Females (n=5,857)	627	.07	324[a]	2,336	3,485	4,878	6,435	.07
MOUNTAIN STATES**								
Males (n=20,753)	891	.05	2,509	4,333	5,367	8,781	10,021	.06
Females (n=11,076)	644	.06	476[a]	1,966	2,839	4,367	6,544	.06
U.S.***								
Males (n=39,848)	1,106	.08	3,294	5,890	7,646	11,928	12,802	.09
Females (n=21,582)	713	.09	900	2,668	3,904	5,961	7,704	.09

*Data analysis uses 1980 U.S. Census, Sample A (5% sample) for Utah.
**Data analysis uses 1980 U.S. Census, Sample B (1% sample) for Arizona, Colorado, Idaho, Montana, Nevada, New Mexico, Utah, and Wyoming.
***Data analysis used 1980 U.S. Census, Sample B (1-in-1,000) for the U.S.
[a]Nonsignificant

Under the linear model portion, the numbers indicate how much money the average man or woman in each geographic location could have expected to receive for each additional year of education. For example, in 1979, an average Utah male could have expected to receive $795 for each year of education. Thus, for twelve years of school he could have expected to receive twelve times $795, or $9,540, because of his education. For having completed four years of college he could have expected sixteen times $795, or $12,720. Under the credential portion, the five columns represent the dollar amounts that the average man or woman in each geographic location could have expected to receive for having attained a given level of education. For example, in 1979, an average Utah man could have expected to receive $2,886 for having completed eleven years of school, whereas a male high school graduate could have expected $4,593, or $1,707 more.

Estimates based on the linear model indicate that each year of education produced $795 for men and $627 for women in Utah during 1979. Males in the mountain states received nearly $100 more in 1979 for each year of education than males in Utah, while each year of education for women in the region earned about $17 more than for Utah women. Nationally, men earned about $1,106 in 1979 for each year of education, over $300 more than men in Utah. Women in the U.S. earned about $713 for each year of education, or about $86 more than women in Utah. Each year of education produced more income for its recipients in Utah's neighboring states than in Utah, and education in the U.S. as a whole produced even greater comparative economic advantages.

The largest differences appeared between men and women. The dollar effects observed under the linear model in Table 5 show that each year of education in Utah produced $165 more for men than for women. Regionally, men received $247 more than women for each year of education, while nationally men earned $393 more in 1979. While educated Utahns were monetarily disadvantaged compared to men and women regionally and nationally, educated women everywhere experienced even greater monetary disadvantages.

Turning to the dollar effects under the credential model, several things should be noted. First, the two nonsignificant effects—one for Utah women with some high school education but no diploma; the other for similarly educated mountain states women—imply that full-time employed women in Utah and in the region would have been just as well off financially if they had never attended high school. Second, it appears that there was at least some credential effect. The increases in income for the fourth year of high school and the fourth year of college were larger than the increases for having attended some college but not having received a degree. For women, the effect of completing high school was much larger than that associated with some high school only. Third, Utah men with less than a college degree received slightly more money for their education than men regionally. Men in the mountain states with a college degree or some postgraduate training received higher returns than did Utah men. Again, however, the difference was relatively small. Nationally, education at every level produced substantially greater income than in Utah for both men and women. The differences in returns to education between women in Utah and women in the mountain states were small at every level. Only when women had received some college education or had earned college degrees were the differences significant, with Utah women reporting higher incomes than was observed regionally.

As in the linear model, staggering differences were found between men and women. Regardless of the level of education completed, men received substantially higher returns than women. This was true in Utah, the mountain states, and the United States. It is interesting to note, however, that differences between men and women were smaller in Utah than in the mountain states or the United States, suggesting either that women were subject to less pay discrimination in Utah or that men's incomes were particularly depressed.

The small R-square values shown in Table 5 indicate that both linear and credential models fail to measure important variables other than education that contribute to income. However, the magnitudes of the effects suggest that they are still important. (Dollar effects in the table include both direct and indirect effects.)

In summary, although Utahns spend a sizable portion of their tax dollars on education, data from four U.S. censuses show that Utah residents received less monetary benefit from education than is true elsewhere. In addition, college graduates in Utah received smaller pecuniary rewards than did their peers in the seven neighboring mountain states. Regardless of where they lived in the United States, women received appallingly low returns on their investment in education. However, in relative terms, this was less true in Utah than regionally or nationally.

In a recent radio news broadcast, a Utah economist reported that in 1984 Utah became a net "out-migration" state, attributing much of this to highly educated young people who leave the state in search of better economic opportunity. When Utahns thus expend their state's resources to educate residents who leave the state, they, in effect, subsidize those states which attract Utah's highly trained workers.

The data in this chapter suggest that the problem of comparative economic opportunity for educated Utahns is not just one of perception—the other person's grass really may be greener. The logical conclusion is that unless Utah can do something to cultivate its economic garden, the state may experience a serious drain on its human resources.

REFERENCES

Belanger, Charles H., and Lise Lavallee. "Economic Returns to Schooling Decisions." *Research in Higher Education* 12 (1980): 23-35.

Hossler, Donald R. "College Enrollment: The Impact of Perceived Benefits." *College and University* 58 (Fall 1982): 85-96.

Renshaw, Edward F. "Are We Overestimating the Returns from a College Education?" *School Review* 80 (May 1972): 459-75.

U.S. Bureau of the Census. *Statistical Abstract of the United States: 1954*. Washington, D.C.: U.S. Government Printing Office, 1954.

_____. *Statistical Abstract of the United States: 1964*. Washington, D.C.: U.S. Government Printing Office, 1964.

_____. *Statistical Abstract of the United States: 1974*. Washington, D.C.: U.S. Government Printing Office, 1974.

_____. *Statistical Abstract of the United States: 1984*. Washington, D.C.: U.S. Government Printing Office, 1983.

Webb, LaVarr. "Legislators Produce $2.5 Billion Budget." *Deseret News*, 28 Feb. 1985, A1.

Webb, LaVarr, and Joe Costanzo. "State Budget Ever Ascending, but Utahns Hardly Spendthrifts." *Deseret News*, 31 March 1983, A1.

16.
PUBLIC WELFARE

Thomas K. Martin

Welfare has become "one of the great unifying issues in American politics," observed Lester Salamon, the author of a major 1978 report on public welfare. "Almost everyone is against it." He went on to note:

> Everyone is against it for a different reason. Recipients complain about benefit adequacy, taxpayers about excessive costs, state officials about cumbersome red tape in Washington, federal administrators about noncompliance by the states, policy analysts about inequities, and congressmen about work disincentives.

Since 1980, attempts by the Reagan administration to reduce the federal budget have only intensified the debate over welfare. Whether public welfare is viewed as one of the great "evils" eroding the nation, as a moral imperative of good government, or simply as unaffordable, one cannot question the importance of public welfare as a contemporary social issue.

This chapter compares public welfare in Utah to welfare in the mountain states and in the United States. To facilitate these comparisons, only federal programs are examined. The term "welfare" is herein limited to public nonmedical assistance programs based on need, such as Supplemental Security Income (SSI), Aid to Families with Dependent Children (AFDC), and Food Stamps (FS).

In 1972, the U.S. Congress passed legislation consolidating and federalizing programs providing joint payments from state and federal governments to adults who were aged, blind, or disabled. This program, called Supplemental Security Income, was implemented in 1974 (Havemann and Demkovich 1977). The most recent SSI data are for 1983.

The Social Security Act of 1935 mandated a federal welfare program entitled Aid to Dependent Children, later Aid to Families with Dependent Children.

The program was to provide cash payments to families with disabled or missing fathers. In 1961, the program was expanded to include families where the father was present but unemployed (Salamon 1978). The most current AFDC data are for 1982.

The Food Stamp Act of 1964 was originally enacted as a means of disposing of surplus food, but by the late 1960s it had become a means of helping the poor to "afford an adequate diet" (Havemann and Demkovich 1977, 46). Until 1980, all food stamp recipients were required to purchase stamps from government outlets at discount prices, the discount varying with each participant's income. These stamps were then exchanged for food at grocery stores (Salamon 1978). In January 1980, the Department of Agriculture began giving out food stamps free of charge to those who applied for them and were eligible to receive them. The most recent FS data are for 1983.

PUBLIC WELFARE IN UTAH

Supplemental Security Income

From 1974 to 1983, total expenditures for SSI in Utah rose from $10 million to $15 million, an increase of 50 percent. During the same time, the number of SSI recipients in Utah dropped from about 9,000 to about 8,000. Consequently, the average monthly SSI expenditure per recipient increased about 68 percent from $93 per month in 1974 to $156 per month in 1983 (see Table 1). Despite this increase, average monthly expenditures per SSI recipient in Utah did not keep pace with inflation as represented by the consumer price index (see Figure 1).

Table 1 also indicates that only a small percentage of Utah's population received SSI benefits, ranging from a high of about .8 percent in 1974 to a low of about .5 percent in 1983. However, a welfare program serving only the blind, the disabled, and the aged would be expected to affect only a small portion of the population, particularly in a state with a high fertility rate and a low average age such as Utah.

Aid to Families with Dependent Children

Total expenditures for Aid to Families with Dependent Children in Utah jumped from about $20 million in 1970 to about $49 million in 1982, an increase of 145 percent. The total number of recipients rose from 39,000 in 1970 to an all-time high of 51,000 just two years later. After 1972, the number of AFDC recipients dropped, hovering at around 35,000, except for 1980 when the number climbed to 44,000.

TABLE 1.

Expenditures, Total Numbers of Recipients, Average Monthly Expenditure Per Recipient, and Percentage of Population Receiving SSI Payments in Utah, the Mountain States, and the U.S., 1974-83

YEAR	EXPENDITURES (IN MILLIONS OF DOLLARS)	TOTAL NO. OF RECIP. (IN THOUS.)	AVE. MONTHLY EXPEND. PER RECIPIENT (IN $)*	% OF POPULATION RECEIVING PAYMENTS*
Utah				
1974	10	9	93	.8
1975	11	9	102	.7
1976	11	9	102	.7
1977	10	8	104	.6
1978	10	8	104	.6
1979	10	8	104	.6
1980	11	8	115	.6
1981	13	8	135	.5
1982	14	8	146	.5
1983	15	8	156	.5
Mountain States				
1974	130	120	90	1.3
1975	143	125	95	1.3
1976	148	122	101	1.2
1977	153	120	106	1.2
1978	157	119	110	1.1
1979	169	116	121	1.0
1980	188	116	135	1.0
1981	209	114	153	1.0
1982	223	110	169	.9
1983	239	113	176	.9
U.S.				
1974	5097	3996	106	1.9
1975	5716	4314	110	2.0
1976	5900	4236	116	2.0
1977	6134	4238	121	1.9
1978	6372	4217	126	1.9
1979	6869	4150	138	1.9
1980	7715	4142	155	1.8
1981	8357	4019	173	1.8
1982	8706	3858	188	1.7
1983	9132	3900	195	1.7

*These figures, computed specifically for comparisons in this chapter, may differ from other published figures.

Source: U.S. Bureau of the Census 1976, Tables 498, 499; 1979, Tables 568, 570; 1981, Tables 561, 562; 1982, Tables 556, 557; 1983, Tables 653, 654; 1984, Tables 640, 641.

FIGURE 1.

Comparison of Consumer Price Index and Average Monthly SSI Expenditures Per Recipient for Utah, the Mountain States, and the U.S., 1974-83.

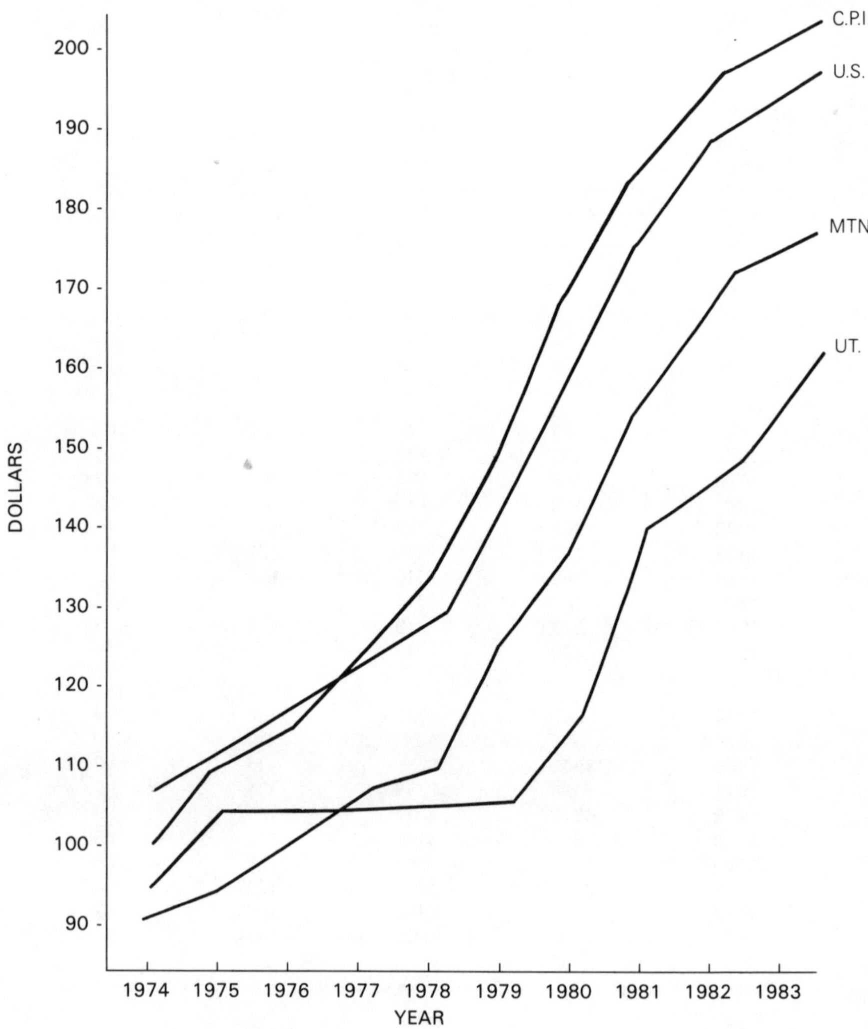

Source: Table 1.

The percentage of Utah's population receiving AFDC payments rose from 3.6 percent in 1970 to a peak of 4.4 percent in 1972 and then dropped to a low of 2.4 percent in 1982, a decline of 33 percent (see Table 2). Table 2 also shows that the average monthly expenditure per AFDC recipient in Utah increased 158 percent from $43 in 1970 to $111 in 1982. Average monthly expenditures per AFDC recipient increased faster than the consumer price index in 1972-73 and in 1980-81. However, from 1976 to 1979, expenditures rose at a slower rate than the CPI. From 1979 to 1980, average monthly AFDC expenditures per recipient dropped, and from 1981 to 1982, average AFDC expenditures per recipient remained unchanged. The net result was that changes in average monthly AFDC expenditures per recipient equalled changes in the inflation rate for the thirteen years as a whole.

Food Stamps

Federal expenditures for Food Stamps in Utah increased dramatically from $2 million in 1970 to $42 million in 1983. The largest single increase in food stamp expenditures occurred in 1980 and corresponded to the relaxation of the federal requirement that all participants had to purchase food stamps. From 1979 to 1980, expenditures in Utah rose from $13 million to $21 million, an increase of 62 percent.

During the fourteen years from 1970 to 1983, the total number of Utahns participating in the Food Stamp program grew threefold from 27,000 to 85,000. Average monthly expenditures per Utah food stamp recipient also tended to increase throughout the period. Figure 3 shows that average monthly expenditures in Utah outstripped inflation as measured by the CPI. Average expenditures per recipient increased from about six dollars per month in 1970 to about $41 per month in 1983, nearly a sevenfold increase.

The percentage of Utah's population participating in the Food Stamp program from 1970 to 1983 was slightly higher than the percentage participating in AFDC. On the average, about 3.6 percent of Utah's population participated in the Food Stamp program, compared to about 3.1 percent participating in AFDC and to about .6 percent in SSI.

PUBLIC WELFARE IN THE MOUNTAIN STATES

Supplemental Security Income

As was the case in Utah, the total number of recipients of Supplemental Security Income in the mountain states declined during the ten years

TABLE 2.

Expenditures, Total Numbers of Recipients, Average Monthly Expenditures Per Recipient, and Percentage of Population Receiving Payments for Aid to Families with Dependent Children in Utah, the Mountain States, and the U.S., 1970-82

YEAR	EXPENDITURES (IN MILLIONS OF DOLLARS)	TOTAL NO. OF RECIP. (IN THOUS.)	AVE. MONTHLY EXPEND. PER RECIPIENT (IN $)*	% OF POPULATION RECEIVING PAYMENTS*
Utah				
1970	20	39	43	3.6
1971	24	43	47	3.9
1972	30	51	50	4.4
1973	28	36	64	3.1
1974	28	33	71	2.8
1975	34	37	76	3.0
1976	36	37	82	2.9
1977	38	38	83	2.9
1978	41	37	93	2.7
1979	39	35	94	2.5
1980	48	44	92	3.0
1981	49	37	111	2.4
1982	49	37	111	2.4
Mountain States				
1970	135	308	37	3.7
1971	164	330	41	3.8
1972	182	349	44	3.9
1973	186	322	48	3.5
1974	201	325	51	3.4
1975	218	322	56	3.3

TABLE 2. CONTINUED

YEAR	EXPENDITURES (IN MILLIONS OF DOLLARS)	TOTAL NO. OF RECIP. (IN THOUS.)	AVE. MONTHLY EXPEND. PER RECIPIENT (IN $)*	% OF POPULATION RECEIVING PAYMENTS*
1976	226	300	63	3.0
1977	225	286	66	2.7
1978	227	268	71	2.5
1979	236	268	73	2.4
1980	274	302	76	2.6
1981	289	280	86	2.4
1982	293	289	85	2.4
U.S.				
1970	4,853	9,659	42	4.7
1971	6,203	10,651	49	5.1
1972	6,908	11,064	52	5.3
1973	7,292	10,814	56	5.1
1974	7,991	11,004	61	5.2
1975	9,211	11,404	67	5.3
1976	10,000	11,184	75	5.1
1977	10,139	10,761	79	4.9
1978	10,729	10,349	86	4.7
1979	11,069	10,397	89	4.6
1980	12,475	11,101	94	4.9
1981	12,981	10,535	103	4.6
1982	12,878	10,495	102	4.5

*These figures, computed specifically for comparisons in this chapter, may differ from other published figures.

Source: U.S. Bureau of the Census 1972, Tables 488, 489; 1973, Tables 472, 473; 1975, Tables 490, 491; 1978, Tables 564, 566; 1980, Tables 561, 562; 1982, Table 556; 1983, Tables 653, 654; 1984, Table 641.

FIGURE 2.

Comparison of Consumer Price Index and Average Monthly AFDC Expenditures Per Recipient for Utah, the Mountain States, and the U.S., 1974-82.

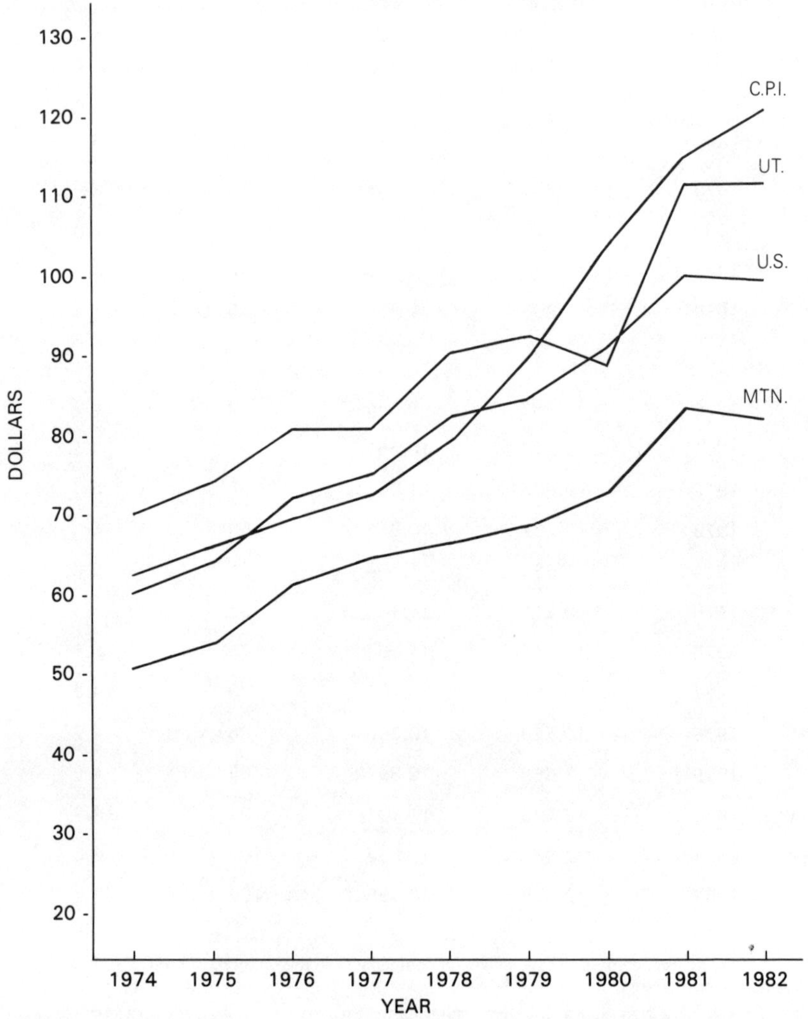

Source: Table 2.

from 1974 to 1983. After a one-year increase from 120,000 in 1974 to 125,000 in 1975, the number of recipients declined to about 110,000 in 1982 and then rose slightly to 113,000 the next year. Total federal SSI expenditures in the Mountain Region increased faster than in Utah, from $130 million in 1974 to $239 million in 1983, an increase of 84 percent regionally compared to a 50 percent increase in Utah.

The fact that the mountain states experienced greater increases in expenditures than Utah, while experiencing declines in participation similar to those in Utah, resulted in greater average monthly expenditures per recipient. In 1974, average monthly SSI expenditures were about 3 percent lower regionally than in Utah. By 1983, expenditures were about 13 percent higher regionally than in Utah and stayed closer to the inflation rate than in Utah.

Average SSI participation rates regionally were 1.7 times higher than for Utah. On the average, about 1.1 percent of the population in the mountain states received SSI benefits compared to about .6 percent of Utah's population. As was the case in Utah, however, the overall trend regionally was one of declining participation.

Aid to Families with Dependent Children

In 1970, the federal government spent about $135 million in the mountain states for Aid to Families with Dependent Children. Government spending for AFDC climbed steadily thereafter to about $293 million in 1982, an increase of 117 percent but less than the 145 percent increase in Utah (see Table 2).

Regional participation in AFDC followed a trend similar to Utah's, which peaked in 1972. As indicated in Table 2, about 308,000 mountain states residents participated in AFDC in 1970. This increased to 349,000 in 1972, and then fluctuated up and down during the next ten years.

From 1970 to 1982, the Mountain Region and Utah had about the same AFDC participation rates. In fact, averaging the percentages of the two populations results in exactly the same mean percentages for the thirteen years, 3.1 percent. The percentage of Utah's population receiving AFDC payments tended to fluctuate more than the region's, but overall rates were about the same.

Utah's AFDC recipients fared slightly better than regional recipients (see Figure 2). While per recipient expenditures in Utah kept pace with inflation, this was not the case regionally, particularly after 1978. The CPI rose about 149 percent from 1970 to 1982 and average per recipient expenditures for AFDC in Utah increased about 158 percent, but average AFDC expenditures in the region increased only about 132 percent from about $37 per month to about $86.

TABLE 3.

Expenditures, Total Number of Year-End Recipients, Average Monthly Expenditure Per Recipient, and Percentage of Population Receiving Benefits for Food Stamps in Utah, the Mountain States, and the U.S., 1970-83

YEAR	EXPENDITURES (IN MILLIONS OF DOLLARS)	TOTAL NO. OF RECIP. (IN THOUS.)	AVE. MONTHLY EXPEND. PER RECIPIENT (IN $)*	% OF POPULATION RECEIVING PAYMENTS*
Utah				
1970	2	27	6	2.5
1971	6	40	13	3.6
1972	7	49	12	4.3
1973	9	45	17	3.8
1974	9	41	18	3.4
1975	11	50	18	4.1
1976	12	43	23	3.4
1977	9	33	23	2.5
1978	9	30	25	2.2
1979	13	44	25	3.1
1980	21	61	29	4.1
1981	29	61**	40	4.0
1982	31	66**	39	4.3
1983	42	85**	41	5.3
Mountain States				
1970	27	290	8	3.5
1971	62	358	14	4.1
1972	68	380	15	4.2
1973	90	454	17	4.9
1974	113	505	19	5.3
1975	177	655	23	6.6

TABLE 3. CONTINUED

YEAR	EXPENDITURES (IN MILLIONS OF DOLLARS)	TOTAL NO. OF RECIP. (IN THOUS.)	AVE. MONTHLY EXPEND. PER RECIPIENT (IN $)*	% OF POPULATION RECEIVING PAYMENTS*
1976	195	594	27	5.9
1977	169	476	30	4.6
1978	156	414	31	3.9
1979	217	586	31	5.3
1980	329	814	34	7.1
1981	416	794**	44	6.8
1982	407	784**	43	6.6
1983	481	864**	46	7.0
U.S.				
1970	550	6,547	7	3.2
1971	1,523	10,549	12	5.1
1972	1,797	11,549	13	5.5
1973	2,131	12,107	15	5.7
1974	2,718	13,524	17	6.3
1975	4,386	19,197	19	8.9
1976	5,327	17,982	25	8.3
1977	5,076	16,134	26	7.3
1978	5,097	15,121	28	6.8
1979	6,478	19,309	28	8.6
1980	8,685	21,990	33	9.7
1981	10,630	22,431**	39	9.8
1982	10,409	22,133**	39	9.6
1983	11,933	23,203**	43	9.9

*These figures, computed specifically for comparisons in this chapter, may differ from other published figures.
**These figures come from preliminary reports and represent annual averages rather than year-end figures.

Source: U.S. Department of Agriculture, Food and Nutrition Service, Annual Statistical Review; U.S. Department of Agriculture, Food and Nutrition Service, "Statistical Summary of Operations."

FIGURE 3.

Comparison of Consumer Price Index and Average Monthly Food Stamp Expenditures Per Recipient for Utah, the Mountain States, and the U.S., 1974-83.

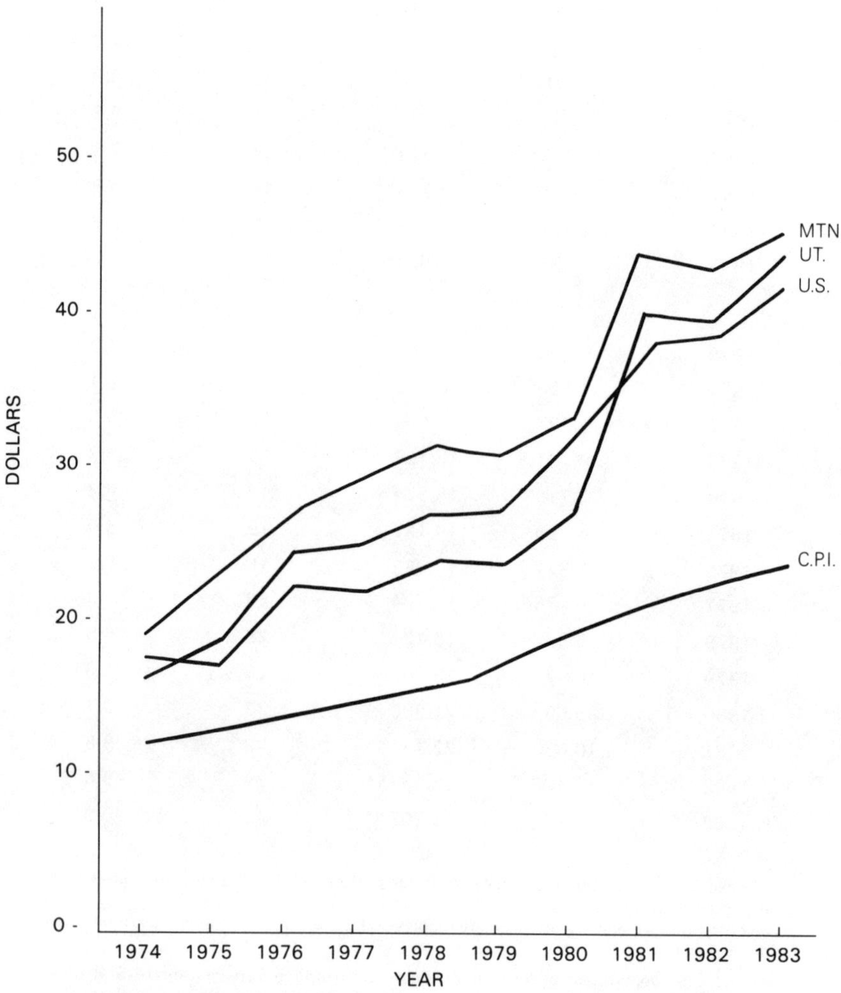

Source: Table 3.

Food Stamps

The U.S. government spent about $27 million on the Food Stamp program in the mountain states in 1970 (see Table 3). Food stamp spending then increased nearly eighteen times to about $481 million in 1983. The percentage increase regionally was slightly less than in Utah during the same period. This probably stems from the fact that the mountain states experienced less growth than Utah in the number of recipients of food stamp benefits. As was the case in Utah, the number of recipients of food stamp benefits tended to fluctuate considerably (see Table 3). The number of recipients regionally increased nearly 200 percent from 1970 to 1983 compared to about 215 percent in Utah. During the same time, about 5.4 percent of the regional population received food stamp benefits compared to about 3.6 percent of Utah's population.

Although total federal expenditures for food stamps in the mountain states rose less than in Utah, the average monthly expenditure per recipient started slightly higher regionally than in Utah in 1970 and remained higher throughout the next fourteen years (see Figure 3). In addition, average monthly expenditures per food stamp beneficiary in the mountain states increased faster than they did for Utah recipients. Regional food stamp benefits also rose faster than inflation during the period under scrutiny.

PUBLIC WELFARE IN THE UNITED STATES

Supplemental Security Income

Overall, expenditures for Supplemental Security Income in the United States rose from about $5.1 billion in 1974 to about $9.1 billion in 1983, an increase of 79 percent (see Table 1). This was slightly less than the 84 percent increase in the mountain states but substantially more than the 50 percent increase in Utah.

In 1974, about 3,996,000 Americans (or about 1.9 percent of the population) received SSI benefits. The number of recipients peaked the next year at about 4,314,000 (about 2 percent of the population) and then declined steadily until 1982 to about 3,858,000 (1.7 percent of the population).

In terms of average monthly expenditures per recipient, SSI recipients fared better nationally than regionally and much better than in Utah. Average expenditures in the U.S. were $106 per month in 1974, $13 per month more than in Utah and $16 per month more than in the mountain states. After ten years, the average SSI expenditure per recipient had risen nationally to $195 per month, about $19 per month more than in the mountain states and about $39 per month more than in Utah. From 1974 to 1978, average monthly expenditures rose slower than inflation (see Figure 1), but from 1978 on, average monthly expenditures in the U.S. paralleled the CPI, while SSI receipts in the mountain states and in Utah continued to fall behind inflation.

Aid to Families with Dependent Children

National expenditures for AFDC rose 167 percent between 1970 and 1981, from $4.9 billion to about $13 billion. The total number of AFDC recipients nationally increased from 9.7 million in 1970 to a high of 11.4 million in 1975, an increase of 10 percent in six years. As Table 2 indicates, however, the number of participants declined for five of the seven years after 1975. The net result was a 9 percent increase from 1970 to 1982.

Table 2 also shows that, as a whole, higher percentages of the U.S. population participated in AFDC than in Utah or the mountain states. About 4.7 percent of the U.S. population received Aid to Families with Dependent Children in 1970. By 1975, the peak year for AFDC participation, this had risen to 5.3 percent, but then dropped to about 4.5 percent by 1982.

In 1970, the average monthly expenditure per AFDC recipient in the U.S. was $42. By 1981, this had peaked at $103, a 145 percent increase—more than in the mountain states but less than in Utah. Inflation during the same period increased about 149 percent (see Figure 2).

Food Stamps

The federal government spent about $550 million on the food stamp program in 1970. By 1983, total federal expenditures had mushroomed more than twenty-one times to about $11.9 billion. This same trend was observed in both Utah and the mountain states.

In regards to the number of food stamp recipients in the United States, the trend from 1970 to 1983 was even more marked than that observed in Utah and the Mountain Region. While the number of food stamp beneficiaries increased nearly 200 percent regionally and about 215 percent in Utah, the number increased 260 percent nationally, from 6.5 million to 23.2 million.

Table 3 indicates that the percentage of the U.S. population receiving food stamp benefits rose from 3.2 percent in 1970 to a high of nearly 10 percent in 1983. Over the entire fourteen-year period, an average of 7.5 percent of all U.S. residents received food stamp benefits. By comparison, an average of 5.4 percent of all mountain states residents and 3.6 percent of Utahns received food stamp benefits.

As was the case in Utah and in the mountain states, average monthly expenditures per recipient for food stamps increased faster than inflation from 1970 to 1983 (see Figure 3). In 1970, the average monthly expenditure per recipient in the U.S. was about $7. By 1983, this had increased 514 percent to about $43 per month compared to an increase of 157 percent in the CPI. By contrast, average food stamp expenditures per recipient in the mountain states increased by 475 percent and in Utah by 583 percent.

SUMMARY

Total spending for public welfare in Utah has tended not to increase as fast as it has nationally. Since 1974, federal spending for SSI rose 50 percent in Utah and 80 percent in the U.S. In the case of AFDC, federal spending increased about 145 percent in Utah compared to 167 percent nationally. Federal food stamp spending in Utah increased slightly less than in the U.S. Comparing Utah to the mountain states, spending in Utah outstripped spending in the region for AFDC and food stamps, but SSI expenditures in the mountain states increased faster than in Utah.

In terms of the number of people receiving welfare benefits, Utah experienced less growth than the nation and did not differ significantly from regional trends. From 1974 to 1983, Utah's participation in SSI declined by about 11 percent compared to a 2 percent decline for all Americans. While Utah AFDC participation fell by about 2 percent from 1970 to 1982, nationally the number of recipients grew by about 9 percent. The number of Utah residents receiving food stamp benefits increased by about 215 percent from 1970 to 1983 compared to 254 percent throughout the United States. Participation in SSI declined slightly more in Utah than in the region; but changes in AFDC participation were about the same, and increases in food stamp participation were greater in Utah.

Comparing average monthly expenditures per recipient in each of the three programs, SSI recipients in Utah did not fare as well as they did regionally or nationally. However, AFDC recipients in Utah experienced greater gains than was true either nationally or regionally. In the case of average monthly expenditures per food stamp recipient, all three areas—Utah, the mountain states, and the U.S.—fared well compared to inflation.

In general, Utah tended to have lower percentages of its population receiving welfare benefits than did the U.S. or the mountain states. From 1974 to 1983, Utah's population had the lowest average participation rate in SSI, while regional rates averaged nearly twice as high and national rates averaged nearly three times as high. Utah and the mountain states experienced AFDC participation rates about 63 percent lower than national averages from 1970 to 1982. The percentage of Utah's population participating in the food stamp program from 1970 to 1983 averaged about 67 percent less than in the mountain states, while the percentage of the population nationally receiving food stamp benefits was about twice as high as in Utah.

REFERENCES

Havemann, Joel, and Linda E. Demkovich. "Making Some Sense Out of the 'Welfare Mess.' " *National Journal* 9 (8 Jan. 1977): 44-51.

Salamon, Lester M. *Welfare: The Elusive Consensus—Where We Are, How We Got There, and What's Ahead.* New York: Praeger, 1978.

U.S. Bureau of the Census. *Statistical Abstract of the United States: 1972.* Washington, D.C.: U.S. Government Printing Office, 1972.

_____. *Statistical Abstract of the United States: 1973.* Washington, D.C.: U.S. Government Printing Office, 1973.

_____. *Statistical Abstract of the United States: 1975.* Washington, D.C.: U.S. Government Printing Office, 1975.

_____. *Statistical Abstract of the United States: 1976.* Washington, D.C.: U.S. Government Printing Office, 1976.

_____. *Statistical Abstract of the United States: 1978.* Washington, D.C.: U.S. Government Printing Office, 1978.

_____. *Statistical Abstract of the United States: 1979.* Washington, D.C.: U.S. Government Printing Office, 1979.

_____. *Statistical Abstract of the United States: 1980.* Washington, D.C.: U.S. Government Printing Office, 1980.

_____. *Statistical Abstract of the United States: 1981.* Washington, D.C.: U.S. Government Printing Office, 1981.

_____. *Statistical Abstract of the United States: 1982-83.* Washington, D.C.: U.S. Government Printing Office, 1982.

_____. *Statistical Abstract of the United States: 1984.* Washington, D.C.: U.S. Government Printing Office, 1983.

_____. *Statistical Abstract of the United States: 1985.* Washington, D.C.: U.S. Government Printing Office, 1984.

U.S. Department of Agriculture, Food, and Nutrition Service. *Annual Statistical Review; Final Report; Food and Nutrition Programs*. Washington, D.C., Fiscal Years 1970-75.

_____. "Statistical Summary of Operations, 1976-83." Unpublished reports. Washington, D.C.

17.

ALCOHOL CONSUMPTION AND ABUSE

Stan Albrecht

> Alcohol is undoubtedly the most widely used—and abused—drug in America. In 1981, the latest year for which figures are available, the equivalent of 2.77 gallons of absolute (pure) alcohol was sold per person over age 14. Translated into alcoholic beverages, this is about 591 12-ounce cans of beer or 115 bottles (fifths) of table wine or 35 fifths of 80 proof whisky, gin, or vodka. (U.S. Department of Health and Human Services 1984, xiii)

The use and abuse of alcohol have far-reaching economic, social, health, and family-related consequences. It is estimated that at least 78 million Americans drink, 10 million of whom can be considered alcoholics (U.S. Department of Health and Human Services 1984, xiii). Alcoholism has been described as one of the three most serious public health problems in the United States today, surpassed in magnitude only by cancer and heart disease (Phillips 1975). Because each alcoholic may have close personal or family ties to at least four or five other persons, the problem may affect at least 40 or 50 million people in this country alone.

While it is not feasible to describe all the problems associated with alcohol and alcoholism in this brief chapter, some of them may be summarized as follows.

1. Traffic accidents are the fifth leading cause of death in the United States and the leading cause among those under the age of 35. In 1981, traffic accidents killed 49,000 people nationally and permanently disabled another 150,000. The consensus is that alcohol is responsible for half of these tragedies (U.S. Department of Health and Human Services 1984, xiii).

2. Estimates suggest that alcohol may play a role in as many as one third of all reported cases of child abuse. And, while there are no statistics linking alcohol with spouse abuse, studies indicate that as many as 50 percent of all cases of marital violence may involve alcohol.

3. Between 3,000 and 6,000 births in 1980 evidenced the fetal alcohol syndrome characterized by mental retardation, slow growth rate, small head, distinctive facial features, and heart and genital organ defects (U.S. Department of Health and Human Services 1984, xiii).

4. The economic costs of alcoholism are enormous. For example, if one considers lost production, health and medical costs, motor vehicle accidents, violent crime, and the cost of social responses, annual costs can run as high as $43 billion (National Clearinghouse for Alcohol Information 1981).

5. Besides adult alcoholics, the National Institute on Alcohol Abuse and Alcoholism estimates that 19 percent of adolescents are problem drinkers. Adolescent problem drinking is defined differently because problems among young people tend to be acute rather than chronic. For example, they usually involve drinking-driving episodes and belligerence rather than alcohol-related medical illnesses and addiction (National Clearinghouse for Alcohol Information 1981).

6. Although there have been numerous attempts to associate alcohol use and criminal behavior, a direct causal relationship is difficult to establish. Nevertheless, several studies have shown that a majority of murderers, their victims, or both had been drinking prior to the committing of the crime. While alcohol may only be a contributing cause, it does appear to play some role.

7. As many as four out of five people attempting suicide are drinking at the time. Alcoholics commit suicide from six to fifteen times more frequently than the general population (U.S. Department of Health and Human Services 1984, xiii).

8. The annual U.S. divorce rate has climbed significantly in recent years. Evidence suggests that the rate of separation and divorce among alcoholics and their spouses is seven times that of the general population (National Clearinghouse for Alcohol Information 1981).

These and other figures support the contention that alcohol abuse constitutes a significant social problem. However, Americans are far from equal in their consumption of alcoholic beverages. Young adults are most likely to drink, with the highest percentage of drinkers among men ages 18 to 29. Women are less likely to drink. The smallest percentage of drinkers is among people over age 65; relatively few heavy-to-excessive drinkers live that long (see Figure 1).

There are also significant geographic differences in the consumption of alcohol. These form the major focus of this chapter. The basic question we

FIGURE 1.

Percentage of Drinkers by Age Group and Sex Averaged for the Period 1971-1976

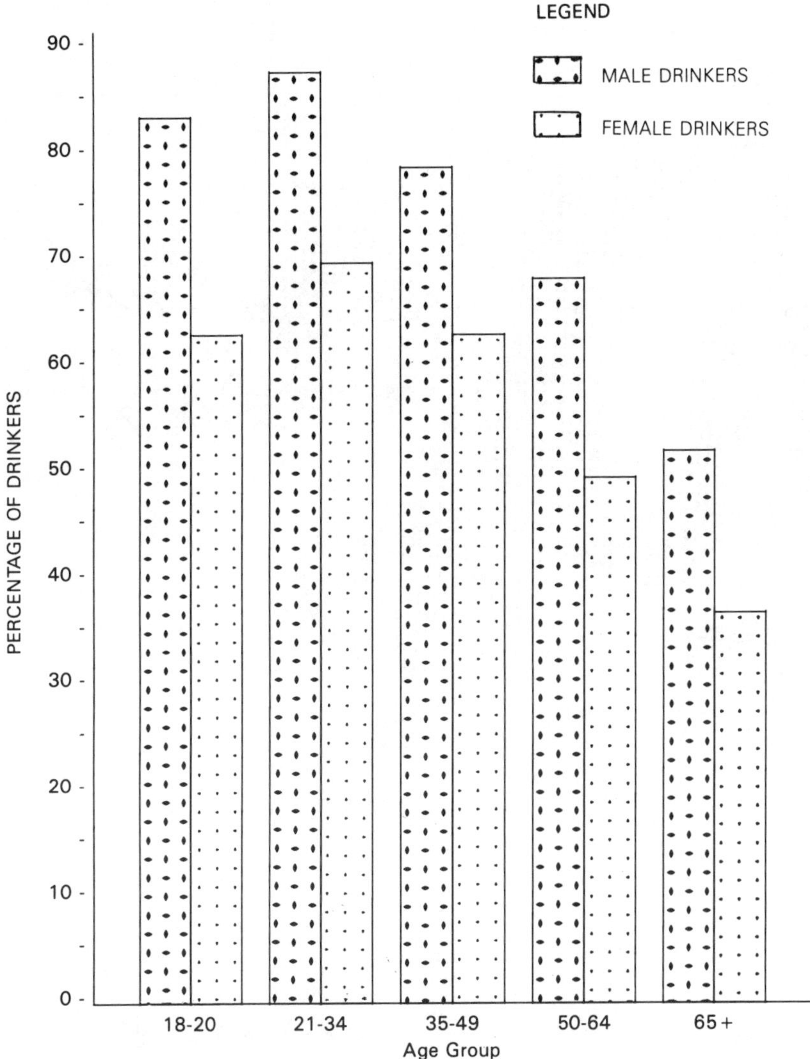

Source: Clark and Midanik 1979.

FIGURE 2.

Apparent Consumption of Ethanol from All Alcoholic Beverages in U.S.—Gallons Per Capita of the Population Age 14 and Older, 1981

U.S. = 2.77

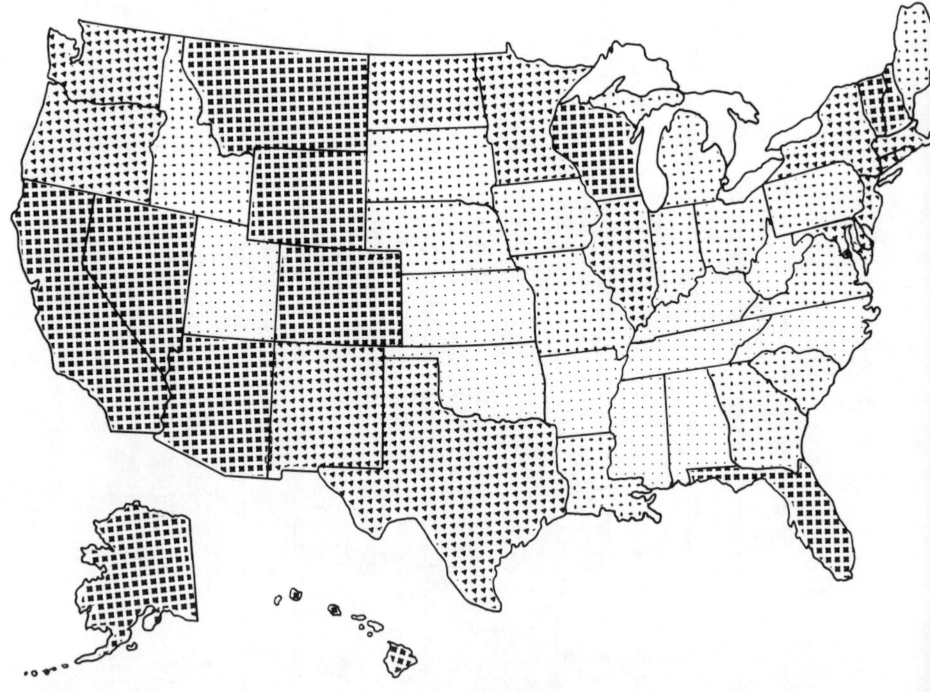

QUARTILES 1.70-2.24 2.25-2.79 2.80-3.20 3.21-5.60

Source: Clark and Midanik 1979.

will attempt to address is how Utah residents compare to other Americans regarding patterns of alcohol consumption.

ALCOHOL CONSUMPTION

Historically, Utah has had one of the lowest rates of alcohol consumption in the nation. This pattern can be observed from the data summarized in Figure 2. The per capita consumption of alcohol in Utah is less than two-thirds of that nationally. Perhaps more interestingly, the pattern for Utah is even more different than for the other western states where patterns have been higher than elsewhere. The Utah rate is only about half that of Arizona, California, Colorado, and Wyoming and less than a third that of Nevada.

Tables 1 through 3 summarize alcohol consumption rates for the nation and for the mountain states for the years 1972, 1977, and 1982 (the last year for which summary data are available). Table 1 summarizes per capita consumption of malt beverages; Table 2, distilled spirits; and Table 3, wine.

As can be seen from Table 1, per capita consumption of malt beverages in Utah is consistently lower than the national average. In 1972, the national rate was 19.3 gallons per capita, while the Utah rate was 12.3. By 1977,

TABLE 1

Per Capita Consumption Of Malt Beverages In Gallons, Total Population, 1972-82

	YEAR		
STATE	1972	1977	1982
Arizona	23.9	27.6	30.2
Colorado	21.0	24.4	27.5
Idaho	21.6	24.6	24.2
Montana	25.0	30.9	31.5
Nevada	29.0	33.6	35.3
New Mexico	21.6	26.7	28.2
Utah	12.3	14.9	15.6
Wyoming	22.9	30.0	30.0
United States	19.3	22.4	24.4

Source: U.S. Brewer's Association 1984, Table 45.

the national rate had climbed to 22.4 gallons per capita, while the Utah rate was 14.9. In 1982, the national rate had again risen to 24.4 gallons, while Utahns consumed an average of 15.6 gallons. For each year, the trend was toward higher rates of consumption; however, the Utah rate remained only about 64 percent of the national rate. In 1972, Utah's per capita malt beverage consumption rate was 49th; only Alabama's rate was lower. In both 1977 and 1982, Utah's rate was the lowest in the nation.

Regionally, Utah stands out as deviant. Within the Intermountain Region, Utah is the only state with rates consistently below national rates. Indeed, other regional states show rates consistently above national averages, both for the total population and for the adult population.

Regarding the consumption of distilled spirits (see Table 2), Utah's per capita rates are even further below the national average. For example, in 1972 Utahns consumed less than one gallon of distilled spirits per capita, less than half the national rate of 1.88 gallons. This pattern is also observed in 1977 and in 1982. For each of these years, Utah's rate is the lowest of all fifty states.

As is true with malted beverages, several of Utah's neighboring states exhibit consumption rates for distilled spirits that are higher than national averages. States like Idaho are closer to Utah's pattern, but other states such

TABLE 2.

Per Capita Consumption Of Distilled Spirits, Total Population, 1972-82

	YEAR		
STATE	1972	1977	1982
Arizona	1.79	1.89	1.99
Colorado	2.20	2.26	2.27
Idaho	1.27	1.39	1.41
Montana	1.80	2.06	1.93
Nevada	5.73	6.77	4.87
New Mexico	1.60	1.65	1.59
Utah	0.93	0.98	0.92
Wyoming	2.01	2.39	2.22
United States	1.88	1.96	1.89

Source: U.S. Brewer's Association 1984, Table 47.

as Wyoming, Nevada, and Colorado consume at rates more than double Utah's. For the region as a whole, Utah, Idaho, and New Mexico have rates below the national average; Arizona's are comparable to the national average; Colorado's, Montana's, and Wyoming's are higher; while Nevada's are the highest in the nation.

The per capita consumption of wine in Utah is also much lower than nationally (see Table 3). For each of the years included, the per capita consumption of wine in Utah was less than half of that nationally. National rates have climbed steadily in the past ten years, while Utah's have remained stable. Utah ranks near the bottom of the fifty states in per capita wine consumption, though several (particularly Alabama, Mississippi, Kentucky, Arkansas, Indiana, and Iowa) show patterns that are as low and sometimes lower than for Utah.

Regionally, the consumption of wine in Utah is substantially lower than in neighboring states. With the exception of Montana, each of the other intermountain states have rates about twice or more than Utah's.

Table 4 presents information on the per capita consumption in gallons of absolute alcohol for 1979 through 1982. As can be seen, Utah ranks last among

TABLE 3.

Per Capita Consumption Of Wine In Gallons, Total Population, 1971-82

	YEAR		
STATE	1972	1977	1982
Arizona	1.69	1.93	2.45
Colorado	1.87	2.13	2.82
Idaho	1.37	1.44	1.77
Montana	0.82	1.17	1.95
Nevada	3.63	4.65	3.61
New Mexico	1.69	1.81	2.02
Utah	0.71	0.72	0.79
Wyoming	0.97	1.20	1.39
United States	1.56	1.77	2.21

Source: U.S. Brewer's Association 1984, Table 49.

TABLE 4.

Ranks of the States for Apparent Per Capita Consumption in Gallons of Absolute Alcohol, 1979-82

STATE	1979 GALLONS	1979 RANK	1980 GALLONS	1980 RANK	1981 GALLONS	1981 RANK	1982 GALLONS	1982 RANK
Arizona	3.42	8	3.09	17	3.29	11	3.13	14
Colorado	3.52	6	3.36	9	3.32	9	3.28	7
Idaho	2.65	29	2.61	32	2.67	28	2.60	31
Montana	3.29	13	3.21	12	3.28	12	3.26	13
Nevada	6.44	1	5.83	1	5.60	1	5.26	2
New Mexico	3.02	17	2.87	20	2.90	20	3.00	16
Utah	1.75	50	1.70	50	1.73	50	1.71	50
Wyoming	3.38	10	3.41	7	3.42	6	3.25	9
United States	2.78	—	2.81	—	2.77	—	2.81	—

Source: Compiled from Alcohol Epidemiological Data System 1984.

the fifty states in per capita consumption of absolute alcohol for each year—about 60 percent the national rate in absolute gallons.

In sum, Utah shows much lower alcohol consumption rates than the rest of the nation. Utah's rates are the lowest in its region in every category. In 1982 Utah ranked 50th in the per capita consumption of malt beverages and distilled spirits and 47th in the per capita consumption of wine. However, both in Utah and in the United States, alcohol consumption per capita has increased (see Figure 3). While Utah's rate remains lower than the national rate, the trend in both cases is nonetheless towards higher levels of consumption.

ALCOHOLISM

Data on alcohol consumption clearly indicate that drinking is an accepted part of American life. However, while drinking is accepted by a majority of the population, "abusive drinking," or alcoholism, constitutes a serious social problem in this country. Yet, there is much about it that is not known. To quote from a 1984 government report on alcoholism: "No other national health problem has been so seriously neglected as alcoholism. Many doctors decline to accept alcoholics as patients. Most hospitals refuse to admit alcoholics. Available methods of treatment have not been widely applied. Research on alcoholism and excessive drinking has received virtually no significant support." (U.S. Department of Health and Human Services 1984, x)

Since that report, some progress has been made. Still, there is much to learn. Statistics on alcoholism tend not to be reliable. The condition of many alcoholics rarely becomes public—their drinking is said to be "under control" or their excesses remain "hidden" to all but a few close friends. Less than 5 percent of alcoholics are included among the stereotyped "skid row" unemployable social isolates (Bahr 1973).

How many alcoholics are there, then? A recent report from the Secretary of Health and Human Services has warned that "when the term 'alcoholic,' 'alcohol abuser,' or 'problem drinker' is used to designate an alcohol abuser, it must be kept in mind that these designations are somewhat less than precise. What is usually meant by an alcoholic is an individual who has been formally diagnosed as such or has (or has had) serious alcohol problems that meet implicit or explicit criteria of alcoholism, whether or not these have ever been formally diagnosed." (U.S. Department of Health and Human Services 1984, xiii)

With these problems in mind, Table 5 estimates the number of alcoholics and the rate of alcoholism for the United States and for the intermountain

FIGURE 3.

Per Capita Consumption of Alcohol—Including Malted Beverages, Distilled Spirits, and Wine

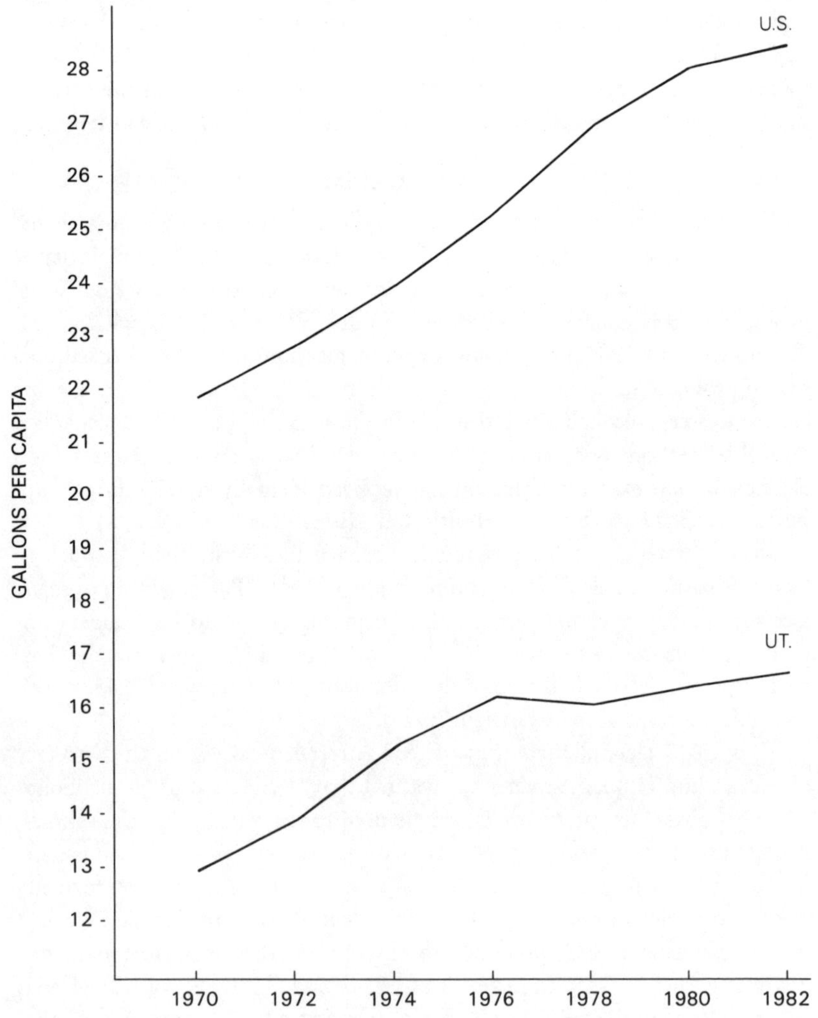

Source: U.S. Brewers Association, Tables 45, 47, 49.

TABLE 5.

Estimate of Alcoholics by Sex for Each State and the U.S., and Rate per 100,000 Adult Population (21 years of age and older)

STATE	POPULATION 21 AND OVER			NUMBER OF ALCOHOLICS			RANK ORDER	RATE OF ALCOHOLISM			RANK ORDER
	MALE	FEMALE	TOTAL	MALE	FEMALE	TOTAL		MALE	FEMALE	TOTAL	
Arizona	629,000	703,000	1,332,000	40,101	6,260	46,361	27	6,375	890	3,481	45
Colorado	759,000	812,000	1,571,000	57,376	12,732	70,108	31	7,559	1,568	4,463	29
Idaho	241,000	247,000	488,000	13,264	3,077	16,341	47	5,504	1,246	1,349	47
Montana	227,000	231,000	458,000	13,881	3,183	17,064	44	6,115	1,378	3,726	42
Nevada	186,000	181,000	367,000	26,220	5,199	31,419	40	14,097	2,872	8,561	2
New Mexico	320,000	341,000	661,000	43,803	5,941	49,744	33	13,688	1,742	7,526	5
Utah	325,000	343,000	668,000	23,752	4,668	28,420	41	7,308	1,361	4,254	35
Wyoming	115,000	116,000	231,000	6,786	2,546	9,332	51	5,901	2,195	4,040	36
U.S.	63,697,000	70,664,000	134,361,000	6,425,453	1,145,116	7,570,569		10,099	1,621	5,634	

Source: Coakley et al.

states. For the United States, there are 5,634 alcoholics per 100,000 population. Utah's rate is lower, with 4,254 alcoholics per 100,000 population.

The Utah data on alcoholism, however, present some interesting paradoxes. One might expect that given the lower per capita consumption of alcohol and the lower percentage of persons who drink at all, the rates of alcoholism would be lower than they are. But while Utah ranks 50th in terms of per capita alcohol consumption, it is 41st in terms of the total number of alcoholics and 35th regarding the rate of alcoholism.

In making regional comparisons, the rate of alcoholism (i.e., number of alcoholics per 100,000 population) in Utah is higher than for Arizona, Idaho, Montana, and Wyoming. The rate in Colorado is higher than in Utah and is substantially higher in New Mexico (in part because of high rates among Native Americans) and in Nevada.

Data on alcoholism in Utah, then, are not entirely consistent in terms of per capita consumption. A far lower percentage of the population drinks than is true for other states. This, in itself, may account for the lower alcohol consumption rates. However, consumption among those Utahns who do drink may actually be higher than is the case nationally. An early study of Mormon drinking (Bacon 1957) argued that while there is little drinking among Mormons generally, the rate of alcoholism among Mormon drinkers is high. The argument is that once abstinence is broken, no institutionalized norm remains to define "appropriate social drinking." Thus, the probability of abuse is much greater. In the absence of additional research, comparative data on per capita consumption and alcoholism rates provide some support for such a contention.

SUMMARY

The abuse of alcohol is unquestionably one of the nation's most serious social problems. Per capita alcohol consumption is rising, and, consequently, the problem of alcohol abuse is also increasing. New research demonstrates the health hazards and other important social problems associated with alcohol. Clinical and experimental research now underscores the threat not only to the drinker but to others. For example, maternal alcohol abuse is now known to represent a serious threat to the fetus, and drinking drivers constitute a major concern in all areas of the country.

The foregoing analysis has indicated that the rate of alcohol consumption varies in different geographic areas. Utah has consistently had much lower rates of alcohol consumption than is the case both regionally and nationally.

Of all fifty states, Utah ranks lowest in the per capita consumption of alcohol when all such beverages are combined. However, Utah follows the national trend of increasing rates of per capita consumption.

When we consider alcoholism, a slightly different picture emerges. While the alcoholism rate in Utah is lower than the national average, it is higher than for many of the other intermountain states. The implication is that while fewer Utahns may drink, those who do are more likely to drink excessively. Consequently, alcohol abuse is a serious social problem both in Utah and elsewhere.

REFERENCES

Alcohol Epidemiological Data System. *U.S. Apparent Consumption, Calendar Year 1982*. Washington, D.C.: 805 15th Street, N.W., Suite 500, 1984.

Bacon, Selden D. "Social Settings Conducive to Alcoholism: A Sociological Approach to a Medical Problem." *The Journal of the American Medical Association* 164 (1957): 177-81.

Bahr, Howard M. *Skid Row: An Introduction to Disaffiliation*. New York: Oxford University Press, 1973.

Clark, W. B., and L. Midanik. *Alcohol Use and Alcohol Problems Among U.S. Adults: Results of the 1979 National Survey.* Alcohol and Health Monograph No. 1, 1982. DHHS Publication No. (ADM) 82-1190.

Coakley, J. F., W. Holland, and J. Evaul. *Estimates of State Prevalence and Prevalence Rates for Male and Female Alcoholics Based on Cirrhosis Mortality Using the Jellinek Formula*. Working paper no. 2. Washington, D.C.: Alcohol Epidemiologic Data Systems Laboratory of Epidemiology and Population Studies, 24 March 1978.

National Clearinghouse for Alcohol Information. *Fact Sheet: Selected Statistics on Alcohol and Alcoholism*. Rockville, MD: National Clearinghouse for Alcohol Information, 1981.

Phillips, Lorne A. "Alcohol Use." In Armand L. Mause, *Social Movements*. New York: J. B. Lippincott, 1975, pp. 281-318.

U.S. Brewer's Association. *Brewers Almanac.* Washington, D.C.: U.S. Brewer's Association Inc., 1984.

U.S. Department of Health and Human Services. *Fifth Special Report to the U.S. Congress on Alcohol and Health*. Rockville, MD: Secretary of Health and Human Services, U.S. Department of Health and Human Services, National Institute on Alcohol Abuse and Alcoholism, 1984.

18.
ADOLESCENT DRUG USE

Stephen J. Bahr
Anastasios C. Marcos

During the past twenty years drug use among adolescents has become a growing national concern. D. I. Macdonald (1984) refers to adolescent drug use as a national disaster. He maintains that "virtually all alcoholics and drug addicts begin their use as adolescents" (Macdonald 1984, 12). National data show that during the past decade there have been substantial increases in the proportion of adolescents using drugs and that initiation to drugs is occurring at earlier ages (Keyes and Block 1984; Johnston et al. 1985).

How much drug use is there among Utah adolescents and how do they compare to adolescents regionally and nationally? Some researchers say there is an epidemic; others think the problem has been exaggerated. Without reliable data, misconceptions may develop and resources could be misallocated. The purpose of this chapter is to assess the extent of adolescent drug use in Utah and to compare it with adolescent drug use in the Western Region and the United States.

RESEARCH PROCEDURES

A sample survey was used to collect relevant data; this is the most efficient and accurate method for estimating drug use. There is substantial evidence that if the survey is anonymous and voluntary, individuals tend to respond truthfully. A more complete discussion of the validity of survey methodology will be given later.

A questionnaire was developed which included items in four major areas: (1) amount and frequency of drug use, (2) problems associated with drug use, (3) attitudes toward school, parents, and peers, and (4) general background information. In developing the questionnaire, input was provided by teachers, educational administrators, school counselors, parents, narcotics officers, drug counselors, and students. The questions were designed to be similar to those in a national survey conducted annually by the National Institute of Drug Abuse. The questionnaire went through numerous drafts and was pretested on two hundred high school students in Utah and 2,600 high school students in Arizona.

A letter from the Utah State Office of Education was sent to Utah's forty school districts explaining the purpose of the survey and encouraging cooperation. Seventeen of the forty districts participated.

Packets with instructions, questionnaires, answer sheets, and pencils were prepared for each school. At the assigned time, a teacher or school official read the instructions to the students and administered the survey. The administrator stated that participation was voluntary and responses would be anonymous. The survey was administered in April 1984, and all students in a school were given the survey during the same hour. The completed surveys were picked up, sorted, and transferred to computer tape.

A total of 48,818 students in grades 7-12 participated in the survey. About 13 percent (6,264) of the questionnaires were excluded because they were incomplete or had illogical response patterns, leaving a final usable sample of 42,554.

The seventeen participating districts are not a random sample of Utah's school population. However, as shown in Table 1, the students surveyed are similar to Utah's student population in gender, ethnic group, grade, and proportion from metropolitan areas, with only a slight underrepresentation of students from grades 10 to 12 and from metropolitan areas.

Geographically, the districts represented all areas of the state. The sample included five out of ten districts from the central region (Wasatch Front) and three from each of the other four regions (northeast, northwest, southeast, and southwest). School districts from every major Utah city participated. In terms of district size, small, medium, and large districts were included. Five districts had student populations greater than 10,000; five had populations between 5,000 and 10,000; and seven had less than 5,000 students. Six of the ten largest and two of the ten smallest districts participated.

In summary, the seventeen school districts included in the survey represented the state well demographically and geographically. Nevertheless, these seventeen districts are not a statistically random sample and may or may not represent all forty districts in other areas.

Validity

Can valid information on student drug use be obtained from a questionnaire? To encourage students to be truthful, the survey was voluntary and anonymous. Evidence that most students answered truthfully and accurately follows:

(1) A fictitious drug was included on a similar questionnaire administered to 2,600 Arizona students. Only 1.7 percent reported that they had taken it. This indicates that intentional overreporting was minimal. Other researchers have also found extremely low response rates to non-existent drugs (Whitehead and Smart 1972).

TABLE 1.

A Comparison of Survey Respondents With Utah School Population in Grades 7-12, 1984

		UTAH SCHOOL POPULATION*	SCHOOL SURVEY RESPONDENTS
Gender	Percent Male	51.1	49.3
Race	American Indian	1.9	2.4
	Asian	1.7	1.8
	Black	0.5	1.0
	Hispanic	3.8	4.1
	White	92.1	90.7
	Total	100.0	100.0
Grade	7	18.4	21.2
	8	18.2	20.5
	9	16.8	17.4
	10	16.1	15.1
	11	15.4	14.2
	12	15.2	11.7
	Total	100.1	100.1
Percent in Metropolitan Area		75	69

*These figures are from Fall Enrollment Report 1983.

(2) In a pretest of 151 students a social desirability scale was administered along with twelve items on drug use. Correlations between social desirability and drug use were small. This indicates that students did not underreport or overreport drug use in order to respond in a socially acceptable manner.

(3) Prevalence rates obtained from different sampling and data collection methods are similar (Johnston et al. 1985; Whitehead and Smart 1972). For example, Bauman et al. (1982) found that reports of cigarette use were valid when checked against a bio-chemical measure using an airbag.

(4) There are substantial relationships between self-reported drug use and various deviant behaviors. For example, students with poor grades and favorable attitudes toward theft reported higher levels of drug use. This is evidence of construct validity.

(5) Test-retest data were collected from 139 junior and senior high school students in central Utah. Ten items on drug use were included in two different questionnaires which were administered one week apart. Ninety-four percent of responses from the second test were identical to those from the first. This suggests that junior and senior high school students are able to respond consistently over time to drug-use questions.

Overall, there is a substantial amount of evidence that the responses of high school students to questions regarding drug use are valid. Given the limitations of official or clinical records, self reports may be the best single measure of adolescent drug use.

Frequent drug users are more likely than other students to be absent or to drop out of school. Overreporting tends to be minimal, and students who respond inconsistently are eliminated from the sample. Therefore, actual adolescent usage rates are likely to be at least as high as those reported in the surveys.

NATIONAL DATA

Each year a survey of high school seniors is conducted by the University of Michigan for the National Institute of Drug Abuse (Bachman et al. 1983, 1984; Johnston et al. 1985). These national data provide a comparison for the Utah survey. The latest survey year available is 1984, and questionnaires were administrated in 134 public and private high schools to more than 16,000 seniors, thereby providing an accurate cross-section of high school seniors throughout the United States. Procedures were similar to the Utah survey in that questionnaires were administered in classrooms during normal class hours. Many of the items in the Utah survey were similar to those in the national survey.

Johnston et al. (1985) provided descriptive results by geographical region. They included all the mountain and pacific states in the Western Region which includes Montana, Idaho, Wyoming, Colorado, New Mexico, Arizona, Utah, Nevada, Washington, Oregon, and California.

RESULTS

Alcohol

The most commonly used drug among adolescents is alcohol. A comparison of alcohol use in the United States, the Western Region, and Utah is shown in Table 2. Over 90 percent of U.S. high school seniors have tried alcohol at least once; 67 percent had drunk alcohol within the past month. This compares to 91 percent and 64 percent regionally. The proportion of Utah seniors having tried alcohol is considerably less, only 56 percent. In fact, the proportion of Utah seniors having ever tried alcohol is less than the proportion of seniors regionally and nationally having drunk alcohol within the past month. Only one-third of Utah seniors had used alcohol within the past month compared to two-thirds of seniors nationally.

Tobacco

Tobacco is the next most commonly used drug. Comparisons among Utah, the Western Region, and the United States in cigarette use is shown in Table 2. Seventy percent of seniors in the United States have smoked cigarettes at least once compared to 65 percent in the Western Region. Only 44 percent of Utah seniors have ever smoked cigarettes.

Twenty-nine percent of U.S. seniors report having smoked cigarettes during the past month compared to 23 percent of western seniors. For Utah seniors cigarette smoking is considerably less—only 12 percent report use during the past month.

Marijuana

The third most commonly used drug among teenagers is marijuana. Table 2 provides a comparison of marijuana use among seniors in the nation, Western Region, and Utah. Rates in the west are similar to those reported by the nation's seniors. Fifty-five percent of seniors in the United States have tried marijuana compared to 60 percent in the west. By contrast, the proportion of Utah seniors having tried marijuana is only 34 percent.

The proportion of seniors having used marijuana during the past month is 25 percent for the United States and 26 percent for the Western Region. In Utah current marijuana use is substantially lower—only 16 percent report having used marijuana during the past thirty days.

TABLE 2.

Percent of High School Seniors Who Reported Use of Various Drugs Ever and During the Past Month

	UNITED STATES 1984		WESTERN REGION 1984[a]		UTAH, 1984	
	EVER	PAST MO.	EVER	PAST MO.	EVER	PAST MO.
Alcohol	92.6	67.2	90.7	63.6	55.8*	34.3*
Cigarettes[b]	69.7	29.3	65.3	22.9	44.2*	11.8*
Marijuana	54.9	25.2	59.8	25.9	33.6*	16.2*
Amphetamines	27.9	8.3	27.9	7.4	19.9*	7.3
Barbiturates	9.9	1.7	8.9	1.2	8.5	3.3*
Tranquilizers	12.4	2.1	11.4	1.3	9.0*	3.4*
Cocaine	16.1	5.8	25.3	9.0	10.3*	4.8
Heroin	1.3	0.3	1.1	0.1	1.4	1.1*
Inhalants	14.4	1.9	15.4	1.8	11.3*	2.7
LSD[c]	8.0	1.5	8.7	0.9	10.5	4.0
PCP[c]	5.0	1.0	5.8	1.4	2.6	1.2
Pain Medications[d]	—	—	—	—	19.6	8.4
Sample Size	(15,900)		(2,900)		(4,901)	

[a]The Western Region includes Arizona, California, Colorado, Idaho, Montana, Nevada, New Mexico, Oregon, Washington, and Wyoming.

[b]Utah students were asked if they had ever used any tobacco products, while in the U.S. survey students were asked if they had ever smoked cigarettes. In both surveys the questions-concerning 30-day use asked about cigarettes.

[c]The items on psychedelics varied among the surveys. In the U.S. survey there was one question on LSD and one on other psychedelics. In Utah, there was one on psychedelics like LSD and one on PCP.

[d]An item on pain medications was not included in the U.S. survey.

*Difference between Utah and United States was significantly different ($p<.05$).

Amphetamines and Tranquilizers

The findings for amphetamines are shown in Table 2. Again, rates for the nation and the region are similar, while use among Utah seniors is substantially less. Twenty-eight percent of all seniors in the United States and in the Western Region have tried amphetamines without a physician's prescription compared to 20 percent of Utah seniors. Illegal amphetamine use during the past month among the three groups was similar: 8 percent of seniors nationally, 7 percent regionally, and 7 percent in Utah.

Another commonly used drug is tranquilizers. Twelve percent of U.S. seniors, 11 percent of western seniors, and 9 percent of Utah seniors report having used tranquilizers without a doctor's prescription. About 2 percent of seniors in the United States and 1 percent of seniors in the Western Region had used tranquilizers illegally within the past month. By comparison, 3 percent of Utah seniors report the illegal use of tranquilizers during the past month (see Table 2).

Cocaine

During recent years the use of cocaine among adolescents has substantially increased (Johnston et al. 1985). Cocaine is the only drug in which use is noticeably higher in the Western Region than in the nation. Sixteen percent of U.S. seniors have used cocaine compared to 25 percent of seniors regionally and to 10 percent of Utah seniors.

Current cocaine use in Utah is almost the same as nationally. During the past month 6 percent of U.S. seniors and 5 percent of Utah seniors admitted to having used cocaine. In the Western Region 9 percent of seniors reported having used cocaine during the past month.

Other Drugs

For the remaining drugs, differences among the United States, the Western Region, and Utah are small. The percentages of seniors having used these other drugs is shown in Table 2.

For barbiturates there are no significant differences among the three groups. About 10 percent of seniors in the United States have used barbiturates illegally compared to 9 percent among western seniors and almost 9 percent among Utah seniors. During the past month the percentage of seniors using barbiturates is 2 percent in United States, 1 percent in the Western Region, but 3 percent in Utah.

Heroin use is extremely low. Only about 1 percent of all seniors have ever used heroin. During the past month about 1 percent of Utah seniors reported heroin use compared to .2 percent and .1 percent nationally and regionally.

Usage rates regarding inhalants, LSD, and PCP are similar among the three groups. Fourteen percent of seniors in the United States have tried inhalants compared to 15 percent and 11 percent of seniors in the west and in Utah, respectively. The use of inhalants during the past month is 2 percent among seniors in the United States and in the Western Region and 3 percent in Utah.

The use of LSD is slightly higher in Utah than in the United States or in the Western Region, while PCP use appears to be slightly lower in Utah. However, the questionnaire items regarding LSD and PCP are slightly different in the Utah survey, which may account for the differences. In the U.S. survey there was one question on LSD, while the Utah question asked about psychedelic drugs such as LSD. Similarly, the national survey had one question on psychedelics other than LSD, while in Utah the question was restricted to PCP.

SIGNIFICANCE OF DIFFERENCES

There are two important questions regarding the differences between United States and Utah seniors. First, are they statistically significant? Second, how important are they in practical terms?

It is impossible to answer the first question definitively because the seventeen Utah school districts were self-selected rather than randomly selected. Statistical tests assume that the sample is drawn from the population in a probabilistic way, which was not the case. Nevertheless, we computed significance tests, assuming that the seventeen school districts were similar to a cluster sample.

Computing significance tests for cluster samples is complex. L. Kish (1965) recommends using a design effect to determine the "effective N"—an adjusted sample size to compensate for the lower precision of cluster samples compared to simple random samples. We estimated our design effect to be 4, and therefore our "effective Ns" are one-fourth of the actual sample sizes. Using the tables from Johnston et al. (1981), we estimated which percentage differences in Table 2 are statistically significant ($P<.05$).

Lifetime and past month use of alcohol, cigarettes, and marijuana are significantly lower in Utah than in the United States. Lifetime use of amphetamines, tranquilizers, cocaine, and inhalants is significantly lower in Utah than in the United States. But past month use of barbiturates, tranquilizers, and heroin is significantly higher in Utah than in United States. All other differences are not statistically significant. (Significance tests for LSD and PCP were not computed because the questions were different.)

Although past month use of heroin is significantly higher in Utah than in the United States, the difference is only 0.8 percent. Such a small percentage difference has no practical significance, particularly since our sample was not selected randomly. Similarly, the differences for past month use of barbiturates and tranquilizers are relatively small, 1.6 and 1.3 percent, respectively.

ANALYSIS WITHIN UTAH

Up to this point we have confined our analysis to comparing Utah to the United States and the Western Region. In the following section we provide a more extensive analysis of adolescent drug use within Utah.

One frequently asked question is whether adolescent drug use is increasing or decreasing. During the 1970s, adolescent drug use, particularly with regard to marijuana, increased substantially in the United States. During the early 1980s rates of adolescent drug use stabilized, and for some drugs the level of use decreased. For example, the percentage of students regularly using marijuana decreased during the past five years (Johnston et al. 1985; Macdonald 1984). On the other hand, cocaine is one drug where adolescent use has increased in recent years (Johnston et at. 1985; Bachman et al. 1984).

TABLE 3.

Percent of Utah Seniors Ever Using Various Drugs, 1972 and 1984

DRUG	1972	1984
Alcohol	65.9	55.8
Marijuana	27.0	33.6
Amphetamines	15.0	19.9
Psychedelics	10.7	10.5
Inhalants	7.5	11.3
Narcotics	3.4	—
Heroin	—	1.4
Cocaine	—	10.3
(n)	(10,846)	(42,556)

Source: Utah State Board of Education 1974.

Reliable trend data on adolescent drug use in Utah are not available. However, during 1972 the Utah State Board of Education conducted a large survey of adolescents. The results from this survey have been compared to our 1984 data to estimate changes during the decade. This comparison is shown in Table 3.

The data indicate that adolescent alcohol use probably decreased slightly from 1972 to 1984. Sixty-six percent of Utah seniors in 1972 reported alcohol use compared to 56 percent in 1984. But the proportion having used marijuana and amphetamines appears to have increased. Twenty-seven percent of seniors in the 1972 survey said they had tried marijuana, while in 1984 this had increased to 34 percent. Similarly, amphetamine use among Utah's seniors increased from 15 percent to 20 percent, as did inhalant use—from 8 percent to 11 percent. There appears to have been no change in the reported use of psychedelic drugs.

The questions on narcotics in the two surveys are not directly comparable. In the 1972 survey there was one question on narcotics. In 1984 this was divided into two questions, one on heroin and one on cocaine. In 1984 the percentage of seniors reporting the use of cocaine was three times greater than that reported for all narcotic drugs in 1972. This suggests that among Utah adolescents the use of cocaine increased substantially from 1972 to 1984.

CORRELATES OF DRUG USE

We now turn to an analysis of some of the social correlates of adolescent drug use. We will focus primarily on alcohol and marijuana use. Alcohol was chosen because it is the most widely used drug among adolescents. Marijuana was chosen because it is the most frequently used illicit drug, and most adolescents try marijuana before they experiment with other drugs (Kandel 1980).

Grade

An analysis of alcohol and marijuana use in Utah by grade is presented in Table 4. As would be expected, the proportion of students having used or currently using alcohol or marijuana increases with grade level. The largest increases tend to occur between seventh and ninth grades. The increases between grades ten and twelve tend to be modest. This suggests that eighth and ninth grades are pivotal regarding adolescent drug use, for it is here that many students apparently begin experimenting with drugs. Parents and teachers should be particularly sensitive to opportunities for drug use and provide adequate support and drug education during this period.

Gender

Another important correlate of adolescent drug use is gender. For alcohol and all illegal substances males tend to consume more than females (Kandel 1980). There is some evidence that gender differences regarding drug use have been decreasing (Green 1979; Kandel 1980). Although some studies have found small gender differences in the proportion having tried alcohol or marijuana, males tend to use these drugs more frequently and consume greater quantities (Green 1979).

In the national high school survey conducted by Johnston et al. (1985) the proportions of male and female seniors having had alcohol are 93 and 92 percent, respectively. During the past month 71 percent of males consumed alcohol compared to only 63 percent of females. Fifty-eight percent of males reported having tried marijuana at least once compared to 51 percent of females. Twenty-eight percent of males and 21 percent of females had used marijuana during the past month (Johnston et al. 1985).

A comparison of gender differences among Utah high school students is shown in Table 5. The differences are not large, but males typically use more alcohol and marijuana than females. For example, during the past month 20 percent of females had drunk alcohol compared to 25 percent of males. Seventeen percent of females had tried marijuana at least once compared to 22 percent of males.

TABLE 4.

Percent of Adolescent Alcohol and Marijuana Use in Utah By Grade

GRADE	7	8	9	10	11	12
Alcohol Use						
Ever	26.0	36.2	45.4	51.4	56.1	55.8
Past Month	9.2	16.2	23.4	29.4	32.7	34.3
8+Days/Mo.	2.4	3.7	5.4	6.9	8.2	9.3
Marijuana Use						
Ever	7.0	12.2	18.7	24.9	30.2	33.6
Past Month	3.4	6.3	10.3	13.5	15.8	16.2
8+Days/Mo.	1.3	2.6	3.8	5.6	6.8	6.7
(n)	(9,090)	(8,703)	(7,309)	(6,308)	(5,900)	(4,914)

For amphetamines and barbiturates there are no gender differences among Utah adolescents, but females are more likely than males to have used tranquilizers. In other research females have been found to use more amphetamines and barbiturates (Green 1979).

Ethnic Group

Kandel (1980) and Green (1979) have reviewed existing data regarding ethnic differences in drug use. They report that the use of alcohol, tobacco, marijuana, and pills is more prevalent among whites than blacks, but that heroin use is more common among blacks. Other ethnic groups have not been adequately studied in large scale surveys. Available data indicate that American Indians may have the highest rates of use for all types of drugs, while Orientals appear to have the lowest rates (Green 1979; Kandel 1980).

In the national high school survey conducted by Bachman et al. (1984), blacks were less likely than whites to use alcohol, tobacco, or marijuana. For example, 73 percent of white high school seniors had drunk alcohol during the past month compared to 40 percent of black seniors. Sixty percent of whites had tried marijuana at least once compared to 53 percent of blacks. For all other drugs except heroin, Bachman et al. (1984) report that whites

TABLE 5.

Percent of Adolescent Alcohol and Marijuana Use in Utah By Gender

	FEMALE	MALE
Alcohol Use		
Ever	39.6	46.4
Past Month	19.7	25.1
8+Days/Month	4.4	6.5
Marijuana Use		
Ever	16.6	21.7
Past Month	8.4	11.6
8+Days/Month	3.1	5.2
(n)	(21,749)	(20,310)

had higher usage rates than blacks. For heroin, whites and blacks had almost identical rates.

A comparison of alcohol and marijuana use among different ethnic groups in Utah is shown in Table 6. Consistent with research in other states, Orientals in Utah have the lowest usage rates of any ethnic group. However, Utah adolescents differ from other states in that whites have lower rates than blacks. Also, American Indians in Utah do not have the highest rates of alcohol and marijuana use.

Utah's teenage Hispanics and blacks have the highest proportion ever using alcohol. More blacks than any other ethnic group report regular alcohol use, followed by Pacific Islanders, "Other," and Hispanics. American Indians rank fifth among the seven ethnic groups in the proportion using alcohol regularly.

Over 43 percent of Hispanics have tried marijuana compared to 40 percent of blacks and 31 percent of "Other." By comparison 29 percent of American Indian students, 18 percent of whites, and 13 percent of Orientals have used marijuana at least once. Again, regular use among adolescents is more common among blacks than any other ethnic group—15 percent of blacks use marijuana eight or more times a month compared to 12 percent among Hispanics and 7 percent among Indians. Slightly more than 3 percent of whites and less than 3 percent of Orientals use marijuana eight or more times a month.

TABLE 6.

Percent of Adolescent Alcohol and Marijuana Use In Utah By Ethnic Group

	WHITE	HISPANIC	BLACK	INDIAN	ORIENTAL	ISLANDER	OTHER
Alcohol Use							
Ever	41.6	66.0	62.5	47.1	41.8	43.1	57.7
Past Month	21.5	37.8	35.1	21.9	17.4	27.1	36.1
8+Days/Mo.	5.1	10.1	14.9	6.2	3.5	13.7	13.6
Marijuana Use							
Ever	17.6	43.2	39.9	29.3	13.2	26.6	31.0
Past Month	9.0	24.8	25.0	14.7	7.0	16.0	18.0
8+Days/Mo.	3.4	11.6	15.4	6.5	2.6	10.5	12.5
(n)	(38,169)	(1,565)	(387)	(935)	(570)	(218)	(424)

Consistent with other research, Orientals in Utah have very low usage rates for all drugs. However, in contrast to other areas, American Indians do not have the highest rates of drug use and whites do not have higher rates than blacks. Black and Hispanic adolescents in Utah tend to use alcohol and marijuana more frequently than adolescents in other ethnic groups. Among the seven ethnic categories, American Indians rank fifth, whites sixth, and Orientals seventh in the consumption of alcohol and marijuana.

Utah's ethnic composition is different from that elsewhere, which may account for some of the differences between the Utah findings and other research. Utah's population is over 90 percent white. Hispanics are the largest minority group, making up less than 4 percent of the total population. American Indians are second and comprise about 2 percent of the population. Orientals account for slightly more than 1 percent of the population, while blacks comprise less than 1 percent.

Region

How does adolescent drug use in Utah vary by region? To make this comparison we have divided the state into five regions: (1) northwest, (2) northeast, (3) central, (4) southwest, and (5) southeast. The central region includes what is commonly called the Wasatch Front. A comparison of student drug use by these five regions is shown in Table 7.

TABLE 7.

Percent of Adolescent Alcohol and Marijuana Use in Utah By Region

	NORTHWEST	CENTRAL	NORTHEAST	SOUTHWEST	SOUTHEAST
Alcohol Use					
Ever	42.0	42.6	55.1	39.8	38.6
Past Month	21.9	22.4	28.4	19.9	19.0
8+Days/Month	5.4	5.4	7.5	4.9	4.9
Marijuana Use					
Ever	19.3	19.3	22.4	16.6	15.5
Past Month	9.6	10.3	11.5	8.5	7.6
8+Days/Month	4.0	4.2	5.1	3.5	2.8
(n)	(7,288)	(25,872)	(3,221)	(3,910)	(2,079)

Differences among the regions are not large. For all drugs the northeast has the highest usage rates, the central and northwest regions fall in the middle, while the two southern regions have the lowest rates. The southeast region is consistently the lowest of the five.

Some might expect the central region to be the highest in adolescent drug use since it includes the state's two major metropolitan areas. But it consistently ranks second among the five regions in amount of adolescent drug use. Why is the northeast region the highest even though it is a rural area? One explanation is that it has had a rapid influx of people in recent years because of energy development. This has created characteristics that tend to be associated with higher rates of crime and drug use, such as a ''boomtown'' atmosphere, a highly mobile population, and an increase in the proportion of the population between the ages of 18 and 30. It should be noted that the northeast region also has a relatively high crime rate (see Chapter 19).

Research has shown that crime and drug use occur more frequently in urban than in rural areas (Green 1979; Kandel 1980). The Utah data are generally consistent with this finding, although the differences between urban and rural areas are relatively small. There is no difference between metropolitan and non-metropolitan areas in Utah for the student use of tobacco, barbiturates, heroin, and psychedelic drugs. The use of alcohol, amphetamines, tranquilizers, cocaine, and inhalants is slightly higher in the metropolitan areas, but the only drug that is noticeably higher in metropolitan areas is marijuana. For example, 16.6 percent of students in non-metropolitan areas have tried marijuana compared to 20.3 percent of students in metropolitan areas. For past month use of marijuana the comparable percentages are 8.5 and 10.6, respectively.

SUMMARY

This chapter compared Utah, the Western Region, and the United States in terms of adolescent drug use, examining trends in Utah and identifying differences in use according to grade, gender, ethnic group, and region. The Utah data came from a survey of 42,000 students, grades 9 to 12, conducted in 1984. The national and regional data were obtained from an annual survey of high school seniors conducted by Johnston et al. (1985).

Alcohol, tobacco, marijuana, and amphetamines are used much less frequently by Utah adolescents than by adolescents in the United States. Utah students are somewhat less likely than United States adolescents to have reported ever using tranquilizers, cocaine, or inhalants, but there are only small differences regarding past month use of these substances. Differences between Utah and United States adolescents regarding the use of barbiturates, heroin, and psychedelics are small, but current use of these substances does appear to be higher in Utah than elsewhere.

Reliable trend data for Utah are not available. A comparison of 1984 data with a 1972 survey suggests that adolescent drug use has increased, particularly for marijuana and cocaine. The use of alcohol appears to have decreased somewhat, however.

The proportion of students experimenting with drugs and using them regularly increases with age. Eighth and ninth grades appear to be critical years when students experiment with drugs. For almost all drugs, use is somewhat greater among males than females. Ethnic comparisons reveal that black and Hispanic adolescents are the most likely to use drugs in Utah, followed by American Indians, whites, and Orientals. Geographic differences within Utah are small, although the northeast region is consistently higher than the other four areas of the state. Differences between metropolitan and non-metropolitan areas are small, but marijuana use is more common in metropolitan areas.

The data suggest that adolescent drug use is less a problem in Utah than in the west or in the United States as a whole. On the other hand, there is evidence that drug use has increased and that substantial numbers of youth are becoming involved in the illicit use of drugs.

In Utah, adolescent drug use may not be epidemic, but large numbers of youth are experimenting with drugs, and many become regular users. The negative consequences associated with drug use make it an issue of concern for all parents, teachers, and youth.

REFERENCES

Bachman, J. G., L. D. Johnston, and P. M. O'Malley. *Monitoring the Future: A Continuing Study of the Lifestyles and Values of Youth, 1982*. Ann Arbor, MI: Inter-University Consortium for Political and Social Research, 1983.

_____. *Monitoring the Future: Questionnaire Responses from the Nation's High School Seniors, 1982*. Ann Arbor, MI: Survey Research Center, Institute for Social Research, University of Michigan, 1984.

Bauman, K., G. G. Roch, and E. S. Bryan. "Validity of Self reports of Adolescent Cigarette Smoking." *International Journal of Addictions* 17 (1982): 1,131-36.

Fall Enrollment Report of Utah School Districts. Salt Lake City: Utah State Office of Education, 1 Oct. 1983.

Green, J. "Overview of Adolescent Drug Use." In G. M. Beschner and A. S. Friedman, eds., *Youth Drug Abuse*, pp. 17-44, Lexington, MA: Lexington Books, 1979.

Johnston, Lloyd D., Jerald G. Bachman, and Patrick M. O'Malley. *Student Drug Use in America, 1975-1981*. Rockville, MD: National Institute on Drug Abuse, 1981.

_____. *Use of Licit and Illicit Drugs by America's High School Students: 1975-1984*. Rockville, MD: National Institute on Drug Abuse, 1985.

Kandel, D. B. "Drug and Drinking Behavior Among Youth." *Annual Review of Sociology* 6 (1980): 235-85.

Keyes, Susan, and Jack Block. "Prevalence and Patterns of Substance Use Among Early Adolescents." *Journal of Youth and Adolescence* 13 (1984): 1-14.

Kish, L. *Survey Sampling*. New York: John Wiley and Sons, 1965.

Macdonald, D. I. *Drugs, Drinking, and Adolescents*. Chicago: Year Book Medical Publishers, 1984.

Utah State Board of Education. *Utah 1972 Statewide Drug Assessment*. Salt Lake City: State Board of Education, 1974.

Whitehead, P. C., and R. G. Smart. "Validity and Reliability of Self-reported Drug Use." *Canadian Journal of Criminology and Corrections* 14 (1972): 83-89.

19.
CRIME

Richard E. Johnson

It has become commonplace in today's media to read of "the crime problem" facing the country. We are persistently confronted with stories detailing specific crimes or containing statistics about the vast number of crimes. From such reports it is tempting to conclude that crime is more serious now than ever before and perhaps even more serious locally than elsewhere. The purpose of this chapter is to provide some perspective for the seriousness of crime in Utah today compared to the United States, to the mountain states, and to the recent past.

THE MEANING OF "CRIME"

Before examining the data, we should first define what is meant by "crime." By far the most commonly employed measure—and therefore meaning—of crime in America is the Federal Bureau of Investigation's Crime Index. Most of the data presented in this chapter are based on Crime Index offenses, including murder, forcible rape, robbery, aggravated assault, motor vehicle theft, larceny-theft, and burglary, with arson added to the list in recent years. But to equate these "street crimes" with "the crime problem" would be a mistake. Most criminologists agree that the harm done to society by street crime—measured in lost dollars, in deaths, and in injuries—is exceeded by the harm done by white-collar and organized crime.

While the public hears most about Crime Index offenses and experts point to the greater damage done by "suite crime" (i.e., white-collar and organized), most of the arrests in America are for other types of crime. These include "victimless" offenses such as disorderly conduct, drug-related violations (primarily alcohol), prostitution and vice, and juvenile offenses such as running away from home. Unfortunately, the data needed to make useful state, regional, and national comparisons for non-Index crimes are not available. So at best the following FBI statistics comprise an incomplete picture of the total crime problem.

More troubling than the incompleteness of the data is the argument by many criminologists that the persistent focus on street crime serves to bias our perceptions against the poor and minorities as the "criminal element" in society, while deflecting our attention away from the crimes of the middle and upper classes. Reiman (1984), for example, cites evidence for the position that our image of what constitutes dangerous crime in America is distorted, much to the benefit of white-collar and corporate criminals. In his view, the very definition of crime, when it is biased or unjust, is just as "criminal" or immoral as the acts of muggers and thieves.

Thus, defining crime is no simple task. It is one of the major controversies in criminology today. The data in this chapter focus primarily on one kind of crime—FBI "street crime"—because that is the type of crime for which data are available and because most people perceive these crimes to merit greatest public concern and attention. Whether the public is correct in its perception remains debatable.

THE FBI CRIME INDEX

Even with our analysis restricted to data from the FBI's annual reports, some caution about the accuracy of these reports is in order. The FBI compiles the information it receives from thousands of sheriffs and police chiefs throughout the United States. There is no requirement that every law enforcement agency even submit a report. In 1983, for example, crime figures were not submitted by agencies with jurisdiction over 1.6 percent of the population in Standard Metropolitan Statistical Areas (SMSAs), 6.2 percent of the population in other cities, and 10.3 percent of the population in rural areas. Figures for these areas had to be estimated (FBI 1984, 43). Furthermore, it is commonly known among criminologists that agencies define and keep records of crimes in different ways, sometimes intentionally inflating or depressing crime rates for political or public relations reasons.

The FBI's basic report of "offenses known to the police," therefore, more accurately consists of offenses categorized in different ways and reported on a volunteer basis by cooperating law enforcement agencies. Moreover, surveys of crime victims reveal that most Index offenses are never reported to the police (see, for example, Bureau of Justice Statistics 1983). And among cities for which both FBI statistics and victim survey data are available, there are great discrepancies between the two measures as to which cities have the greatest amounts of the various offenses (Cohen and Land 1984). Apparently, the likelihood of a citizen reporting a crime varies significantly by offense and by location. Just how these factors affect the validity of Utah's crime statistics is not known. In the first place, there are no state or regional victim surveys to compare with national surveys. Second, there are no studies indicating how the reporting procedures of Utah's police compare to procedures elsewhere. In our comparisons of crime statistics, we must assume that the reporting behavior of both citizens and police in Utah is similar to that in other parts of the region and nation. And when arrest data are utilized, which constitute only about one-fifth of offenses known to police, one must further assume that the efficiency and biases of the criminal justice system are similar across areas. With these cautions and assumptions, we will now consider the numbers.

Table 1 compares the rates of 1983 Crime Index offenses known to police in Utah, the mountain states (including Arizona, Colorado, Idaho, Montana, Nevada, New Mexico, Utah, and Wyoming), and the United States. The Index is divided into violent and property crimes. Robbery is listed as a violent

TABLE 1.

1983 FBI Index Crime Rates Per 100,000 Population

	UNITED STATES	MOUNTAIN STATES REGION	UTAH	UTAH'S RANK AMONG FIFTY STATES	UTAH'S RANK AMONG EIGHT MT. STATES
Total Index	5159	5884	5118	18	5
Violent Crime	529	442	256	36	5
Murder	8	6	4	40	7-8
Rape	34	37	25	30	5
Robbery	214	113	64	38	5
Aggravated Assault	273	286	163	35	8
Property Crime	4630	5442	4862	15	5
Burglary	1334	1411	1016	34	4
Larceny-theft	2886	3715	3610	8	4
Motor Vehicle Theft	429	316	236	29	5

crime because it involves taking property by force or threat of force that is in the immediate possession of another. Burglary involves illegal entry in order to commit a crime, and larceny-theft involves theft of property other than a motor vehicle without personal confrontation or illegal entry. The other offenses are self-explanatory.

At first glance, Table 1 appears to depict Utah as high in crime. Even though its total crime rate per population is below the national average, Utah ranks 18th among the fifty states. A closer look, however, reveals that Utah's high ranking is due solely to one offense—larceny-theft. For every violent offense and for every other property crime, Utah ranks below both the national median and the combined national rate. But because larceny-theft is by far the most often reported offense (56 percent of the total nationwide), its rate alone largely determines the total crime rate. In terms of violent crimes, Utah's murder rate is only half of that nationally, with only ten states having lower rates. Similarly, combined violent crime in Utah is less than half of the national rate, with only fourteen states being lower.

Over the past few years, the nation, the region, and Utah have all experienced declines in crime rates. The national Crime Index in 1983 was down 7 percent from 1979, with a 2 percent drop in violence and an 8 percent drop in property crime. The mountain states declined 9 percent in total, 10 percent in violence, and 9 percent in property crime. And Utah dropped 7 percent in total, 16 percent in violence, and 6 percent in property crime. Most politicians attribute this to "get tough" crime policies, while criminologists point to the aging of the "baby boom" generation out of the high-crime ages. For whatever reasons, Utah in 1983 was a safer place than Utah in 1979 or the United States in either 1979 or 1983.

Comparing Utah's street crime to that nationally may be unfair, however, as there are significant regional variations. Perhaps a better indicator of Utah's "criminal climate" can be derived from comparisons with the other states in the Mountain Region. As shown in Table 1, the region ranks above the national average in Index crime, but again this is due to property crime and not violence. While the mountain states region ranks second among nine regions in property crime, it ranks sixth in violent crime.

Within a regional context, neither Utah's high property offense rate nor its low violence rate appears to be unusual. Among the eight mountain states, Utah is consistently nestled in fifth place in total Index crime, in violence, and in property crime. Utah's relatively high larceny-theft rate is below the mountain states' combined rate and ranks fourth among the eight states. In fact, no Crime Index offense is known to occur with a higher rate in Utah than in the mountain states as a whole. Utah's greatest departures from regional rates occur for murder and aggravated assault, for which Utah ranks as the safest place among the mountain states.

Within Utah, some areas are much safer than others, of course. Of Utah's twenty-nine counties, only three have total Index crime rates exceeding the statewide rate of 5,118 per 100,000 residents shown in Table 1. Salt Lake County tops the list with a rate of 6,931, followed by Uintah County with 5,922 and Weber County with 5,736.

Compared to 1979, these rates represent decreases for Salt Lake and Weber counties of 19 percent and 21 percent, respectively, and a crime increase for Uintah County of 85 percent. The high crime rates in Salt Lake and Weber counties, therefore, are not evidence of a "crime wave" in those areas over the past few years. Furthermore, their rates compare to similar urban counties nationwide. The crime rate in Uintah County, however, is exceptionally high for its level of urbanization and has recently risen dramatically. Probably due in large part to its "boomtown" environment, with new energy-related developments and accompanying transient populations, Uintah County has more of a "crime wave" or "crime problem" than any other county in Utah.

Along with geographic location, the level of urbanization is one of the best predictors of Index crime. For the United States as a whole, metropolitan areas have a total Crime Index rate of 5,852 (per 100,000 population), which overshadows the "other cities" rate of 4,629 and far exceeds the rural rate of 1,881. To place Utah's crime rates in perspective one needs to examine more closely the data regarding levels of urbanization. It is possible, for example, that a low-crime state like Utah is low because it is rural, but that its small towns are just as criminal as other small towns and that its few urban areas are just as criminal as urban areas anywhere.

According to Table 2, the level of urbanization in Utah (as categorized by the FBI) parallels the nation's. Utah's population is 77 percent metropolitan, 12 percent in the "other cities" category, and 11 percent rural. This compares to 76 percent, 10 percent, and 14 percent nationally. So Utah's crime rate would not jump if the state were to reflect exactly the nation's urbanization. In fact, with Utah's crime rates and the nation's urbanization, Utah's expected rate would be 2 percent lower than its actual rate. To the extent that Utah is low in crime, it is not because it is low in urbanization.

A closer look at Table 2 shows that violence in metropolitan and other cities in Utah is lower than is true nationally, while rural Utah is more violent than rural America. For property crime, the differences are not as striking. However, Utah surpasses the nation in both metropolitan and rural areas while it falls short in other cities.

The picture once again changes when comparing Utah to the mountain states. The region as a whole is substantially less urbanized than either Utah or the United States, with only 63 percent of its residents in metropolitan areas, 18 percent in "other cities," and 19 percent in rural areas. When Utah's crime rates are compared to the region's rates by categories of urbanization, Utah's rates are uniformly lower. When the region is compared to the nation, however, its rates are below national rates only in metropolitan violence. For violence in "other cities" and in rural areas, and for property crime in metropolitan areas, "other cities," and rural areas, the mountain states are more criminal than America generally. In other words, levels of urbanization fail to "explain away" high crime in the region. In fact, regional rates would increase 4 percent if the urbanization-specific rates of the nation were applied to the mountain states.

TABLE 2.

1983 FBI Index Crime Rates Per 100,000 Population, by Level of Urbanization

	UNITED STATES	MOUNTAIN STATES	UTAH
Metropolitan			
(% of population)	(75.7)	(62.8)	(77.2)
Total Index	5852	6796	5726
Violence	627	504	272
Property	5225	6291	5454
Other Cities			
(% of population)	(9.9)	(18.5)	(11.9)
Total Index	4629	5991	3937
Violence	315	413	181
Property	4314	5578	3755
Rural			
(% of population)	(14.4)	(18.6)	(10.9)
Total Index	1881	2706	2094
Violence	161	260	220
Property	1720	2447	1874

Within the mountain states, however, levels of urbanization are useful in predicting crime rates. Table 3 shows the rankings of the mountain states in terms of the percentage of the population in metropolitan areas and in total Index crime. The correlation between urbanization and crime is strong, with only Utah and Idaho disrupting a uniform pattern. These two states are less criminal than would be expected given their levels of urbanization, Idaho by one ranking and Utah by two. Once again, Utah appears to have a relatively crime-free environment within the mountain states.

The third variable having an important influence on aggregate crime rates is the age structure of the population. This is due to the fact that teenagers and young adults seem to commit more than their share of Crime Index offenses. People of comparable ages in two states could be equally criminal, but because one state has an abundance of youth, it might appear to be more criminal. It should be noted here that police have no way of knowing the ages of criminals who are not caught, so age data necessarily consist of arrest statistics. This, of course, diminishes one's confidence in the accuracy of the data, since approximately four out of five Index offenses do not result in an arrest.

TABLE 3.

Mountain States Ranked by Percent Metropolitan and by Total 1983 FBI Index Crime

STATE	RANK IN PERCENT METROPOLITAN	RANK IN TOTAL FBI INDEX CRIME
Nevada	1st	1st
Colorado	2nd	2nd
Utah	3rd	5th
Arizona	4th	3rd
New Mexico	5th	4th
Montana	6th	6th
Idaho	7th	8th
Wyoming	8th	7th

Gamma = .79

Using 1983 arrest-by-age data and 1980 census data for the age composition of the American population, one can measure the percentage of arrests for each five-year age grouping. For example, 15 to 19 year-olds constitute 9.3 percent of the American population, but they contribute 30.1 percent of Crime Index arrests. If all age groups contributed equally to arrest figures, 15 to 19 year-olds could contribute 9.3 percent of all arrests, but their proportion is more than three times what it should be. Using the criterion of proportion of arrests versus proportion of population, age groups can be classified as high, medium, or low in crime. High-crime age groups are those with more than 1.5 times their share of arrests, low-crime age groups have less than .5 their share of arrests, and medium-crime age groups fall in between.

Table 4 shows the age structures of the United States, the mountain states, and Utah in terms of crime-level age groupings. Both Utah and the region have more than their share of high-crime-age groups (15 to 29 year-olds). If age-specific arrest rates were available on a state-by-state basis, Utah would drop in its apparent criminality based on age structures relative to the mountain states, while the region would not look so criminal compared to the nation. But age-specific arrest rates are only available nationwide, so the best one can do is calculate that if the nation retained its age-specific rates and inherited Utah's age structure, arrests nationally would increase by 3 percent. The net effect of age structure is therefore real, but it is diminished in its impact by

TABLE 4.

Percent of Population in High-, Medium-, and Low-Crime Age Groupings, Based on 1983 FBI Index Crime Rates and 1980 Population Figures

	UNITED STATES	MOUNTAIN STATES	UTAH
High-Crime Ages (15-29)	27.3	28.8	29.4
Medium-Crime Ages (10-14, 30-44)	27.3	27.5	25.7
Low-Crime Ages (0-9, 45+)	45.6	43.6	45.0

Source: FBI 1984; The Numbers News 1981.

the fact that Utah has a disproportionate number of low-crime 0 to 9 year-olds to counterbalance its large group of high-crime 15 to 29 year-olds.

Within the mountain states, differences in age are smaller and less reliable in predicting crime rates than are differences in levels of urbanization. In contrast to the strong correlation between the rankings of the eight states in Index crime and percent metropolitan clusters (Table 3, gamma=.79), there is practically no relationship between the states' rankings in arrests and percent in high-crime ages (gamma=.07). Age structure, then, does little to change one's perception of Utah's crime profile relative to that regionally.

NON-INDEX CRIME

As discussed earlier, the FBI Index reveals only a narrow and perhaps misleading picture of crime. And unfortunately, reliable data on other types of crime at the state, regional, and national levels do not exist. In spite of these limitations, two kinds of crime have recently received much attention in Utah and should be mentioned.

Utah has been described by reporters and experts alike as the "fraud capital of the nation." Yet never has this description been supported by facts or figures. The reputation may be real, but it is based largely on speculation and on the perception that Utah's religious population is unusually trusting and naive and therefore easy to defraud. The problem was considered serious enough that in 1984 Utah's governor established a special task force to examine securities fraud in the state. The following excerpt from the task force's report summarizes the extent of our knowledge of this issue:

> Several articles stated that Utah is the "stock-fraud capital of the nation" or the "sewer of the securities industry." Controversy exists on whether or not such reputation is deserved. The United States Attorney for the District of Utah believes that a serious problem exists. . . .
>
> Norman S. Johnson, a local securities attorney, stated that such reputation was undeserved and that the securities industry in Utah was no worse than [in] other areas in the nation of comparable size. Whether or not Utah is, in fact, the "stock-fraud capital of the nation" is open to discussion. (Governor's Securities Fraud Task Force 1984, 11)

It is probably the case that honesty is emphasized and expected to such a degree in Utah that dishonesty strikes a higher profile locally than it does in other areas of the country. And crimes committed by those who talk and dress like pillars of the community receive considerable attention because they are unexpected. In short, if Utah citizens are really more naive, this might encourage not only susceptibility to fraud but also an inflated response to a small or average amount of fraud.

There are FBI arrest statistics for fraud, although arrest data have limited accuracy as a measure of actual crime. The national arrest rate for fraud in 1983 was 130.5 per 100,000 population (FBI 1984, 172). By comparison, Utah's rate was 64.1 per 100,000, less than half the national rate (Utah Bureau 1984, 32). If Utah is a fraud capital, this is not reflected in arrests for fraud. Parenthetically, those same reports show that national and Utah arrest rates for related offenses such as forgery, counterfeiting, and embezzlement are almost identical. At this point, Utah's image as a hotbed of fraud remains just that—an unverified image.

The dynamics and incidence of child abuse, one of the most tragic aspects of crime, are discussed in Chapter 11. According to arrest records for "offenses against family and children," the U.S. rate is 23.0 per 100,000 residents (FBI 1984, 172), while Utah's is 14.8 (Utah Bureau 1984, 32). Like fraud, if Utah experiences a disproportionate amount of child abuse, it is not apparent in arrest statistics.

SUMMARY

The measurement of crime is elusive, involving ideological disputes over the appropriate meaning of crime, uncertainties about the accuracy of official law enforcement crime reports, and the absence of data for many types of crime. If one focuses on FBI reports of "street crime," taking them at face value, Utah appears to be among the safest states in the nation in terms of violent crime. And with the exception of larceny-theft (usually the least serious FBI offense), property crime rates are also low in Utah. Furthermore, the rates for both violence and property offenses declined from 1979 to 1983.

Compared to the nation, the mountain states are relatively low in urban violence but high in property crime and rural violence. Within that regional context, Utah has lower than average rates of every FBI offense, with an exceptionally low murder rate.

The level of urbanization and age structure are known correlates of crime rates. Urban areas and areas with high numbers of 15 to 29 year-olds have higher crime rates. Controlling for level of urbanization and age structure causes Utah's environment to appear even less criminal. In general, the mountain states benefit statistically by having low levels of urbanization and an approximately average crime-prone age structure. Utah, on the other hand, maintains lower raw rates in spite of levels of urbanization and an age structure that are conducive to higher crime. Utah's crime rates would probably rank even lower regionally and nationally if Utah mirrored the nation's or the region's older and more rural populations. Thus, controlling for these factors improves Utah's already favorable crime position nationally.

There are no numbers that support the idea that Utah has exceptionally high rates of fraud or child abuse. The only available arrest data indicate that Utah's rates are below national averages. In short, it is difficult to make a case for the position that Utah is experiencing a crime wave of any sort.

REFERENCES

Bureau of Justice Statistics. *Report to the Nation on Crime and Justice: The Data*. Washington, D.C.: U.S. Department of Justice, 1983.

Cohen, Lawrence E., and Kenneth C. Land. "Discrepancies Between Crime Reports and Crime Surveys: Urban and Structural Determinants." *Criminology* 22 (Nov. 1984): 499-530.

FBI. Federal Bureau of Investigation. *Crime in the United States: Uniform Crime Reports—1983*. Washington, D.C.: U.S. Government Printing Office, 1984.

Governor's Securities Fraud Task Force. *Report*. Salt Lake City: State of Utah, 1984.

Reiman, Jeffrey H. *The Rich Get Richer and the Poor Get Prison*. 2nd Ed. New York: Wiley and Sons, 1984.

The Numbers News. "Supplement to *American Demographics*." Vol. 10 (19 Oct. 1981).

Utah Bureau of Criminal Identification. *Crime in Utah—1983*. Salt Lake City: Utah Department of Public Safety, 1984.

20.
UTAH'S UNIQUE POPULATION STRUCTURE

Yung-Ping Chen

As noted in Chapter 3, Utah has long been noted for its high fertility. The state's average family size is larger than in the rest of the country: one child more than in the Intermountain Region and more than one child greater than in the United States. This difference is large and is expected to persist for some time into the future. One important consequence of high fertility is a youthful age structure. With the youngest population of any state, Utah's population structure provides an interesting basis for the study of dependency ratios and their policy implications.

Dependency ratios are generally classified into three types: the youth dependency ratio, referring to the number of young people as a proportion of the working-age population; the aged dependency ratio, or the number of older persons as a proportion of the working-age population; and the total dependency ratio, which is the sum of the two. Dependency ratios are important. For whether the young and the old are cared for within the family or by society, it is the working population that supports them. A high youth dependency ratio means that extra resources must be placed in child care, child socialization, and education, if youth are to be cared for and trained adequately. When the aged dependency ratio grows there are proportionately fewer people of working age to care for the elderly. Additional resources are required for social security, hospitals, nursing homes, and for the children of the aged. The resources of families, states, and nations may be stressed if youth or aged dependency ratios become too high.

This chapter uses dependency ratios based solely on population sizes in selected age groups. These ratios do not capture the effects of such related demographic and economic factors as incidence of disability, early retirement, size of the female labor force, family structure, and unemployment rates. Despite their imperfections, however, crude measures of dependency are still useful in analyzing the implications of broad changes in population subgroups such as the young and the old.

The youth dependency ratio in this chapter is the population under age 20 divided by the population between the ages of 20 and 64. The aged dependency ratio is computed by dividing the population age 65 and over by the population between the ages of 20 and 64. The total dependency ratio is the sum of the youth and aged ratios. Table 1 displays dependency ratios in Utah, the Intermountain Region, and the United States for decennial years from 1940 through 1980 based on actual figures, and for 1990 and 2000 based on population projections. These projections are the first of the State Population Projections released by the Census Bureau based on the 1980 census results. They are consistent with the middle series of national population projections published as *Current Population Reports, Series P-25, No. 922* (U.S. Bureau of the Census 1983).

As shown in Table 1, the youth ratio has been consistently higher in Utah than in the United States for the period 1940 to 1980. From 1980 to 2000, projections show that not only is the youth ratio in Utah much higher than in the U.S., but it is also increasing in Utah while declining nationally.

With regard to the aged ratio, paralleling the experience in the U.S., Utah's ratio increased from 1940 to 1980, although the ratio was lower in Utah than nationally. According to projections for the period from 1980 to 2000, the aged ratio in Utah will decline somewhat, whereas it will increase in the United States.

Finally, in Utah the total dependency ratio rose from 91 in 1940 to 107 in 1970. Although the total ratio increased as well for the United States from 1940 through 1970, it was only 69 in 1940 and 90 in 1970, much lower than in Utah. From 1980 to 2000, it is projected that the total dependency ratio in Utah will rise from 95 in 1980 to 103 in 1990, then subside to 100 in the year 2000. By contrast, the United States is projected to experience a declining total dependency ratio, from 75 in 1980 to 69 in 1990 and 68.5 in 2000.

Compared to other states in the region and the U.S., Utah's youth ratio has been and is estimated to be higher from 1940 to 2000, the only exceptions being in 1940 and 1950 when New Mexico had a higher ratio (see Table 2).

While the aged ratio in Utah rose from 1940 to 1970, the percentage increase was not as large as in many other states regionally and nationally.

TABLE 1.

Dependency Ratios in Utah, Intermountain Region, and U.S.: Selected Years 1940-2000

		UTAH	REGION	U.S.
1940	Youth Ratio	80.0	68.2	57.6
	Aged Ratio	10.5	10.8	11.3
	Total Ratio	90.5	79.0	68.9
1950	Youth Ratio	80.4	69.8	58.3
	Aged Ratio	11.8	12.9	13.8
	Total Ratio	92.2	82.8	72.1
1960	Youth Ratio	97.7	85.0	74.1
	Aged Ratio	14.3	15.4	17.4
	Total Ratio	112.0	100.4	91.5
1970	Youth Ratio	91.5	79.9	71.7
	Aged Ratio	15.1	16.5	18.4
	Total Ratio	106.6	96.4	90.1
1980	Youth Ratio	80.0	61.0	55.5
	Aged Ratio	14.5	16.6	19.4
	Total Ratio	94.5	77.6	74.9
1990	Youth Ratio	88.0	55.4	48.0
	Aged Ratio	14.5	18.1	21.3
	Total Ratio	102.5	73.5	69.3
2000	Youth Ratio	87.5	53.5	46.5
	Aged Ratio	12.8	18.4	22.0
	Total Ratio	100.3	71.9	68.5

Youth ratio is population under age 20 divided by population age 20-64 times 100. Aged ratio is population age 65 and over divided by population age 20-64 times 100. Total ratio sums youth and aged ratios.

Source: Social Security Administration for U. S. data and Bureau of the Census for all other data.

TABLE 2.

Dependency Ratios in the Intermountain Region: Selected Years 1940-2000

		UTAH	ARIZONA	COLORADO	IDAHO	MONTANA	NEW MEXICO	NEVADA	WYOMING
1940	Youth Ratio	80.0	73.9	60.3	69.4	58.5	87.9	47.3	61.5
	Aged Ratio	10.5	8.7	13.4	10.9	11.0	8.6	9.7	8.5
	Total Ratio	90.5	82.6	73.7	80.3	69.5	96.0	57.0	70.0
1950	Youth Ratio	80.4	72.4	61.5	73.8	64.0	83.2	51.8	64.7
	Aged Ratio	11.8	10.8	15.4	13.9	15.5	9.3	11.2	11.0
	Total Ratio	92.2	83.2	76.9	87.7	79.5	92.5	63.0	75.7
1960	Youth Ratio	97.7	84.1	78.1	89.0	83.9	94.4	64.2	80.9
	Aged Ratio	14.3	13.7	17.7	18.1	19.8	11.1	11.3	15.4
	Total Ratio	112.0	97.8	95.8	107.1	103.7	105.5	77.5	96.3
1970	Youth Ratio	91.5	78.7	74.4	82.0	80.1	88.5	67.4	77.6
	Aged Ratio	15.1	18.0	16.2	19.1	19.8	14.1	11.3	17.8
	Total Ratio	106.6	96.7	90.6	101.1	99.9	102.6	78.7	95.4
1980	Youth Ratio	80.0	59.1	53.8	68.0	59.4	65.7	49.6	61.0
	Aged Ratio	14.5	20.3	14.4	18.5	19.2	16.2	13.4	13.8
	Total Ratio	94.5	79.5	68.2	86.5	78.6	81.9	63.0	74.8
1990	Youth Ratio	88.0	51.2	45.5	67.1	52.5	57.8	42.0	61.3
	Aged Ratio	14.5	24.8	13.9	17.8	19.5	19.5	17.7	11.2
	Total Ratio	102.5	76.0	59.4	84.9	72.0	77.3	59.7	72.5
2000	Youth Ratio	87.5	48.7	42.9	65.0	49.0	56.3	41.5	61.4
	Aged Ratio	12.8	26.5	13.3	15.3	18.3	21.6	20.2	9.0
	Total Ratio	100.3	75.2	56.2	80.3	67.3	77.9	61.7	70.4

Youth ratio is population under age 20 divided by population age 20-64 times 100. Aged ratio is population age 65 and over divided by population age 20-64 times 100. Total ratio sums youth and aged ratios.

Source: Social Security Administration for U. S. data and Bureau of the Census for all other data.

Approaching the year 2000, the aged ratio in Utah is projected to decline, along with Colorado, Idaho, Montana, and Wyoming, whereas in Arizona, New Mexico, Nevada, and in the U. S., it is estimated to rise (see Table 2).

Because the working-age population bears the costs of supporting old and young dependents, the total number of dependents (i.e., the total dependency ratio) is an important consideration. In Utah, the total ratio is projected to grow from 94.5 in 1980 to more than 100 in 1990 and 2000. When the total ratio exceeds 100, there are more potential dependents than potential workers. In contrast, the total dependency ratio in the United States was only 74.9 in 1980 and is projected to decrease to 68.5 by 2000.

A high dependency ratio has important implications in other areas. It may be that Utah will witness an increase in labor force participation rates among women and older persons in order to reduce the burden of dependency. But accommodating these employees will probably require job redesign and other modifications to the work environment.

Because of the predominance of young people in Utah, financing education will continue to be a major issue. Since education costs are principally financed by state and local governments, financial pressure will grow in these political jurisdictions. And because society supports its young dependents through the institution of the family, the demand on private resources will remain strong.

Lest Utah's relatively small aged ratios mask the significance of the increase in the absolute number of older persons, it should be pointed out that according to projections the number of persons age 65 and over will increase 37,000 from 1980 to 1990, and an additional 31,000 from 1990 to 2000. The increase of 68,000 from 1980 to 2000 is greater than the total size of this group in 1965. The care and support of the older population will be increasingly important for both the private (i.e., family) and public sectors. Health care, especially longterm, is a complex issue that must be addressed.

In analyzing the dependency ratios from 1940 to 2000 for Utah, one is struck by the similarity between 1940-70 and 1980-2000. Of course, the former is fact, and the latter is a projection. But if history repeats itself it could be instructive for young and old alike to review how Utah dealt with the large youth ratios and total ratios from 1940 to 1970 in hopes of preparing the state for virtually identical trends from 1980 to 2000.

TABLE 3.

Population Subgroups and Dependency Ratios in Utah, 1940-1980 (Actual) and 1990-2000 (Projected)

	1940	1950	1960	1970	1980	1990	2000
(0-19) Young Age Population	231,185	288,070	410,508	469,156	600,733	886,600	1,213,600
(20-64) Working-Age Population	288,910	358,374	420,162	512,556	751,084	1,007,300	1,386,700
(65 and over) Old Age Population	30,215	42,418	59,957	77,561	109,220	146,400	177,100
Total Population	550,310	688,862	890,627	1,059,273	1,461,037	2,040,300	2,777,400
Youth Ratio	80.0	80.4	97.7	91.5	80.0	88.0	87.5
Aged Ratio	10.5	11.8	14.3	15.1	14.5	14.5	12.8
Total Ratio	90.5	92.2	112.0	106.6	94.5	102.5	100.3

Source: Bureau of the Census.

REFERENCES

U.S. Bureau of the Census. *Provisional Projections of the Population of States, by Age and Sex: 1980 to 2,000. Current Population Reports, Series P-25, No. 937*. Washington, D.C.: U.S. Government Printing Office, 1983.

NOTES ON CONTRIBUTORS

Stan L. Albrecht is dean of the College of Family, Home, and Social Science at Brigham Young Univeristy, Provo, Utah.

Stephen J. Bahr is director of the Family and Demographic Research Institute at Brigham Young University, where he is also a professor of sociology.

Bruce A. Chadwick is a professor of sociology at Brigham Young University.

Yun-Ping Chen is Frank M. Engle Distinguished Chair for Economic Security Research at the American College in Bryn Mawr, Pennsylvania.

Rita Edmonds is a core faculty member of the Comprehensive Clinic at Brigham Young University.

Kristen L. Goodman is a research assistant for the Research and Evaluation Division of the Correlation Department of the Church of Jesus Christ of Latter-day Saints, Salt Lake City, Utah.

Tim B. Heaton is a professor of sociology at Brigham Young University.

Cardell K. Jacobson is a professor of sociology at Brigham Young University.

Richard E. Johnson is a professor of sociology at Brigham Young University.

Jinnah Kelson executive director of the Phoenix Institute, Salt Lake City, Utah.

Jean M. Larsen is a professor of family sciences at Brigham Young University.

Anastasios C. Marcos is a research associate of the Family and Demographic Research Institute, Brigham Young University.

Craig Manscill is a graduate student in Family Studies at Brigham Young University.

Thomas K. Martin is director of the Office of Institutional Research and Planning at the Utah Technical College, Provo, Utah.

Jerald W. Mason is a professor of family sciences at Brigham Young University.

Vanessa Moss is a graduate student in education at Brigham Young University.

Boyd C. Rollins is a professor of sociology at Brigham Young University.

James E. Smith is a systems analyst for the Westat Corporation, Washington, D.C.

Ralph B. Smith is dean of the College of Education at Brigham Young University.

Adrian Van Mondfrans is a professor of education at Brigham Young University.